The New Plantation

The New Plantation

Black Athletes, College Sports, and Predominantly White NCAA Institutions

Billy Hawkins

Softcover reprint of the hardcover 1st edition 2010 978-0-230-61517-5

First published in 2010 by
PALGRAVE MACMILLAN®
in the United States—a division of St. Martin's Press LLC,
175 Fifth Avenue, New York, NY 10010.

Where this book is distributed in the UK, Europe and the rest of the world,
this is by Palgrave Macmillan, a division of Macmillan Publishers Limited,
registered in England, company number 785998, of Houndmills,
Basingstoke, Hampshire RG21 6XS.

Palgrave Macmillan is the global academic imprint of the above companies
and has companies and representatives throughout the world.

Palgrave® and Macmillan® are registered trademarks in the United States,
the United Kingdom, Europe and other countries.

ISBN 978-1-137-03534-9   ISBN 978-0-230-10553-9 (eBook)

DOI 10.1057/9780230105539

Library of Congress Cataloging-in-Publication Data

Hawkins, Billy.
    The new plantation: black athletes, college sports, and predominantly
white NCAA institutions / Billy Hawkins, Ph.D.
        p. cm.
    Includes bibliographical references and index.

        1. African American athletes—Social conditions. 2. African American
college students—Social conditions. 3. National Collegiate Athletic
Association. 4. College sports—United States. 5. Racism in sports—United
States, 6. Racism in education—United States. 7. United States—Race
relations. I. Title.

GV706.32.H38 2010
796'.08996073—dc22   2009024404

A catalogue record of the book is available from the British Library.

Design by Newgen Imaging Systems (P) Ltd., Chennai, India.

First edition: February 2010

10 9 8 7 6 5 4 3 2 1

Transferred to Digital Printing 2011

CONTENTS

Contents

TABLES

FOREWORD

We are living in a changing and complex society. The world of sport can be viewed as a mirror while reflecting on social issues related to race, gender, homophobia, human rights, social responsibility, and accountability. The illumination of these areas leads to multiple discourses in the analysis. While some scholars view sports as a microcosm of society, others contend that sports are ahistorical. The historical and chronological context of racism and the Black athlete must not be disregarded. The suffering of those oppressed Blacks by the structures of injustice must be felt and we as a society must learn to feel that pain as if it was our own and be willing to bear personally some of the costs of the removal of this pain.

Dr. Billy Hawkins does an excellent analysis while focusing on the role of sport in our society as it relates to the Black athlete. He acknowledges the multiple historical and institutional instruments that have been implemented to maintain the commodification of the Black male. Using the internal colonial model, Hawkins examines the experiences of Black athletes at predominantly White institutions. He provides an alternative analysis into the controversial and critical relationship that exists between the Black athlete and these institutions. His critiques are profound, compelling, and provocative. His inquiry into the structural variables and inheriting inequalities facing Black athletes is refreshing and informative. Investigations into the historical precedence of race and ethnicity in relationship to career opportunities illuminate unique circumstances associated with the sociocultural, sociopolitical, and economic indicators of commodification. These are seminal pieces of his scholarship. Hawkins connects the past, uncovers history, and provides a template for attempting to understand how this history is influencing our current issues in sport.

Dr. Billy Hawkins is considered one of the foremost scholars in focusing on the role and implications of the Black athlete in sociology. He combines his own personal experiences as a former student athlete with his extensive formal education to create an eminently qualified perspective. For everyone interested in gaining unique insights into the institutional makings of a system that commodifies as well as exploits the college athlete and more specifically the Black athlete, Hawkins' *The New Plantation* is a must read.

FRITZ G. POLITE, Ph.D., MPA
Director, Institute for Leadership, Ethics and Diversity (I-LEAD)
Director, Community Service and Global Outreach

PREFACE

A statement to contemplate is that at some level and to some degree, we are all colonized individuals. The Emancipation Proclamation did not end the plantation system or the internal colonial process; it released it. It was the Emancipation Proclamation that enabled the plantation system to transcend the South and influence other corporate and institutional practices throughout this nation. Therefore, when we do not control the decisions about our productivity and creativity, we are internally colonized. When our career activities are not motivated by a desire for inner freedom, self-expression, and a desire to contribute to human development, we are functioning like internally colonized individuals.

A second comment to marinate on is from Professor Derrick Bell's, *And We Are Not Save: The Elusive Quest for Racial Justice*, "We have made progress in everything, yet, nothing has changed." Despite the racial progress we have made in this nation, the Black Body[1] continues to be used as a valued commodity to generate revenue for capitalist endeavors.

Yet, I want to use this quote with an optimistic twist because within each of us is the potential and greatness to be agents of change in our respective fields in alleviating various inequalities and multiple forms of oppression and exploitation. Thus, we can leave an imprint and make a difference in the earth that will benefit those who will follow so that progress and change will be synonymous.

★　★　★

Now, in the larger social scheme of things, there are more pressing issues to engage that are challenging our collective consciousness than the topic of intercollegiate athletics. Wars, natural disasters, human neglect are some of the challenges we are encountering during this era in time. The National Collegiate Athletic Association (NCAA) Division I athletics poses no immediate threat to our national security. It does not have any enormous bearing on the gross national product. It does not assist in solving the national problems of healthcare, poverty, crime, and so on. Yet, intercollegiate sports draw the attention of millions of spectators and command the participation of thousands. Although intercollegiate athletics faintly registers on the radar of social concerns, it warrants inquiry because the power relations and inequalities endemic in the larger society are reflected and reinforced in this contested terrain.

More specifically, intercollegiate athletics has a long history of controversy, unethical practices, and issues associated with inequitable treatment, which has required governmental intervention. In October 1905, Theodore Roosevelt convened several meetings at the White House with presidents from Harvard, Yale, and Princeton universities to discuss the state of college athletics. The formation of the NCAA (formerly IAAUS) in 1906 was the result of these meetings, and it had the charge of addressing the issues of player safety, professionalism/amateurism, and academic integrity. Over the years, there have been additional challenges that demanded this governing body's undivided attention.

At a time when the Democratic Party is embracing its first biracial candidate—Black by social norms— and when the United States has elected and is celebrating its first Black president, race still matters. Therefore, to extend W. E. B. Du Bois' proclamation of race being the problem of the twentieth century, it continues to remain relevant and a challenge in the twenty-first century. Race is entrenched in the sociocultural configurations of this country, and hinders many from transcending inequalities and barriers assigned to groups based on the superficiality of phenotypical differences. Despite the progress of the Democratic Party in endorsing its first biracial candidate and the United States in electing its first Black president, race continues to be a thorn in the side of NCAA member institutions. From the years of desegregating to the current years wherein Black males are disproportionately competing in revenue-generating sports, these institutions reflect patterns of behavior toward Black males, specifically, that resemble practices witnessed in other institutions' interaction with Black males in the United States, for example, slavery, sharecropping, and the prison industrial complex.

Our purpose as Black males in this country has largely been defined by structural demands and institutional needs, which has mainly required our physicality. Therefore, to a significant degree, our experiences are shaped within the context of these demands and needs. The current racial demographics of NCAA revenue-generating sports provide an example of how millions of Black males' experiences have included either using sport or being used by sport to obtain a desired end; unfortunately the latter more frequently occurs. Again, history finds us burdened by our Blackness and physicality; toiling to build so that others can occupy, performing so that others can enjoy, and sacrificing for the benefit of others. Therein resides the significance of engaging the topic of Black athletes, college sports, and predominantly White NCAA institutions, because in the words of Reverend Dr. Martin L. King, "Injustice anywhere is a threat to justice everywhere." This will be the mantra flowing through the chapters of this book.[2] Therefore, reforming college athletics must be about justice and not about merely penalizing the victim. Nor can it be about providing a Band-Aid to mask deep wounds or about administering an analgesic for temporary relief.

ACKNOWLEDGMENTS

It is always appropriate to give thanks. There is not enough space to sufficiently express my gratitude for the many contributions that were necessary to complete this project. I acknowledge the Creator who lives in all, loves all, and who has placed unlimited splendor and greatness in us all to be released. I am learning that nothing is impossible.

I express eternal gratitude to the following: my parents, Joe Will and Rachel Hawkins who provided me with a foundation to believe in the impossible; to my sisters, Phyllis, Ann, Valerie, Sandra, and Clinita who were a constant source of encouragement; to my children who are the source of my motivation and inspiration, Marcus, Dorjon, Daquon, Courtnee, and Imani; to my brother-in-law, Tommie Sampson, thank you for your support. To Dr. Valerie McCray, I greatly appreciate your emotional support and ingenious insight—you are truly a Godsend.

The professional support I received requires considerable recognition. Dr. Michael Lomax, I greatly appreciate the example and standard you are setting as a scholar, and the support, prayers, and ear you have given as a colleague and friend. To Dr. Fritz Polite, thanks for encouraging me to put this project forward, again. Your mentorship and expertise has been a blessing—thank you. Dr. Akilah Carter, I greatly appreciate your assistance as a graduate student, your story as a former collegiate athlete, and now, as a colleague, your research focus on Black women athletes. Much thanks to Dr. Gary Sailes for the wisdom, guidance, and the lunches during my visits to Indiana. To the great shoulders I stand upon: Drs. Dana Brooks, Earl Smith, Doris Corbett, Othello Harris, Yvonne Smith, Dee Pearson, and Professor Linda Greene, I have gleaned so much from your scholarship, your leadership, and your presence—thank you. I greatly appreciate Drs. Jay Coakley and Allen Sack for taking the time to read this manuscript and provide feedback. To Drs. Rose Chepyator-Thomson, Derrick Alridge, Jerome Morris, Louis Harrison, Keith Harrison, Leonard Moore, Algerian Hart, Jacqueline McDowell, Reuben May, Boyce Watkins, John Singer, Emmett Gill, and Deborah Stroman, I greatly appreciate the times we have communicated about broader social issues and about race and sport, and I am inspired by your scholarship and activism—thank you. To my colleagues (Fellow NASSSers) and friends I greatly appreciate your insight, advice, and scholarly support. Dr. Richard Southall, as director of College Sport Research Institute, thank you for prevailing on the road less traveled and breaking the process of domestication. Thanks to Marlee Stewart for your editorial services. I am indebted to the many Black athletes who read a version of this manuscript and thanked me for telling their story. In their silent protest of balling to get a degree or to make it to the next level, I understand your struggle and dilemma of remaining voiceless. Your time will come to reach one and teach one how to maneuver the collegiate athletic milieu.

BJH

Introduction

The Context: A Background

Birthed into a world,
Socialized into a system of beliefs;
Shaped my behavior, my attitude—
Told me what to think, what to want, what to do, who to be. . . .
Herein begins the unlearning,
My undoing.

—Sadiki, *My Pen, My Pain, My Healing*

The context that shaped my frame of reference for this work started in a small southern town in the late '60s and early '70s, where the options to become upwardly mobile for young Black males were extremely limited and routinely restricted. Racial segregation was the prevailing social condition that regulated Black life and determined our mobility. The legal roads most traveled by my predecessors and peers consisted of the following: as manual laborers in the local factory or as seasonal laborers (tobacco or peach fields, etc.)—a byproduct of the sharecropping systems that my grandparents endured; we could join the armed forces, where the majority were assigned to infantry divisions; or an athletic scholarship in the sports of basketball, football, and sometimes baseball (however, very rare in baseball).

My hometown was a perfect example of how the Black body has been a valued commodity in generating revenue and wealth for the White establishment. I remember our summers involving seasonal patterns of labor where we rotated from tobacco to peach fields, to catching chickens at night, or to construction work when available, all for meager wages. Though these positions were an inadequate source of income, they provided a fear of being trapped in a lifestyle that relegated us to a subservient status, mistreatment, and exploitation from employers who never knew our name. In retrospect, the wages were more of a burden than a blessing in that we never made enough to invest in improving the quality of our lives. And, unfortunately this forced some of my peers to participate in "alternative," generally illegal, career paths to augment their income and increase their means. These alternative occupations were also options for those young Black brothers seeking survival against the odds and social barriers they inherited at birth. Therefore, they became employees of the private and externally funded open-air drug markets that are pervasive in Black communities throughout the United States. Others participated in other criminal activities (e.g., petty robbery, etc.) that ultimately led to a life ensnared in the prison system. Thus, in order to leave this town, (voluntarily or involuntarily) we were mainly funneled through the following tracks: the military, athletics, or by way of the prison system.

High-school dropout rates were generally high for Black males in my community. Part of it due to the perception we had about education and the nerds who excelled at it, and also because we viewed it as a long route to achieve the American Dream we witnessed White citizens in our town achieving and enjoying. This dream for us seemed too distant and elusive to achieve through the normal chain of command: get good grades, graduate from high school, go to college, get good grades, graduate from college, get a good job, get married...and live happily ever after. Although education was preached to us as a means of social mobility, the majority of my peers, including myself, did not view it in a similar fashion.

In retrospect, in our conversations about education, we politicized it as a system of indoctrination and assimilation that further bound Blacks to the system of White supremacy. Especially when we did not find our presence or contributions situated anywhere in the curriculum. We only read how Europeans either discovered, invented, or created everything. The salient message propagated by this Eurocentric curriculum was that Europeans were the superior race, and that Blacks' major contributions to this nation were as slave laborers. Therefore, the last thing we cared to be deceived into thinking was that this educational system would somehow nullify racism and place us in equitable standing with Whites. Our method of rebellion was to drop out, or do just enough to get by. Besides, by doing too good academically would call into question the validity of our Blackness and masculinity. Our logic was obviously loose and misguided.

As I grew older, I began to understand that the White power structure that ran this town was a major factor in our social mobility. We were only allowed to go so far up the economic ladder, move so close in adjourning neighborhoods, and to interact socially with extreme caution. I remember summers working with my Dad in his masonry business having to eat lunch in the kitchen of restaurants among the Black cooks and dishwashers or out back under the shade of trees. At a young impressionable age during my preteen years, while sitting in the kitchen of those restaurants near the door that led to the main dining area, I often wondered why we were not allowed to eat in the cool dining area. Furthermore, the beautiful homes my Dad constructed from his physical labor in the exclusive White neighborhoods provided me with images to dream and hope as well as images to reinforce the gap between the worlds of the White power structure and the Black community.

Despite our limited options, we all had one thing in common: sport was a common denominator and a rite of passage in our coming into manhood. The majority of the Black males in my small town were filtered through the culture of sport and played until they either dropped out of school because there was a substantial decrease in academic interest and performance, or because reality set in and priorities shifted because they realized that they did not have enough talent to make it to the next level.

★   ★   ★

It was seven of us that hung tight. Like typical male youth, we were preoccupied with the predictive behaviors of preteen and teenage males: we had evolved from playing marbles to playing "streetball" (football, basketball, and sandlot baseball—given the respective seasons); hanging out at the pool hall—hustling; or simply trying to start or find a fight. Our world was small but our dreams were big. We had limited access to the larger sociocultural issues outside of our community, so we were naïve about the challenges that awaited us because of our race and gender. Despite living in the aftermath of the turbulent sixties and the racial desegregation it birthed, we still lived in intensely racially segregated communities. We accepted this racial social ordering and sought to overcome it through sport, or to remain unconscious of it through our perpetual occupation with playing sport. The latter was a type of escapism that gave us some sense of control over our existence. In the pickup games, we made the rules, picked the teams, and decided on the location to compete. At the age of 14, our small worlds were a playground and most of our waking moments were consumed with some type of athletic activity: afterschool or on the weekends. We did not hang out at the library—did not know the hours of its operation; nor were we participants in some of the formal organizations that sought to socialize boys into men (e.g., Boy Scouts).

As with many small southern towns, sports are a staple. Sports provided us with a context for racial and masculine identity development. In other words, in this southern town with a population of about 14,000, sports provided us with momentary experiences to express our physical prowess, to be sexually promiscuous, and to transcend race. As Henry Bassinger has expressed in *Friday Night Lights*,[1] the lives in these communities are strangely interwoven around these seasonal events. Our small town could have easily replaced the Permian Panthers of Odessa, Texas. During sporting events, our racially and economically segregated community was afforded the opportunity to temporarily transcend its racial and class differences and forge a sense of unity, a communal identity, and a common enemy—the opposing team. Athletics was the main space we shared where race did not matter—we competed equally and together—a team, a united community.

Unfortunately, some of these experiences were a source of miseducation because it created an assembly of unrealistic racial relationships and assumptions about masculinity. The interracial relationships and interaction were shallow because they were based on only one dimension of who we were—athletes. The "Friday Night Lights" created an illusion for us as athletes and the fans. It was our athleticism that drew the cheers from a predominantly White audience. Who we were as young men, our career goals, or life dreams were never engaged, because these relationships rarely developed beyond the façade created by athletic events. This false adoration was both intoxicating and delusional. Outside of school and school activities, before desegregation filtered to our small town, our worlds were predominantly Black—no cheering White fans or no social interaction. These mixed messages were often points of confusion and dissonance because we were accepted because of our athleticism, but outside of the context of athletics, we were ostracized, ignored, and rejected as Black males: conveniently rendered invisible.

Furthermore, the development of our masculine identity through sports was faulty because ideals of athletic achievement and dominance carried over into our interaction with women. Thus, they became our quest to develop and insulate our faulty ideals of what it means to be a real man. Apparently, our logic was twisted because the more girls we sequestered the more masculine we were perceived to be among our peers. The reality was that we did more lying about our sexual accomplishments to construct and maintain an image of manhood. We did not consider the fact that our efforts to construct these masculine identities were based on damaging the reputation of some woman's or man's daughter or some girl's or boy's sister.

★   ★   ★

It started with little league baseball and evolved to competing for a starting spot on the varsity football and basketball teams. Although I considered myself to be a better baseball player, most of my friends played basketball and football. Furthermore, there were no girls attending the baseball games, and I was one of the only two or three Blacks who consistently played up to the senior league level. Though there were Blacks excelling in baseball at the professional level, it was not a very popular sport among my peers nor did it hold the glamour of football and basketball; besides, football ruled in this region of the country with basketball coming in at a distant second.

We had individuals like Hank Aaron, Bob Gibson, Reggie Jackson, Vida Blue, and so on, but the majority of our role models were professional football players (Jim Brown, O.J. Simpson, Walter Payton, etc.) and basketball players (Bill Russell, Julius Erving a.k.a. Dr. J., George Gervin, etc.). We gravitated toward these sports because we saw ourselves in those sports and saw those sports as being avenues for success. The glamour and fast-paced tempo and frequent opportunities for explosive in-your-face moves appealed more to us than the slower-paced game of baseball. We modeled ourselves after these players and embodied all that they represented athletically; thus, in our pick-up basketball games I was the silky-smooth scoring George Gervin or the gravity-defying Dr. J.; in street football, I became the unstoppable Walter Payton or the acrobatic receiver, Lynn Swan.

Without a doubt, we dreamed of becoming professional athletes; as most kids (males) do growing up. For me, I do not recall if it was about making a lot of money or becoming famous, but about the opportunity to be in a space where I thought I had some control over my life; a place were racism would be suspended and I would be valued and accepted as equal. Sports held that power over my life and the life of many of my Black male peers. It was a drug for us, we were addicts—athletic junkies needing our daily fix of sport; all the while, dreaming of making it to the pros; dreaming of being free from the burdens of poverty and the limitations this town placed on us because of our skin color.

In the Black community of this small town, excellence in education and sports was important, but often sexualized: Black girls were expected to excel educationally and Black males encouraged and expected to excel athletically and do only enough to get by educationally. Females that performed well athletically were not an anomaly, but they were viewed differently: they were cool among the boys, and envied among less athletic girls. Our level of knowledge about alternative lifestyles or sexual orientations never permitted us to question their sexuality. We were in a religiously conservative community where we received a weekly dose of "fire and brimstone" messages. Therefore, understanding of sexuality was rooted in a strict religious tradition coupled with a heavy dose of southern patriarchy: in sum, God created man and woman—man was expected to be the provider (the breadwinner) and the woman was the nurturer (the homemaker)—end of story.

Sports was merely an extension of these patriarchal masculine ideals, where girls were not expected to excel athletically as much as boys. If you ever were "schooled" by a girl on the court, you might as well relocate and change your identity because your "man-card" would be revoked indefinitely or until you redeemed yourself. Not against her, because that would not have sufficed. You had to pull a "hyper-masculine" athletic feat of sorts—like block someone's shot in some humiliating fashion, dunk over someone older, or while playing football, hit someone so hard that they get a glimpse of the afterlife.

As a male, if you did not compete in athletics, your masculinity was questioned; consequently, if you made "too many"[2] good grades, your masculinity was questioned. In school and throughout the various neighborhoods, our manhood was put to the test, either in defining our masculinity through dehumanizing or demasculinizing performances or reinforcing our masculinity by engaging in frequent bouts of violence. We were not given "street creds" among our peers for making all "A's" or being on the debate team. It was admirable for young Black males to excel in both academics and athletics, but the athletic piece gave us the most "props."

Rewarding our athletic performances indirectly reinforced our ideals of sports being a means of expressing our masculinity. We played harder and more physical and talked among ourselves about the hard hits we made or how we tried to take someone out with an elbow. Being on an athletic team gave us a sense of identity, and unfortunately to some degree, a false sense of self. Yet, it was a rite of passage for us; providing us with an extended family, father figures in the coaches, and a system of rules and regulations to harness our raging hormones.

By the time of graduation, my athletic skills did not mature enough to get me any intercollegiate considerations; therefore, a week after graduation, with diploma in hand, I was on a chartered bus on my way to a military boot camp. Unaware of this path and the demands of military life, during my time in the military I gravitated toward sports to make friends, to find solace, to make peace with myself. I carried my dream of being a professional athlete and addiction to sport throughout my tour in the military.

Basketball was the sport that I gravitated to the most. I was selected for several all-base teams or all-star teams and played consistently in competitive military leagues. This was enough to cultivate my esteem and feed my addiction, and encourage me to pursue a chance at college athletics after my military term ended. This led me to the local junior college where I was able to walk-on my first year and receive a scholarship my second year. For my junior and senior years, I committed to a small private school that had a history of mainly recruiting Black athletes[3] for athletic entertainment, which I learned during my senior year. This was evident when you noticed that all the Black males and all except two Black females were on athletic teams (one was from the Caribbean and the other was from a wealthy family). Regardless of my purpose of entertaining the predominantly White student body and faculty, I saw it as an opportunity to further my education.

At this private institution, I noticed the irony and contradictions of this arrangement at games where there would be five Black players performing before a predominantly White cheering audience; similar to my youth and high-school experiences. This experience was interesting in that this audience consisted of fellow classmates who did not interact with us normally and treated us with contempt outside of the sporting context. It was as if we were invisible when we were not donned in uniforms and entertaining them athletically. Did this sporting event disarm them enough to look beyond our skin color and admire our athletic abilities? Or, did it put them at ease and make them feel comfortable seeing Black males in a prescribed role of using our physicality to amuse a White audience?

On one occasion, I "respectfully" confronted a couple of White female students who had a poster of Michael Jordan in their room about their ambiguous behavior. I asked how they could admire this Black male and hold us in contempt. Their response was: "Because he is different." Different, I wondered? Different athletically, yes—well, most definitely! Different financially—most definitely! Nevertheless, I thought, "wasn't he Black like us?" "Was he not subject to the same Black experiences; especially if he ended up in the wrong side of town or crossed the paths of a skinhead or Klansman." "How was he different from us in their eyes?" My curiosity continued to probe for answer. "What place did they elevate this Black male so that he was different from all other Black males, especially the ones they saw everyday in class and throughout campus?"

I did not know at the time of how the dynamics of sports, Jordan's athletic excellence, his monetary value, and his photogenic personality allowed him to transcend race—made him "race neutral." To them, I suppose, he was in a different racial category; not Black like me; something more acceptable, palatable, or tolerable. Despite their pseudo-acceptance of Michael Jordan, my gut told me that Mr. Jordan still would have limits in their racially segregated circles; he would not be invited home for dinner to meet the parents. Despite his wealth and status, I doubt if he would have been invited to join their fathers' country club. It is interesting to witness how sports and more specifically, athletic excellence, could evoke such racial contradictions, where individuals who have been enslaved and brutally ostracized in a society can be ennobled and deified. More specifically, there is this racial compartmentalization, where in a sporting context Black males can be esteemed and glorified, and outside of the arena, we are racially profiled to be menaces to society.

★   ★   ★

During my collegiate experience, a fellow teammate and I received athletic honors in my junior year by being named to the small college all-American team. We were selected to travel to Europe to represent our institution by playing in several tournaments. The key was that our school had to sponsor us by financing the cost of the trip. To the president, this was out of the question. Knowing his stance on race and athletics, I imagine he cringed at the fact of having "his" college represented internationally by two Black males. It was a mere five years earlier that an all-Black basketball team had brought national attention to this institution by winning the national championship. How ironic this is today, when we have many predominantly White universities known nationally and internationally because of Black athletic excellence. It is a major contradiction and a twisted irony to have institutions of higher learning known by the American public more for their football and basketball teams, specifically, than their academic exploits. The greater irony is that it is not until universities have public service announcements during the broadcasting of these sporting events (mainly football) that many Americans get a glimpse of the academic expertise of these institutions.

Regardless, this award fed my addiction more and pumped my ego into believing that I would be and should be noticed by at least one of the pro scouts who frequented our games. At the end of my senior year, I had my bachelor's degree, nagging injuries, and only a local agent tempting me with an offer to play in a professional league in South America. This was not the way I envisioned my athletic dream unfolding, therefore, I decided to take a year off to rehabilitate a body that I had demanded so much of from consecutive years of playing since little league. The year-to-year pounding and stressing became noticeably irritating each morning, at the age of 25, waking up stiff and aching. It sounds masochistic, but I loved every minute of it—the wins the losses; the breaks and bruises. Most importantly, walking across that stage, and receiving my bachelor's degree with my Mom and Dad in the audience was extremely gratifying because it defied the odds of the statistical prediction of Black males in the United States. I had something in hand, heart, and mind, that justified being weekend entertainment and invisible during the week.

I must admit who being an athlete can be extremely beneficial if one learns to navigate the system effectively. Some of the ways include, first, taking advantage of the educational opportunities, by networking and developing relationships with individuals one has contact with because of sports, by always having options beyond the playing fields and arenas, keeping an open mind, and by keeping things in perspective. These are some of the ways to increase one's human capital, as well as one's social capital, which can prevent the experience of being one-dimensional and a burden to the community. Some athletes experience direct upward social mobility by being drafted into professional sports leagues. For others, there are indirect opportunities for becoming upwardly mobile: that is, their recognition provided them with job opportunities after they graduated; it could be working in the company of a wealthy supporter of the program; or it could extend to having an opportunity to further their education at the graduate level. The key is in recognizing the structural arrangements and manipulating them to ones advantage.

Fortunately, sports provided me with the opportunity to meet a variety of people. It was a means of indirect upward social mobility where I was able to develop relationships with individuals from other institutions. One of these relationships was fruitful and led me to graduate school at a university in the north Midwest region of the United States. At the time, a bachelor's degree was the only degree on my radar scope; it was the only degree I could grasp in my small town mind. Besides, within my social circle, I did not personally know anyone who went to graduate school and obtained a master's degree. This was all new to me, and I give partial credit to the athletic experience that enabled me to meet the right people who were able to provide me with valuable information about graduate school.

This educational venture was a perfect escape to defer my dreams of playing beyond college, to take a physical sabbatical from organized sports, and to physically and mentally rehabilitate from those yearly routines and rituals of competitive sports. I received a graduate assistantship that allowed me to work in strength and conditioning and coaching. I thought coaching was the career path suitable for my passion for the game. It was rewarding, but not as rewarding as my academic studies. Graduate school was the first time I was able to focus quality time on academics. I did not have to worry about a game at the end of the week, nor was I tired from practice. I actually had time to engage the subject matter. I thoroughly enjoyed it and developed a love and passion for wanting to "inquire into things."

I began to immerse myself more and more into the academic life as my dream of making it in professional sports slowly faded away. This newfound passion for learning led me to continue my education and work on a doctorate degree. It was while I was working on my doctorate that I was afforded the opportunity to work in athletic administration—in athletic student services. I worked with the athletes who were labeled "at risk" academically—this group was incoming freshman and predominantly Black male. This was an eye-opening experience for me because it was a major university that had one of the top athletic programs in the nation. Although the level of intensity and demands were different, the Black experience was similar to my experience at the small private college I attended. I was again able to witness some of the contradictions and controversies between higher education and athletics, especially as it relates to Black athletes. There were many success stories, where athletes worked against the odds, navigated the structural barriers in the institutional arrangements, and excelled academically to receive a bachelor's degree. Nevertheless, there were too many Black males, specifically, that were not, and are not, navigating successfully through this system. For them, the maze of deception, the academic rigor, the enormous time demands, and so on, created barriers to their success.

During this opportunity I began to reflect on the historical context of my collective experiences, began to shape my views toward activism; my desire to inquire into intercollegiate athletics was also birthed at this time. Writing about the experiences of Black athletes in intercollegiate athletics has been a way to channel my frustration and disappointment in a system with such potential, as well as providing me with an opportunity to speak for the voiceless Black male athletes caught in this maze. For example, athletes like Jason[4]: an extremely talented teammate on my junior college team, who had several athletic scholarship offers to major universities. Unfortunately, he could not get past his freshman year academically. He was able to read defenses and calculate eminent traps, but lacked the confidence in basic academic skills—education was simply not a priority for him. Little effort was made to assist him beyond the basketball court, because there was always a new crop of athletes (Black) who was waiting in the wings and could run just as fast and shoot just as good. I was one of those in the new crop waiting on my opportunity to take the place of those who transferred to four-year colleges or to replace the larger percentage of those athletes who succumbed to the demons of academic neglect. Little did I know that my opportunity to advance and compete would come at a price of another athlete having to be discarded because his eligibility expired or his value depreciated. This perpetual system sustains a competitive environment and limits the opportunity for collective bargaining because ultimately your teammate is also your competitor.

Ralph Ellison best captures this fracturing competitive environment in the "battle royal." In the *Invisible Man*, Ellison illustrates how young Black men were placed in a ring to fight for prize money (coins), but most importantly, for the entertainment of White men. Like Ellison's young Black males in the battle royal, the perceived value of the prize prevented any conscious assessment of the particular arrangements or any convergence and activism around a common plight. We simply competed and fought for the prize.

★   ★   ★

Sport has been described as a microcosm of the larger society. It has also been depicted as a barometer for racial progress. However, sports is a powerful institution that provides a context for critical examination because it informs dominant cultural practices and informs ideologies that help to shape social interaction. Thus, I dare not attempt to approach this subject lightly. Nor would I do justice to the many voices of Black athletes who have been silenced if I merely intellectualize their (our) experiences or simply provide a scholarly exegesis to a worthy topic. Examining the experiences of Black athletes participating in intercollegiate athletics at predominantly White National Collegiate Athletic Association (NCAA) Division I institutions (PWIs will be used) is more than a line of research and scholarly inquiry. It has been a lived experience for me that ranged from being a former collegiate athlete to being a tenured faculty member at major research institution, which happens to have a nationally ranked athletic program, both financially and competitively. I am also a spectator-fan: a spectator of many collegiate sports and a fan specifically to basketball—my prior experiences have biased me. I am also a critic because I love the physical expression of the talent displayed by today's athletes, but I also wish to promote a healthy equitable sporting experience where there is a balanced exchange between educational achievement and athletic output. Though there may be some inherent hypocrisy in being critical, since sports has been a means of me achieving a certain degree of upward mobility, my motives are to promote structural changes that will improve the educational success of Black athletes, and other athletes adversely affected by athletic capitalism.

The system of intercollegiate athletics[5] has remained relatively consistent with other social institutions where the Black body is a valued commodity: a cog or a tool for capitalist expansion. Within the context of intercollegiate athletics, the faces and voices change periodically, yet the goal of capital accumulation remains the same.

It is these recycled faces and voices that I have seen and heard from my various levels of experiences that haunt me. There are versions of lives that resembled the reincarnated experiences of Connie Hawkins, Dexter Manley, Lloyd Daniels, and others that need a voice. Sports was ascribed to be their means of social mobility, and for some, it became their ticket to a collegiate education and a career in professional sports. Nevertheless, for the larger percentage, their narratives are different. They were labeled academically deficient and pathological, and unfortunately, many conformed to this stigma. Once their talents were exhausted and their eligibility ran out, their value decreased and room was available for the new crop of talent who was ready to fill the void they left.

One face and voice in particular that is hard to erase is of a young man recruited out of the state of Texas (predominantly Black community) to a large predominantly White Midwest university—this university had an "athletic" pipeline to Texas for Black football talent. This individual, I will call Reggie for the sake of privacy, was recruited under considerable national scrutiny because it was alleged that his SAT was taken by someone else. I would notice during study tables his lack of academic confidence and distant interest in particular academic subjects. One day I happened to have a copy of the Askia Toure's, *From the Pyramids to the Projects: Poems of Genocide and Resistance*, which piqued his interest, so he requested to borrow it for a class project. I kindly and innocently obliged because I was glad it sparked his interest. Besides, how can you reject anyone desiring to read an "old school" poet expounding on issues of genocide and resistance?

The next day, Reggie came into study table with a slight grin of confidence. He began to recite verbatim various poems contained in this volume without error or hesitation. All I could think of was the power of the self-fulfilling prophecy, where here was a Black male, who was labeled academically deficient, and was conforming to that description. Yet, he had the mental capability and potential, and with the right nurturing, he could have risen above this stigma. I was too late. Reggie was fast, and they needed his speed and mental focus to be developed and fine-tuned for Saturday evenings' performances. He did not last long at this academically rigorous university majoring in eligibility, and he did not obtain a lucrative career in professional sports. This is about him and others like him. Since the Black communities, more specifically, consistently provide a pipeline of athletic labor to meet these institutions' demands for athletic excellence, each year I witness a new group of faces and voices; some ending up like Reggie, a few making it to the professional league, but not enough graduating.

For the few who are navigating the system, it can be a turbulent ride. For example, the experiences of one Black athlete I had the opportunity to work with highlight the occupational hazards encountered on the way to academic success. He grew up with no running water in their home (during the seventies in the United States). His athletic abilities were recognized at a very young age. By junior high school, he had been kindly persuaded to attend a certain high school that would assure him in learning the style of football that would position him to transition smoothly into their collegiate program. He made all the right moves, changing residence to meet the district demands to attend this high school, excelling athletically, and receiving an athletic scholarship. All the right moves resulted in one wrong move that left him requiring reconstructive surgery on his knee, and cast doubt on his dreams of making it to the professional level. Devastated by the incident and disappointed by the treatment he received from members of the athletic staff, he was not without hope and a desire to focus on receiving an education. This young man fought back and competed, although not at the previous level, graduated with the goal of starting his own business. Athletics was a burden and a blessing to his personal desires and career aspirations: it initially equipped him only to see professional sports as his means of social mobility; consequently, it provided him with an opportunity to be successful academically. Despite the bitter taste he had because of the ill treatment he received when he was no longer a productive commodity, and notwithstanding, his dream of making it to the pros being unattainable, he persevered and graduated. It has sometime taken injuries in the form of concussions, spinal cord injuries, reconstructive surgery, and so on, to provide an epiphany.

Both the positive and negative narratives are valuable stories that need attention. The context in which these narratives are constructed make for an interesting terrain for analysis. My inquiry began with trying to understand the structural arrangements of these athletic departments and universities, and their impact on the lives of Black athletes. I began to question, what is a conceptual framework for analyzing these institutions as it relates to Black athletes? Is there a framework that best captures the experiences of Black athletes at PWIs?

★   ★   ★

This book is a critical analysis that examines the relationship between Division I intercollegiate athletic programs at PWIs and Black male athletes, specifically, (the term *student* athlete will not be used because of sociopolitical reasons and the structural dynamics that will be put forth in this book). It provides a conceptual framework for analyzing the intercollegiate athletic experiences of Black athletes.

It is important to note that structural inequalities[6] in the larger society and stereotypical racist beliefs[7] about athletic superiority produce an athletic labor force in Black communities that supply these institutions with a consistent flow of athletic labor. Recruited mainly to play sports and produce winning seasons, too many young Black males are indirectly encouraged to make academics a lower priority because of the athletic rigor required to meet the economic demands of athletic budgets. Despite the dismal percentages (e.g., 1.1 percent of college football players and 1 percent of basketball players will be professional rookie players), there is still a pervasive system of channeling[8] young Black males, specifically, down the narrow path of athletics. For many, this channeling leads them into relationships with predominantly White NCAA Division I institutions that may not provide equitable returns for them. These institutions of higher learning have performed poorly in their relationship with many Black athletes who entered naively into a world where they sought acceptance and fame.

The major focus of this book will examine the controversial relationship between PWIs and Black athletes. It seeks to position Black male athletic experiences within the broader historical and social context of exploitation endured by internally colonized people in the system of slavery. This analysis will examine how these institutions' athletic departments, like colonizers, mainly prey on the athletic prowess of young Black males, recruit them from predominantly Black communities, exploit their athletic talents, and discard them once they are injured or their eligibility is exhausted. In the case of the athletes who are discarded after an injury, it reinforces Oliver Cromwell Cox assessment of the master-slave relationship, where "the master may consciously decide to use up his slaves because their replacement is cheaper than their conservation."[9] An internal colonial framework, the plantation model, will be used to examine how the structures of these institutions and athletic departments work economically, politically, socially, and culturally, to shape the experiences of Black athletes. Thus, the basic premise is that these institutions continue a heritage of White supremacy, which is inherent in the American culture, where racist practices are embedded in these institutions' relationship with Black male athletes.

It is important to state at the onset that in this relationship there is a shared responsibility regarding the academic success or failure of Black athletes. These institutions, more specifically the athletic departments, are not solely responsible for the academic success or failure of Black athletes. However, with the resources they have available, they have not unreservedly worked to improve these results either. This is especially the case when they recruit student athletes that they know will be challenged academically at many premier academically rigorous universities. Yet, their profit-driven motives and interests in the athletic abilities of these student athletes overshadow the student athletes' academic challenges, thus, resulting in academic assistance that focuses on maintaining eligibility. Despite the creation and implementation of policies that require athletes to make successful progress toward a degree, or the policies that have been constructed to encourage athletic departments to recruit, retain, and graduate athletes, the practice of majoring in eligibility pre-vails (e.g., the Academic Progress Rate or APR—is the current piece of legislation to assist in the image construction and public relation of these institutions; it will be discussed in a later chapter). Even when athletes graduate, their degree informs me of whether they majored in eligibility or not (this will be discussed in a later chapter).

To expound further, on the issue of institutional responsibility and accountability for the educational achievement, the educational success rate, as measured by graduation rates, speaks volumes to a structural issue and not just an individual default. Several accounts that have chronicled the experiences of Black athletes have blamed the lack of Black academic achievement solely on the shoulders of Black athletes. When we criti-cally examine graduation rates within the context of intercollegiate ath-letics, using C. Wright Mills' concepts of personal troubles and public issues,[10] the consistently low rates speak to concerns beyond the character and cognitive abilities of the individual. There are inherent structural contradictions that contribute to the lack of educational achievement of Black athletes. This message begins to take shape when kids in the eighth grade are being courted by major shoe companies and Division I coaches because of their athletic potential. Kids are also being ranked as top pros-pects as early as the sixth grade.[11] It is perpetuated throughout the subcul-ture of youth and interscholastic sports, where athletic talent is awarded over academic abilities, and it is further exacerbated at the intercollegiate level.

When the NCAA indirectly reports that 58 percent of Black basketball players and 51 percent of Black football players (Football Bowl Subdivision or BCS and Football Championship Subdivision schools combined) did not graduate in 2008,[12] in which 56 percent of the basketball players and 50 percent of football players at NCAA member institutions are Black, this cannot simply be attributed to racial intellectual shortcomings. Thus, according to Mills, "An [public] issue, in fact, often involves a crisis in institutional arrangements, and often too it involves what Marxists call 'contradictions' or 'antagonism.'" (p. 9). This "crisis in institutional arrangement" is the topic under examination throughout this text. Furthermore, the fact that these institutional arrangements are consistent with the historical expropriative arrangements White institutions have had with Black people is paramount to this discussion.

In order to negotiate strategies to navigate successfully in this current culture of intercollegiate athletics, it is imperative that young Black ath-letes understand that the playing fields and arenas at these institutions have replaced the cotton and tobacco fields that their ancestors toiled in from sun up to sun down. The slave-masters and overseers have also been transformed into positions where their identities are concealed and are not easily recognizable. During the recruiting process and the initial visits, these individuals appear to have Black athletes' best interest at heart, and like wolves in sheeps clothing their true agendas are undetected amidst the promotional promises of how great of an educational opportunity this will be for the recruiting prospect.

This is not to imply that all athletic administrators and coaches at this level are only there to oppress and exploit the talents of Black athletes. I personally know of several coaches and administrators who have a genuine concern about the lives of Black athletes (and all athletes in general) on and off the field and even after their eligibility has expired. Unfortunately, the pressures produced from the commercialization of collegiate sports have often forced many athletic administrators and coaches to focus mainly on the athleticism and nurturing the physicality of Black athletes.

Because winning equates to economic gains and increased job security, lucrative endorsements, and TV contracts for head coaches and other members of their coaching staffs, a premium is placed on enhancing the athletic abilities of Black athletes in sacrifice of their academic pursuit. This is evident when we see coaches' salaries escalating in the past ten years, where in 2007 the average salaries for coaches at major level Division I NCAA institutions was $950,000; with the highest total salary, including bonuses, peaking out at $4 million.

Furthermore, increased commercialization in the form of multibillion dollar TV contracts and multimillion dollar endorsements has created hidden agendas that often cause these athletic departments/institutions to neglect the minds of Black athletes while exploiting their athletic talents. Thus, to foster successful navigation, young Black athletes need to be aware of the institutional arrangements that place pressure on athletic administrators and coaches to win games, conference championships, bowl games, and the like. Within this framework, where "winning is the only thing," academics will be given a "lower" priority unless athletes take full responsibility in obtaining an education. Coaches that once cared about the well-being, mental welfare, and human development of athletes are being replaced by athletic entrepreneurs, and athletic departments are being directed by MBA-trained corporate executives whose corporate mission supersedes the educational mission.

Regardless of these institutions' efforts to hide behind the veil of amateurism, intercollegiate athletics reflect the values of professional sports. Professional sports are profit driven; they are outcome oriented and winning is heavily valued and in most cases, "winning is the only thing." Similarly, intercollegiate athletics at the Division I level reflect this profit-driven motive, where images, careers, and money are at stake when teams do not win games and appear in bowl or championship games. Simply stated, winning and winning big is the only thing, with graduation rates of their players being a necessary distraction. In the age of corporate athletics, very few, if any, intercollegiate athletic programs can afford unsuccessful programs. It is unfortunate, but often times, the way some athletic programs develop success requires them to put a greater premium on athletic development and performance and less on academic performance.

As an ideology, amateurism assists in maintaining these institutional arrangements and works paternalistically in keeping athletes in revenue-generating sports exploitable. As with most ideologies (i.e., dominant or prevailing systems of ideas that direct ones thinking and behavior), they are imperative for systems of oppression and exploitation (e.g., slavery or internal colonialism, etc.). According to the NCAA Manual, amateurism, as defined by the NCAA, declares that:

> Student-athletes shall be amateurs in an intercollegiate sport, and their participation should be motivated primarily by education and by the physical, mental, and social benefits to be derived. Student participation in intercollegiate athletics is an avocation, and student-athletes should be protected from exploitation by professional and commercial enterprises.[13]

Couched within this definition of amateurism is the paternalistic nature of the NCAA and its member institutions. The *Random House College Dictionary* defines paternalism[14] as:

> The system, principle, or practice of managing or governing individuals, businesses, nations, and so on, in the manner of a father dealing with his children.[15]

Mary Jackman further expounds that:

> The traditional father-child relationship on which the term [paternalism] is based was one in which the father authoritatively dictated all the behaviors and significant life-decisions of his children within a moral framework that credited the father with an assailable understanding of the needs and best interests of his children. They, in turn, accepted implicitly and absolutely the authority of their father—occasional bouts of independence were not unexpected, but never tolerated. Good children learned to comply with and defer to the wishes of their father.[16]

These institutions, according to the ideology of amateurism, are working in the best interest of Black athletes by protecting them from other exploiters while providing them with an educational opportunity. Thus, it appears that the welfare of athletes is the main priority, however, preserved in this expropriative arrangement is the exploitation of the Black athlete.

When there are "occasional bouts of independence," the NCAA, in its fatherly manner and in the best interest of the family (many member institutions), provides the necessary discipline to encourage compliance. An example of a program being disciplined by the NCAA, which received national attention in 2007, was the Oklahoma Sooners' football program.

The NCAA sanctions against the Oklahoma Sooners for not monitoring players' employment involved them erasing their wins from the 2005 season, and losing two scholarships for the 2008–2009 and 2009–2010 school years. An example of a player being disciplined by the NCAA is when JaRon Rush of UCLA received a multigame suspension by the NCAA because Rush received monetary benefits from an AAU coach and agent while in high school. The original sentence for JaRon's "unNCAA-like" conduct was a 29-game suspension and a $6,125 fine; after an appeal, it was reduced to 9 games and repayment of the fine.

There are some cases where the institutions (college or university) will discipline their respective athletic departments or a player prior to NCAA disciplinary actions; often to soften the disciplinary actions from the NCAA. An example of this was with St. Johns suspension of Erick Barkley. However, the NCAA went beyond St. Johns suspension and further disciplined Barkley for receiving benefits and other violations. Another example of an institution self-disciplining itself was with the University of Georgia in 2003. In the midst of the academic scandal, they removed the basketball team out of both the Southeastern Conference (SEC) and NCAA tournaments in order to appease the NCAA. However, the NCAA went beyond the University of Georgia's self-sanctioning and included a four-year probation and a reduction of men's basketball scholarships by one for each of the next three seasons.

Another occurrence in which the NCAA flexed its disciplinary muscle happened with the Florida State University cheating scandal where 61 athletes cheated on an online test or received inappropriate academic assistance from academic support staff.[17] The NCAA placed the school on a four-year probation, along with other penalties, and they had to forfeit victories they accomplished during the time of the indiscretion.

These are only fractions of the way the NCAA operates in a father-like (paternalistic) manner to maintain amateurism, or to protect athletes from exploitation by professional and commercial enterprises. This operation further establishes an exploitable relationship between athletes and the NCAA, where the beneficiary of this athletic commodity has mainly been the NCAA. It keeps the Black athlete under the authority of these PWIs, and their talents exploitable to benefit these institutions. Thus, this system of paternalism functions like an iron fist in a velvet glove[18]; providing a "protective" environment for the development and expression of Black athletic talent, yet controlling and exploiting this talent as a commodity in the open market.

Part of the paternalistic nature of PWIs is the support they provide to athletes for academic support. Within the constructs of athletic capitalism, athletic departments are providing academic support services for athletes and the NCAA will legislate rules (e.g., Academic Progress Report—APR) to give the illusion that academics are a priority, however, the fundamental principle of generating revenue prevails. Multimillion dollar facilities are being constructed as academic support centers that house computer labs, resources centers, academic support staff offices, tutorial services, and the like, all to insure athletic eligibility and give the illusion that they promote academic excellence. For example, the following institutions have or are in the process of constructing academic centers specifically for athletes: Louisiana State University spent $15 million, Mississippi State University spent $10 million, University of South Carolina spent $13 million, University of Michigan spent $15 million, Texas A&M spent $8 million, and the University of Georgia spent $7 million. The NCAA reports that Division I athletic departments spend a minimum of $150 million annually on academic support services. The University of Southern California spends $1.5 million on tutors and academic support staff, while the University of Georgia has a budget of $1.3 million for tutors. Clearly, the money is there to support athletes' academic endeavors, and the academic support services are extensive in several top-level athletic departments. The concern is with those programs that function, according to Dr. Linda Bensel-Meyers—former tenured English professor at the University of Tennessee—as "academic evasion centers" instead of academic support centers. Therefore, are they extensions of paternalism that seek to protect and promote the interests of athletes, or mere illusions distracting from their fundamental nature and business practices?

★   ★   ★

In the larger scheme of things, sports mirrors patterns of social interaction that prevail in the larger society, and at times it can be viewed as a barometer of racial progress. Intercollegiate athletics is a subculture of the sports industry that similarly reflects and reinforces race, class, and gender ideologies that are dominant at the macro level of society. Therefore, the challenges Blacks encounter at the societal level (discriminatory practices, racial profiling, exploitation, etc.) are often similar to the encounters they face within other social institutions. Furthermore, the triumphs and progress we have achieved through sports has transcended into other social institutions. Fortunately, many Blacks daily prevailed against the contradictions in institutional arrangements and have had varying levels of success. Similarly, many Black athletes have transformed their negative experiences in predominantly White campuses into productive careers in the following occupations: professors, lawyers, doctors, political leaders, managers, accountants, professional athletes, and other occupations. It is unfortunate that these success stories are not highlighted more in the media as much as the cases of academic and athletic deviance. Regardless, this terrain must continually be contested and manipulated to increase the success rate of Black athletes so that they can go on to be productive citizens.

This book will provide a perspective into the interworking of intercollegiate athletics and race. The focus is on the revenue generating sports of football and men's basketball. It is proposed in this book that many of these institutions function like plantation systems that internally colonize and exploit the athletic resources of Black athletes, and too often they return to their communities either injured (physically or psychologically) or poorly educated, despite the athletic expenditures they have given to these institutions; they then become a burden on the communities that bore the burden of nurturing that athletic talent.

Because of the interworking of this system, the concept of amateurism will be challenged in the chapters that follow; as mentioned previously, amateurism is more of an ideology than a legitimate practice. These programs operate more on a professional or semiprofessional level, and they are more commercial in nature, than they are amateuristic. As professional or semiprofessional leagues, we will explore how the behavior of Black athletes resembles the labor patterns of oscillating migrant laborers.

My perspective has been informed from the following sources: my personal experiences, focus groups, think tanks, after-class discussions, and informal and formal interviews with Black athletes, coaches, academic counselors, faculty members, athletic directors, and administrators from various NCAA Division I institutions. My observation of the patterns of behavior witnessed at the structural level of these institutions, and the experiences of individuals mentioned above will be used to focus on the social constraints and arrangements Black athletes must navigate.

Similar to the military industrial complex and the prison industrial complex that consist of a network of organizations/universities, businesses, corporate vendors, and so on, who collaborate and are driven by a profit motive, NCAA Division I intercollegiate athletics form an athletic industrial complex[19] that functions similarly. In the following pages, this study intends to describe this athletic industrial complex using a plantation model (internal colonial model[20]) to draw similarities between the structures of these institutions (intercollegiate athletics and internal colonialism) and highlight some of the deficiencies of PWIs because, like a plantation system, they are driven by economic motives.

Because internal colonialism has not been a conceptual framework used to analyze the experiences of Black athletes, a variety of historical sources will be used to construct this model. The reason this model was chosen to apply to NCAA Division I intercollegiate athletics is because according to Robert Staples:

> The main concern of the internal colonial model is the structural inequality between racial groups and the dynamics of social institutions and practices that maintain racial differentials in access to social values and participation in society. It focuses on structural variables instead of exploring individual motivations....[21]

Staples also suggests that, "It [internal colonial model] has managed to shift the foci of study from the victims of racial oppression to the oppressor and his exploitative system."[22]

The goal of using this model is to illustrate the structural variables and inequalities of predominantly White institutions—examine the "crisis of institutional arrangements." This model can also be instructive in understanding the institutionalization of social and cultural racism and the political and economic exploitation inherent in PWIs relationships with Black athletes. This will include a look at the ideology of Blacks' purported physical superiority and intellectual inferiority, and also the pattern of oscillating migrant laborers to see how they contribute to these inequalities.

The question may arise as to why White athletes are not included in this study. Although White athletes share some of the same experiences as Black athletes, it is because they have benefited the most from this relationship. For example, they graduate at higher rates and they have more avenues of employment to explore upon graduating. For example, in 2008, the NCAA reported that four-year graduation rates for Black male athletes participating in football and men's basketball were 49 percent and 42 percent, respectively. These rates are considerably lower than the rates of their White teammates. This is important when we examine the racial demographics of the teams and starters, where Black athletes make up the majority of the basketball teams and the majority of starters on football teams at several NCAA universities.

Another reason they have been able to benefit from this arrangement is because of White skin privilege.[23] White skin privilege allows White athletes to blend more into the predominantly White school setting, thus allowing them to have more positive experiences than Black athletes. According to Robert Sellers, "Black athletes are more likely to report experiencing racial isolation than are white athletes."[24] Their ability to assimilate into the campus setting reduces the stress and negative experiences Black athletes are subjected to because of their skin color.

I have noticed in my experiences that the lives of Black athletes on predominantly White campuses are more complex than their counterparts. The simple act of walking across campus, sitting in classrooms where there are very few (if any) Black students, or being vocal in class discussions can be challenging and uncomfortable for some Black athletes. These simple acts, in and of themselves, are stressful for many White students, but race adds another layer within this predominantly White environment. For several Black athletes I have worked with, this has been a contributing factor in their low class attendance and social interaction on campus. White athletes do not have to contend with this level of stress that evolves from racial ignorance; therefore, their experiences are different.

Furthermore, although Black and White athletes are members of the same working class or athletic labor force, Black athletes occupy a different structural position because of their race and other sociocultural factors. Thus, within this working class or labor force group, there exist lines of division based on racial categorization (mainly phenotypic characteristics) and sociocultural factors. This line of division denotes what is known as a *class fraction*.[25] Therefore, Black athletes are a class fraction within this larger working class. According to Phizacklea and Miles, a class fraction is "an objective position within a class boundary, which is in turn determined by both economic and politico-ideological relations."[26] Phizacklea and Miles explain that:

> Class boundaries mark the objectively different structural positions in economic, political and ideological relations but these relations also have independent effects within these boundaries.[27]

Therefore, Black athletes and White athletes exist in the same labor class (working class) and share similar experiences regarding economic exploitation. However, Black athletes are considered a class fraction because they make up a different structural position based on different economic relations (socioeconomic status of family upon entering college) and politico-ideological relations (race, the sports they participate in, and possibly their position on the team, and the low percentage of Blacks that make up the student body).

Studies that have highlighted the different structural positions Black athletes occupy in relation to their White counterparts include the stereotypical belief regarding Blacks' intellectual inferiority and athletic superiority, the differences in their demographic and academic backgrounds, overall college life experiences, mental health issues, and social support.[28] Furthermore, there are several studies that illustrate how the academic performance of Black athletes is lower than that of White athletes once they are on campus.[29] Because of the different backgrounds and experiences of Black and White athletes and despite the common experience of labor exploitation they share, in this analysis Black athletes will be viewed as class fractions.

Consequently, it is important to note that within the class boundary of Black athletes, this concept of a class fraction extends even further because each Black athlete brings different experiences to the university. Therefore, within the labor class and within the class fraction of Black athletes there is stratification among Black athletes where they are layered based on social class, popularity or celebrity status, academic class, and so on. This stratifying was made known to me in a discussion with a couple of Black athletes about an internal conflict several team members were experiencing. I made the assumption that there was a certain level of unity and collective consciousness among the Black athletes on the football team, therefore, I suggested they take the issue to the captain of the team, who was Black, to voice their concerns. They corrected my incorrect supposition by informing me that they did not talk to this individual, and that this person had very limited interactions with other Blacks on the team.

This not only alerted me to the stratification that existed between Black athletes, but it also informed me of the fragmentation that often prevents the development of a collective voice needed in addressing conflicts of interest. Historically, this has been a strategic practice implemented to divide and rule in the colonization process and documented as a process used on plantations to suppress insurrections and maintain control over slave labor. The co-opting of Black leadership in the United States by the White power structure has been documented in the literature and is another example of this as a practice that creates stratification and stifles efforts of organizing around a common goal.

Besides the overt practice that created varying structural positions within a class fraction, there are covert schemes, such as levels of assimilation, geographic regions, socioeconomic status, and so on, that can stratify Black athletes within their class boundary. Therefore, it is hard to make generalizations about the experiences of all Black athletes on predominantly White campuses, even those on the same team. Although they are all subject to have a "Black experience" involving racist verbal attacks or ill-treatment based on racist stereotypes, a small percentage are shielded and have more positive experiences, despite their skin color.

Chapter 1 provides a historical overview of the Black athlete in intercollegiate athletics: This chapter will provide a historical context of the experiences of Black athletes in intercollegiate athletics. It will provide a brief overview of the Black migration from Historically Black Colleges and Universities (HBCUs) to predominantly White colleges and universities. Chapter 2 outlines the internal colonial model—the New Plantation Model. This chapter will outline the various components that will be used to address the experiences of Black athletes. Chapter 3 addresses some of the ideological issues that have provided a lens for labeling Black athletes intellectually inferior and examines how academic clustering reproduces the myth of the intellectually inferior but athletically superior Black athlete. It will examine how academic clustering disproportionately affects Black athletes. Chapter 4 engages the economic burden of the Black body. Because economics is the key reason this relationship has emerged, this chapter will look at the burden placed on the Black athletic body. It will attempt to answer the question put forth by Sidney Willhelm, *Who Needs the Negro?* This chapter will address how Title IX sports that are occupied mainly by White women are benefiting from the Black male athletic labor. Chapter 5 looks at the Black athlete's racialized experiences at predominantly White NCAA institutions. The chapter will look at how racism continues to plague Black athletes covertly and overtly—whether it is the negative assumptions made by faculty members and peers as they walk into classrooms, or the blatant racist verbal attacks endured by many Black athletes. Chapter 6 addresses the environmental factors. This chapter will focus on the sociocultural settings Black athletes are recruited into at predominantly White NCAA institutions. The concept of oscillating migrant laborers will be used to explain the migration process from communities of color with diverse cultural expression to predominantly White communities with a predominantly monocultural environment. Chapter 7 takes into consideration the political component and how Black athletes are oppressed politically because they lack a voice in the political process that governs their lives and the lack of Black athletic administrators and coaches denying them adequate representation at the leadership level. Chapter 8 engages the subject of interscholastic athletics and how it has become a breeding ground for the internal colonial setting. Finally, chapter 9 will address the topic of decolonization and reformation: This chapter will address the concept of how academic reformation must begin with the decolonization of the mind and the ideological processes that are in place to maintain and insulate a system of exploitation.

★ ★ ★

Within the scope of examining the structural inequalities, a consistent theme that emerges throughout this book is a plea for athletic reform. It is a sad dilemma but a mistake that is often made in assuming that moral reasoning can be appealed to in order to alleviate the exploitation and oppression of capitalist expansion. In efforts of reforming intercollegiate athletics, I am making an appeal to the capitalist motives and not the moral consciousness of the administrators and officials who govern intercollegiate athletics to approach this topic with an open mind so that productive and creative solutions will be the end result. The deception that affords the exploitation of athletic labor can only survive but so long. In the words of Frederick Douglass, "The limits of tyrants are prescribed by the endurance of those whom they oppress."[30] An adequate return on investment, which can simply equate to a meaningful educational experience resulting in a functional degree and employable skills, for four years of athletic labor, is the least these institutions can provide for athletes. Thus, within this current intercollegiate athletic configuration there exist questionable practices that warrant examination. I conclude with a unique experience that attempts to capture the essence and irony of the configuration.

In visiting an interstate rival between two nationally ranked teams, I noticed a major paradox where I, and an extremely small percentage of Black fans peppered throughout the stadium, were sitting in a stadium with over 107,000 White fans cheering for two teams manned predominantly by Black athletes. Besides the sold-out facility, this event drew national television coverage. This strange dilemma generated a multitude of thoughts: did the Black athletes laboring in this context fully understand the magnitude of the revenue that was at stake in this event; were other fans oblivious to this glaring contradiction in racial demographic percentages between teams and fans (i.e., did they feel that there was nothing wrong with these arrangements, or did they feel that Black athletes were in the "right" place and should be proud, honored, and happy to be at these institutions and representing them nationally); and finally, were these fans concerned about the career paths of the athletes? What is profound about this experience is that it has been and continues to be replicated every Saturday afternoon during the autumn season of the year. It has become a fixture in the landscape of institutions of higher learning in the United States. Therefore, like the fall season that begins to usher in a winter chill, so too do we witness on campuses and throughout our homes the thrill and excitement of young men challenging themselves and others in athletic competition.

CHAPTER ONE

Brief Historical Overview and the Experience of Black Athletes and Students at Predominantly White Institutions: A Mind Is a Terrible Thing to Waste

> Education and work are the levers to uplift a people. Work alone will not do it unless inspired by the right ideas and guided by intelligence. Education must not simply teach work—it must teach life.
> —W. E. B. Du Bois, *The Talented Tenth*

Education has always been valued in the Black community. The value we place on education pre-dates Blacks' existence in the United States. Scholars of ancient African civilizations have well documented the value these dynasties have placed on education.[1] Their architectural skills, economic systems, and mathematical abilities clearly illustrated the utility and primacy education held in various African cultures. Undoubtedly, the system of colonialism and the Atlantic slave trade disrupted centuries of educational traditions. Furthermore, the institution of slavery provided Africans a peculiar environment where they were forced to learn a new language, acculturate or assimilate into a new culture,[2] and become acclimated to a new country.

Yet there were barriers to Blacks learning in the plantation system. Frederick Douglass best captures the parameters placed on what slaves could or could not learn. Douglass informs us of how Master Hugh insisted to his wife that instructing human chattels (slaves) was unlawful and unsafe, and he further states that:

> If you give a nigger an inch he will take an ell. Learning will spoil the best nigger in the world. If he learns to read the Bible, it will forever unfit him to be a slave. He should know nothing but the will of his master, and learn to obey it. As to himself, learning will do him no good, but a great deal of harm, making him disconsolate and

unhappy. If you teach him to read, he'll want to know how to write, and this accomplished, he'll be running away with himself.[3]

Furthermore, according to Faustine Childress Jones-Wilson, "the African-American population is unique in that its educational history includes as law and public policy the systematic, long-term denial of the acquisition of knowledge."[4] Despite this travesty and regardless of the parameters placed on what Blacks could or could not learn, learning has been fundamental to our experience and survival in this country, and it continues to provide a means of upward social mobility.

Personally, education was consistently championed as a means of empowerment and mobility by my parents. My youth consisted of constant reminders, from my parents, about the benefits of education and how it would improve my quality of life. The expectation was for us (my siblings and I) to go to school, at a minimum graduate from high school, and pursue technical school for a trade or college for an associate's or bachelor's degree. The premise being that education was that our security for social mobility (intergenerational mobility)—a life better than that of our parents. Success for our parents and other members in the Black community was vicariously experienced through our level of educational and career achievements.

This phenomenon is rooted in generations of being denied access to education and the collective belief that it provides self-empowerment, self-definition, and community development. It was also a result of my parents, as offspring of sharecroppers, who were only able to go so far educationally due to work responsibilities. However, they knew the benefits education would provide for us in breaking the cycle of poverty and miseducation. Collectively, within my immediate community, the opportunity to receive an education went beyond the indoctrination that took place in plantation-run churches, where we sought liberation through education from a history and pervasive master-slave mentality that attempted to keep Blacks in their place by keeping them uneducated or miseducated.

This chapter will briefly examine the plight of Black students and Black athletes[5] from their humble beginnings at Historically Black Colleges and Universities (HBCUs), to their migration to predominantly White colleges and universities, and the various challenges they face. This chapter seeks to provide a historical context of the sociocultural settings of these predominantly White institutions (PWIs) to assist in the formulation of the plantation model.

★ ★ ★

Historical Black Colleges and Universities

The need for Black colleges and universities was birthed out of the institutional arrangements of Black Codes during the early 1800s and during Jim

Crow segregation in the late 1800s.[6] Coupled with the dominant ideology that Blacks were intellectually inferior, as well as laws that prohibited slaves from being educated, these legal forms of segregation placed significant restrictions on Blacks' economic, political, and educational mobility after the Civil War. However, Blacks' desire to excel in this country prevailed against these racist practices, and Black institutions of higher education became the reservoirs of Black intellectual and athletic genius during the late 1800s and throughout the early 1900s.[7]

The financial support of these institutions varied from being ventures of Freedmen's Societies, Black and White religious groups/denominations (e.g., Christian Methodist Episcopal, African Methodist Episcopal, Presbyterian, Quakers, etc.), to philanthropists and congressional charters. Therefore, the motives for creating these institutions also varied from a sincere desire to educate Blacks in becoming empowered and functional American citizens to being federally mandated due to the Morrill Act in 1890. This legislation produced large land grant institutions and required all Southern and border states to develop separate public Black and White colleges or Blacks would have to be admitted to existing colleges.[8]

There was also variance in the missions of the first Black colleges where the foci ranged from liberal arts institutions, to teacher-training colleges, to colleges and universities with an agricultural and mechanical or technical focus. Despite the different contributors to the establishment of Black colleges, the variance in motives and missions, it is abundantly clear that Black colleges and universities (will be referred to as HBCUs) became the reservoirs of higher education for Blacks, especially since they were denied the opportunity to attend White institutions of higher education, especially in the South.

Although the first HBCUs were formed in the North prior to the Civil War (Cheyney 1837, Lincoln 1854, and Wilberforce 1856), the majority of the 105 HBCUs (private and public, four- and two-year institutions) were located in the following Southern states: Mississippi, Alabama, Georgia, North and South Carolina; this is undoubtedly due to the fact that the majority of the Black population in the United States after the Civil War lived in Southern states. Consequently, HBCUs were scattered throughout the Southwest (e.g., Wiley College and Paul Quinn College), Midwest (e.g., Wilberforce University and Central State University), Northeast (e.g., Lincoln University and Cheyney University), Mid-Atlantic (e.g., Howard University and Bowie State), South (e.g., Grambling State and Tuskegee Institute), and Southeast (e.g., Bethune-Cookman University and Florida A&M University).

U.S. history documents the practice HBCUs have had in nurturing and producing many of the Black intellectuals, inventors, scientists, clergymen, and political leaders in the United States during the nineteenth century. For example, to name a few: Booker T. Washington attended Hampton Normal and Industrial Institute (currently Hampton University and formerly Hampton Institute); Ida B. Wells, W. E. B. Du Bois, and

John Hope Franklin all attended Fisk University; Zora Neale Hurston attended Howard University; Thurgood Marshall graduated from Lincoln University; and Reverend Martin L. King, Jr. attended Morehouse College. The list of alumni from HBCUs is extensive and their local, national, and international contributions are immeasurable. Even after the *Brown v. Board of Education* decision in 1954, the migration of Blacks to predominantly White colleges and universities, and despite the criticism HBCUs incurred of being anachronistic, they remained vital in meeting the educational needs of Black high school graduates throughout the civil rights era.

The Black Athlete and the HBCUs Sporting Experiences

Regarding athletic contributions, HBCUs provided the major avenue, and many times the only avenue, of intercollegiate competition for athletically talented Black high school athletes who sought to prolong their athletic careers and obtain a college education. Although a few Black athletes attended predominantly White colleges and universities in the late 1800s, the majority competed at HBCUs.[9] They competed in a variety of sports, but the dominant sports were initially football, baseball, and basketball; later, tennis, golf, wrestling, and track were popular intercollegiate sports at HBCUs. The sports HBCUs offered often reflected the demands and interests of the Black community as well as mirrored their White counterparts.

The first athletic competition at Black colleges and universities occurred in 1892 in North Carolina where Biddle Memorial Institute (named Biddle University in 1877) defeated Livingston College. Biddle was established in 1867 and named in honor of Mary D. Biddle and Major Henry J. Biddle who donated $1,400 to the institution. The "naming rights" lasted until 1923, when Biddle University's name changed to Johnson C. Smith. Consequently, Livingston College was a product of a group of Black ministers affiliated with the African Methodist Episcopal Zion Church who in 1879 formed Zion Wesley College. The name of the College was changed in 1882 in honor of Dr. David Livingstone.[10]

This inaugural event created athletic competition between HBCUs, where rivalries began to emerge between institutions across the country. This created a need for the development of conferences to oversee and regulate Black intercollegiate athletics and promote academic and athletic excellence. The Central Intercollegiate Athletic Association (CIAA) was formed in 1912, and it was the first of several major conferences formed during the early 1900s.[11] Each conference was layered with premium talent; however, the CIAA was considered the most dominant conference in football and baseball during this period. Despite CIAA dominance, rivalries emerged in a variety of sports among the HBCUs conferences with a variety of teams winning title championships. For example, in baseball, it was schools like Morris Brown, Morehouse, Alcorn A&M, and Virginia Union; in football it was Hampton, Wiley, Morgan, Morehouse, and Tuskegee; in basketball it was Morehouse, Hampton, Alcorn A&M, and Howard; and in track it was Hampton, Bishop, Southern, and Wilberforce.[12] These respective schools dominated certain sports, during the early to mid-1900s.

Black females also began their athletic excellence at HBCUs. Though ideologies about female physical abilities restricted many of their White counterparts and to a certain degree Black females in general, Black females excelled in a variety of sports at HBCUs.[13] Several of the pioneers in women athletics were Black female athletes from HBCUs. For example, Wilma Rudolph, Wyomia Tyus, Willye White, and Mandeline Manning competed for Tennessee State; Althea Gibson attended Florida A&M; Alice Coachman competed for Tuskegee Institute, and the list of other Black female athletes who excelled at HBCUs is extensive. Not only did they receive conference and national honors and awards, but many also represented the United States in international events such as the Olympic and Pan American Games. Unfortunately, their place in sports literature is nominal, but their voice is being resurrected through current sport studies scholars who see the need in examining the experiences of Black female collegiate athletes.[14]

★   ★   ★

This chapter cannot clearly do justice to the extensive contributions Black male and female athletes from HBCUs have made to the professional sports industry as well as professional amateur athletes who represented their country in international athletic competitions (e.g., Olympics, Pan American Games, etc.). For example, the legendary Grambling University coach, Eddie Robinson, has supplied the National Football League (NFL) with over 200 players during his 57-year career; including Super Bowl XXII's most valuable player, Doug Williams. The list of Hall of Famers that competed at HBCUs is also quite extensive. Highlighting the significant contributions of many Black females athletes who competed at HBCUs and how the HBCUs supplied a pipeline of talent to the professional sports industry is beyond the scope of this chapter. Nevertheless, the point to be made is in illustrating the historical role HBCUs played in nurturing Black athletic talent, specifically, and intellectual ability in general.

It is unfortunate, but unless there is a resurgence of Black athletic talent re-migrating back to HBCUs, naysayers' predictions of HBCUs athletic programs remaining mediocre at best appear imminent. Besides the financial challenges facing higher education in general and HBCUs specifically, the athletic infrastructures (stadiums, arenas, athletic training facilities) needed to attract and enroll blue-chip athletes have not fully evolved. The athletic budgets of HBCUs pale in comparison to the athletic budgets of predominantly White National Collegiate

Athletic Association (NCAA) Division I institutions (PWIs). For example, according to the Office of Postsecondary Education 2006–2007 Division I budget figures, Delaware State is the only HBCU that ranked among the top 200 (out of 339 schools), with an operating budget of $17,289,496; while Alcorn State ranks 337 out of 339 schools, with an operating budget of $3,172,348.[15] It is hard to compete for recruits with PWIs that have operating budgets ranging from $46 million to $100 million. Furthermore, it is also difficult to compete with PWIs without increasing commercialization (i.e., corporate sponsorship, media rights sales, sale of licensing products, etc.), which has prompted criticism from the purveyors of academic integrity. Furthermore, as we will see in later chapters, increased commercialization comes at a risk of alienating and exploiting the athlete and threatens the academic integrity and mission of the institution.

The Migration of Black Students to Predominantly White Institutions

Black students have made a major shift from attending traditional Black colleges and universities in the South to attending predominantly White colleges and universities throughout the United States. At the beginning of World War II, only 10 percent of Black college students attended PWIs.[16] As of 1984, 80 percent of Black students in higher education attended PWIs.[17] Currently, according to the *2007 Status on Minorities in Higher Education Report*, this percentage remains fairly consistent with it fluctuating between stagnation and decline.

Blacks' migration to PWIs has provided social mobility for many, but it has occurred at a cost of enduring challenges inherent in the structural arrangements of PWIs. One of the immediate and re-occurring challenges has been with racism. Barry Beckham has described Black students' experiences at PWIs as "Strangers in a Strange Land." In general, he contends that the PWIs environments are inadequate in meeting the needs of these minority students.[18] One of the prevailing reasons for this is the lack of racial awareness, thus, the increase in racial interaction has resulted in an increase in racial tension.

Furthermore, in a seminal piece examining the experiences of Blacks in college, Jacqueline Fleming highlights that racial tension can contribute to attrition, which works as an obstruction to social mobility.[19] Social and cultural isolation are other challenges Blacks have had to contend with at PWIs. The structures of these institutions cannot be ignored when we consider the matriculation and attrition of Black students; especially when they persevere and graduate.

We will see in this section how Black athletes are not above the law or beyond the scope of having a "Black experience" during their tenure at PWIs. Literature documents that though they are segregated within the athletic culture of the institution, the experiences of the Black male athlete are similar in nature with their racial peers. This section will first provide a brief overview of the experiences of Black athletes and Black students at PWIs, and then summarize the major themes of racism, alienation, and racial or social isolation occurring in the literature.

The Experiences of Black Athletes and Black Students and PWIs

Since their great migration to these institutions, Black athletes have received considerable attention. The media and many research studies have mainly highlighted the negative aspects of Black athletes' experiences—attrition and retention problems, and low graduation rates. Unfortunately, most of the attention is placed on the Black athletes' alleged academic pathology. Emphasizing these negative attributes allows critics of college athletics, researchers, college administrators, etc., to conclude that Black athletes are intellectually challenged—mere dumb jocks.

There is limited research that focuses on how the Black athletes' experiences with racism, racial isolation, and alienation may contribute to their academic success and graduation. Researchers and journalists have concentrated on the recruiting, living conditions, and retention and graduation rates of Black athletes. These studies have examined how Black athletes are highly recruited for their athletic talents and have high attrition rates, and low graduation rates.[20]

Several studies that have addressed discrimination in sports and have positional segregation at the collegiate and professional level. This research highlights how race has been a factor in the position an athlete plays. For example, "thinking" and "nonthinking" positions are the categories used to describe positions in certain sports—mainly football, basketball, and baseball. "Thinking" positions (e.g., quarterback, pitcher, and center) are the leadership positions which a disproportionate amount of White athletes occupied during the '60s, '70s, and '80s, when the majority of the data for this research was being collected. Conversely, Blacks occupied the majority of "non-thinking" positions (e.g., running backs, outfielders, forward).[21]

Patricia A. Adler and Peter Adler, in *Backboards & Blackboards: College Athletes and Role Engulfment*, provide an in-depth analysis of the lived experiences of college athletes competing at one of the nation's top 20 institutions.[22] One phenomenon they observed is the inadequate social settings Black athletes encountered on predominantly White campuses, which fostered alienation and social isolation. In their account, racial and socioeconomic barriers separated Black athletes, and cultural and physical differences distinguished them from other students on campus.

Regarding Black students in general, several researchers and journalists have addressed the issues of racism,[23] alienation, and racial isolation on college campuses.[24] According to Fleming, the academic functioning or "intellectual growth" of Blacks on predominantly White university and college campuses is greatly impaired by the stress of racial tension. Fleming refers to these university and college campuses as "unaccepting environments," where the predominantly White college and university environments lack the essential ingredients to provide for the social and academic prosperity of Black students.[25] Therefore, these environments can be considered inadequate social settings that lack the essential support for Black students' academic success.

These inadequate social settings also involve the inability to identify culturally with the predominantly White campus environment; that is, Black culture is relegated to minute parts of the general education curricula, isolated in Black cultural centers, or only recognized during a cultural diversity event, and/or totally repressed. Both terms, *unaccepting environments* and *inadequate social settings*, best capture the institutional setting of PWIs. A further review of literature on the experiences of Black students, in general, at PWIs will help to lay a foundation for the internal colonial model that will be used to explain the relationship these institutions have with Black male athletes, specifically, in revenue-generating sports. Racism will be the first characteristic to be defined and reviewed as a consistent occurrence for Black students at PWIs.

Racism

To set the stage for this section, it is appropriate to provide some parameters by defining race and racism, and then to examine how Black students have had experiences with racism at PWIs. *Race* is defined as both a genetic and sociological construct. As a genetic construct, race is used to classify people who have collectively similar gene frequencies, and differ consistently from other racial groups. Historically, anthropologists have used three major racial categories to classify human species: the Caucasoid, the Mongoloid, and the Negroid. The Caucasoid are people of European descent. The Mongoloid race includes people with racial heritage from East Asia and the indigenous peoples of the Americas. Finally, the Negroid are people of African descent, especially south of the Sahara. Each racial group shares similar gene frequencies, which are ultimately expressed in various phenotypes: for example, Caucasoids have pale reddish-white to olive-brown skin color, light blond to dark brown hair, light blue to dark brown eyes, and a high bridge nose; the Mongoloid skin color is saffron to yellow or reddish brown, dark, straight, and coarse hair, their eyes are black to dark brown, and a low to medium nose bridge; finally, the Negroid skin color is brown to brown-black, hair is dark and coarse, eyes are dark, and the nose bridge low with broad nostrils.[26]

In U.S. history, race has been a controversial term. Due to the conflicting scientific data that have sought to define race as a biological construct, race as a social construction has gained validity in the context of this country. Therefore, race as a sociological construct suggests that there are certain phenotypical differences (mainly skin color) that are used to justify and rationalize the unequal treatment of groups of people based on these differences and because of these differences. Thus, the collective experience of Blacks in this country is a racialized experience; layered with racism or racist practices.

To be a racist has both positive and negative connotations. In the positive sense, a racist is a person that simply prefers his/her respective race. Racists prefer to marry within their race, live among members of their race, and attend social functions with members of their racial group. In the negative sense, a racist is a person who thinks their race is superior and all other racial groups are inferior, for example, they prefer to live among themselves because of their hatred toward other racial groups; they also prefer to marry within their race because racial mixing or miscegenation reduces their biological quality.[27] The latter has been the most divisive and destructive, and has produced the practice of racism. Within the framework of this book, racism is the local and global power system structured and maintained by persons who classify themselves as Whites to oppress and exploit people of color.[28] Furthermore, it is an ideological system and a behavior dynamic exercised by Whites, specifically, which discriminates based on race and maintains a system of supremacy—*White supremacy*.

The significance of race has been called into question as the United States attempts to embrace its cultural and racial diversity. For example, William Julius Wilson asserts in *The Declining Significance of Race: Blacks and Changing American Institutions* that economic class position trumps race. He states that:

> Race relations in America have undergone fundamental changes in recent years, so much so that now the life chances of individual blacks have more to do with their economic class position than with their day-to-day encounters with whites.[29]

Unfortunately, within higher education race maintains a level of significance and racism remains an annoying occurrence.[30] A recent example illustrating how race and gender are very much significant was expressed by MSNBC syndicated radio host of *Imus in the Morning*—Don Imus. Mr. Imus' description of the University of Rutgers' women basketball players as "Nappy-Headed Hos" speaks to the image the dominant American psyche has ascribed to Black female athletes, specifically, and Black women, in general. These comments demonstrate the significance of race and the persistence of racism naively perpetrated toward Blacks in the United States. Therefore, race and racism, as it relates to Black students, warrants further investigation. Two forms of racism that are common to our society and adversely affect Black students are institutional racism and cultural racism. These will now be discussed.

ɔure (formerly Stokely Carmichael) and Charles V. Hamilton r: *The Politics of Liberation in America* suggests that institutional .. originates in the operations of established and respected forces in society.[31] It is a covert form of racism that is subtle and less identifiable in terms of specific individuals committing the acts; unlike overt racism where there are blatant verbal or physical racial attacks.

The institutional arrangements and practices of the educational system in this country have maintained, to a significant degree, racist institutional policies when it has "determined what is considered knowledge, how it is to be transmitted to new generations, and who will do the teaching."[32] Furthermore, higher education is an institution that has policies that fall within the category of institutional racism. These practices are racist, and although they may be unintentional, they are subtle acts that deny opportunity, oppress, and exploit individuals. Examples of this are the various college admission tests (SAT or ACT), which discriminate against Black students because they are designed to test ability in the context of White society, and have been considered insufficient predictors of success in college.[33]

A 1994 speech given by Francis L. Lawrence, president of Rutgers University, demonstrates how racism prevails at institutions of higher education. In a faculty senate meeting, he naively stated that

> The average S.A.T.'s for African-Americans is 750. Do we set standards in the future so we don't admit anybody? Or do we deal with a disadvantaged population that doesn't have that genetic, hereditary background to have a higher average?

His comments ignited student protest and national exposure and criticism. However, after admitting that his comments were a "verbal slip," and making a public apology, the governing board of Rutgers University reiterated their support for the continual service of President Lawrence.

Regarding cultural racism within the context of higher education, it is also an institutionalized form of racism. In a broad sense, cultural racism occurs when a society's cultural prescriptions are of a dominant group (in this case Whites of European descent) and are predicated on a set of values and a sense of history that places other groups (Black Americans and all people of color in general) at a fundamental disadvantage.[34] Education, specifically higher education in America, has always been centered around and supportive of the dominant White culture. To remedy this distortion, a multicultural curriculum in the U.S. educational system has gained increasing support.[35]

Multiculturalism is an awareness that we live in a culturally diverse society. Multiculturalism in education is an effort toward ameliorating cultural racism by releasing the educational system, and eventually our social system, from its monocultural prison and opening it up to the liberating influences of other cultural perspectives.[36] Despite the objectives of multiculturalism, it has not fully materialized. Thus, the prescriptions of the White culture is the norm at PWIs; it is institutionalized and undoubtedly informs us of what is considered significant and what is to be valued. Within this framework, all other cultures are therefore of minor significance and are of less value in the process of education.

It is important to note that both Black students and Black athletes experience institutional and cultural racism, and regardless of class or athletic status, neither are immune to the racism that exists on predominantly White campuses. At first glance, it would appear that Black athletes would benefit from preferential treatment and experience less racism than Black students (nonathletes) because of their celebrity status and high degree of visibility by the media (print and electronic) as athletes around campus. However, Black athletes have suffered overt forms of racism ranging from being called nigger on campus to being told to sit on the back of the team bus by White teammates.[37] The defamatory remarks and other racial actions are similar to situations that constantly plagued Black nonathletes on predominantly White college and university campuses. Furthermore, the perception of their intellectual abilities[38] is often called into question and presents opportunities for racist assumptions. The fact that they are herded into remedial classes and clustered into majors that are of little interest to them, but have been proven to assist them in maintaining eligibility, are institutional racist practices.[39]

Therefore, in many cases it did not matter how many points they scored, how many yards they ran, how much publicity they received in the local or national media, they were still Black and subject to having a "Black experience."[40] I find it rather ironic, but not surprising, that Black athletes must struggle with the various forms of racism at predominantly White colleges and universities, because every fall and early spring semester they are athletic ambassadors representing these institutions nationally and in some cases internationally.

Institutional and cultural racism are those unseen forces that all Black students and other people of color must continuously work against in order to succeed on these campuses, and in this society. The overt racist acts that I have experienced were not as devastating as the covert acts of not being represented in the curriculum, or having limited representation as students and members of the staff or faculty. Growing up in the South, I had become immune to being called racist names, but I was challenged in adjusting to those forms of racist practices that secretly denied me of my "inalienable rights" as a student, as an American, and as a human being.

Institutional and cultural racism create additional barriers to the academic success of both Black students and Black athletes. Even though they wish to be students with equal opportunity at these institutions of higher education, Black students are constantly reminded of their "twoness" as Blacks and students; and in the case of Black athletes, their "threeness": Black, student, and athlete.[41] In these unaccepting environments, racism in all forms constantly reminds Blacks of "our place" in society. It can also produce other challenges for Black athletes such as, alienation, and voluntary and involuntary social and racial isolation.

Alienation, or estrangement from the dominant group, can develop as a shield to protect Black students from these two unreconciled strivings.[42] It can also be enforced due to the structure and settings of these environments. Therefore, the next topics to be addressed in this historical overview are invisibility, alienation, and social and racial isolation and how Black students and Black athletes experience these on predominantly White campuses.

Invisibility, Alienation, and Social and Racial Isolation

Ralph Ellison best captures the experience many Blacks have encountered at PWIs. In the prologue to *Invisible Man*, he poetically conceptualizes the experiences of invisibility, which fosters alienation and social and racial isolation. He states:

> I am an invisible man. No, I am not a spook like those who haunted Edgar Allan Poe; nor am I one of your Hollywood-movie ectoplasms. I am a man of substance, of flesh and bone, fiber and liquids—and I might even be said to possess a mind. I am invisible, understand, simply because people refuse to see me. Like the bodiless heads you see sometimes in circus sideshows, it is as though I have been surrounded by mirrors of hard, distorting glass. When they approach me they see only my surroundings, themselves, or figments of their imagination—indeed, everything and anything except me.
>
> Nor is my invisibility exactly a matter of biochemical accident to my epidermis. That invisibility to which I refer occurs because of a peculiar disposition of the eyes of those with whom I come in contact. A matter of the construction of their inner eyes, those eyes with which they look through their physical eyes upon reality. I am not complaining nor am I protesting either. It is sometimes advantageous to be unseen, although it is most often rather wearing on the nerves. Then too, you are constantly being bumped against by those of poor vision. Or again, you often doubt if you really exist. You wonder whether you aren't simply a phantom in other people's minds. Say, a figure in a nightmare, which the sleeper tries with all his strength to destroy.[43]

The small percentages of Black students and Black athletes on predominantly White campuses often results in a condition of not only invisibility but also hyper-visibility: they are easily noticed in classrooms and throughout the campus. The incongruity of this hyper-visibility is that it renders all Black students invisible on predominantly White campuses. Therefore, although they are easily noticed when they attend class or absent from class, they are invisible because people refuse to see them for who they are; they are mere figments of others' imagination. The invisibility and hyper-invisibility dilemma suggest that they are so visibly noticed that their true identity of being intellectually equal is invisible; they are simply minority, affirmative action, or special admits. Their invisibility derives from the fact that PWIs are microcosms of the "American World," which W. E. B. Du Bois describes as "a world which yields him no true self-conscious, but only lets him see himself through the revelation of the other world."[44] Often, this invisibility is internalized producing voluntary isolation.

This invisibility becomes greater for Black athletes when they are of no service to the school. Sport sociologist, George Sage, states that:

> When their [Black athletes] eligibility has been used up or they become academically ineligible to compete for the team, they are discarded and ignored by the coaches who recruited them.[45]

If they suffer from injuries that prevent them from competing, they are also rendered invisible to these PWIs' athletic departments.

Another way I have seen this invisibility in action is as a member of an athletic student services department. In the course of my involvement in higher education, I have encountered numerous Black athletes (male and female) dissatisfied with either the classes they were taking or majors they declared. They expressed interest in other areas. However, instead of "bodiless heads" as Ellison described, they were treated as "headless bodies" requiring their academic lives completely orchestrated for them. Many "well-intentioned" academic advisors do not see Black athletes for who they are, instead they see SAT or ACT scores, or some other statistic rather than individuals who have persistence, determination, and are able to work hard and achieve a desired outcome. The noncognitive variables they possess are proven indicators of academic success. Unfortunately, when academic majors are chosen for Black athletes, this is another example of how they are rendered invisible and incapable of making decisions that will affect their educational future.

The invisibility experienced by Black students and Black athletes at predominantly White campuses also exists in the form of alienation, racial and social isolation.[46] Several studies have surveyed students and found that Black and Hispanic students at a California university experience greater alienation and isolation than White students.[47] Similarly, a study of Black and White students at a Midwestern university found that Black students experienced more alienation than their White peers did.[48]

Alienation and isolation have been found to be two of the major predictors of Black student adjustment on predominantly White campuses. The feeling of alienation by Black students and their isolation results in minimal involvement in on-campus activities. Other studies that have investigated Black students' adjustment and achievement also found that alienation and isolation were strong predictors of negative outcomes for Black students.[49]

These studies also suggest that racism or racial tension produces an environment of alienation and isolation. Consequently, alienation and isolation are considered "self-induced" within this type of environment, where Black students choose or are forced to alienate and isolate themselves for comfort, security, and protection from racial tension. "Self-induced" alienation and isolation of Black students is a means of withdrawing into the Black experience.[50]

In a study of Black students on predominantly White campuses in North Carolina, it was concluded that perceptions of racial prejudice result not only in a growing dislike and mistrust of Whites but also in feelings of alienation that arouse a need to seek refuge exclusively among other Black students.[51] It has also been suggested that Black students' feelings of alienation and isolation are a means for them to avoid racial ignorance. Therefore, Black students take refuge with other Blacks to shield themselves from racial prejudices. Thus, self-induced alienation and isolation become mechanisms to remedy them from the ills of the hostile environment experienced by Black students on predominantly White campuses.

Another form of alienation and isolation that exists for the Blacks on predominantly White campuses occurs between Black students and Black athletes. A study cited in *The Chronicle of Higher Education*, found that enrolling a higher percentage of Black athletes and a lower percentage of Black students results in alienation and isolation; thus, Black athletes are more likely to alienate and isolate themselves (by choice or necessity) from the student body.[52] William Rhoden, a journalist for the *New York Times*, interviewed Black students and Black athletes at several PWIs across the country and found that many athletes retreat into their athletic communities.[53] According to Rhoden, many schools with major revenue-earning athletic programs increase the alienation of Black athletes by sequestering them in athletic dorms. He further states that, "Athletes, with a team-oriented mentality to begin with, often become a self-contained social unit."[54] This appears to be an experience common to both Black and White student athletes, and one remedy the NCAA implemented was in abolishing the concept of "athletic" dorms in 1996.[55] This has removed the physical barriers of alienation and mainstreamed athletes into the larger student body housing, but it did not remove the team-oriented mentality that exists among student athletes, which also contributes to self-induced alienation and isolation.

Furthermore, social and racial isolation could be products of the recruitment process Black athletes go through. Another historical account by Jack Olsen illustrates how Black athletes are:

> Recruited into a society for which he [or she] has no cultural or educational preparation, and isolated by its unwritten codes, the typical

Negro athlete discovers an immense gap between himself [herself] and the college community.[56]

The fact that this statement was written over 40 years ago, speaks to the issue of how some Black athletes recruited by these institutions were from families where few, if any, members had attended college. Therefore, they lack the social and cultural background and the educational preparation that are specific for the community they are entering. However, today, in spite of culturally diversifying PWIs, Black students and Black athletes are still entering environments that are distinctly different socially and culturally from their social and cultural backgrounds.

★ ★ ★

This brief review of literature illustrates the challenges Black students, in general, have faced at PWIs. It informs of how both Black students and Black athletes experience alienation, and racial and social isolation at PWIs. Either they are invisible, displaced property on predominantly White campuses, or their social isolation and alienation cause them to experience predominantly White campuses passively. Black athletes are not immune to these experiences, despite the publicity they receive and the exposure they provide. In either case, attrition rates increase for Black students and Black athletes, unless they learn to merge the different identities into one or assimilate into the dominant culture, or unless these institutions expand the educational experience by creating a much more inclusive environment that will embrace and implement diverse cultural perspectives, learning styles, and broader measures of assessing achievement.

Education should be a process where Black students are able to merge their identities without losing either of their identities. For the Black athlete, obtaining a college education by way of an athletic scholarship should be a balanced exchange. However, this hope has been too often unfulfilled, and this balanced exchange has not been sufficiently realized for many Black athletes. For a large percentage of Black male athletes who do not graduate or make it to the professional level, there is this unequal exchange.[57] From a historical analysis, this unequal exchange appears to be inherent in the White–Black relationship.

In conclusion, this chapter informs us of the structural arrangements of PWIs and the limitations they have had in embracing culturally diverse populations. It is the structural arrangement that racially, culturally, and socially isolate Black athletes, which allows an internal colonial analysis to best capture their existence and relationship with these PWIs.

The internal colonial or plantation model will be discussed as an alternative tool of analysis for examining the experiences of Black athletes at PWIs. In outlining this model, the goal is to develop a conceptual framework that draws upon similarities that exist between colonized individuals and Black athletes, and to connect Black athletes' experiences in a broader social context where the exploitation of the Black body has been a re-occurring theme in U.S. history. Another goal of this model is to inform on discrepancies in structural arrangements and institutional practices where reform is needed to enhance equity in the unequal exchange between Black athletes and PWIs.

CHAPTER TWO

The New Plantation Model: A Conceptual Framework for Diagnosing the Experiences of Black Athletes at Predominantly White NCAA Division I Institutions

What matters is not to know the world but to change it.
—Franz Fanon, *Black Skin, White Masks*

The historical overview provided insight into the experiences Black students and Black athletes have had at Historically Black Colleges and Universities (HBCUs) and their migration to predominantly White institutions (PWIs). Their transition has been met with racial and cultural challenges that continue to create a very segregated experience for many Black students in general, which ultimately affects the quality of their educational experience and overall collegiate tenure. Each semester I am constantly reminded of the racially segregated experiences of Black students. In classrooms, during various events,[1] in the dining hall, and so on, students racially cluster together out of familiarity, common interest, or safety. Although, racial desegregation of PWIs has occurred, racial integration is a reality yet deferred.

To capture the structural arrangements of PWIs as it relates to Black athletes, an internal colonial or plantation model will be constructed. The review of literature to formulate this model would be considered dated under normal research agendas; however, given the scope of this topic, the literature pertinent for the construction of this model was during the period of 1960s–1970s. Chapter 1 provided insight into Black athletes' experiences, which will also be useful in shaping this model. Each component will be discussed to illustrate how internal colonialism is much more than a system of racial oppression, but a system that oppresses and exploits politically, economically, socially, and culturally. Because internal colonialism borrows from colonialism, it will be addressed briefly as a foundation for the internal colonial model.

★   ★   ★

According to Albert Memmi, colonialism is a system for political and economic exploitation.[2] Blauner further suggests that:

> Colonialism traditionally refers to the establishment of domination over a geographically external political unit, most often inhabited by people of different race and culture, where this domination is political and economic, and the colony exists subordinated to and dependent upon the mother country.... Classic colonialism involved the control and exploitation of the majority of a nation by a minority of outsiders.[3]

For Lerone Bennett, "Colonialism is a mass relationship of exploitation based on inequality and contempt and perpetuated by force, cultural repression, and the political ideology of racism."[4] Furthermore, colonialism results in "A systematic negation of the other person and a furious determination to deny that person all attributes of humanity."[5]

Colonialism is often depicted as a group of people relocating into another geographical area where the natives' labor, the land and its natural resources are exploited by the newcomers or colonizers. An example of colonialism is the European colonization of Africa, Asia, and the original territory of the Americas. In these countries, Europeans created a colonial system that politically, economically, and culturally exploited the non-Europeans.[6] Therefore, colonialism is related to a relocation of a people, the colonialist or colonizer, to a new geographical area where the natives of this area are subjugated by these newcomers.

The colonial situation develops when there is political, economic, and racial exploitation *within* a geographical area by one group of people (non-citizens or non-natives) over citizens or natives of that area (e.g., the European and indigenous American situation in North and South America or the colonization of African territories by Europeans).

In order to analyze the conditions of Blacks in the United States, colonialism has been reformulated into the conceptual framework of *internal* or *domestic colonialism*. The conceptual formulation of domestic or internal colonialism has provided several researchers with a framework for analyzing the living conditions of Blacks in America.[7] Bennett further suggests that:

> All colonialism is internal in the sense that control is exercised by people on the scene, whether they represent a distant metropolitan power or a metropolitan center within a country's borders.[8]

Examples of this in the United States are the ghettoization of Black people and the "reservationization" of Native Americans by colonialists who are "on the scene." In addition, the case in Ghana, where the British colonialists operate out of a key city or location within the colonized territory, is an example of internal colonialism. Colonialism is generally considered to exist when control and exploitation of a native majority is performed by a minority of outsiders, whereas, internal colonialism involves the oppression of people who are either transplanted or original natives, and they are a numerical minority in the land; the majority is the dominant group.[9]

The fundamental element of internal colonialism is group relations within a society, not the mother country/colony separation in geography.[10] Thus, the relationship White Americans have with Black Americans is an internal colonial relationship that does not involve Whites colonizing a territory that was predominantly Black. Two ways in which Blacks have been and continue to be internally colonized are slavery and ghettoization.

In conclusion, colonialism and internal colonialism have two common elements: (1) There is a power relationship between the colonized and the colonizer, and this relationship is a continual reciprocity (e.g., the colonized exist because of the colonizer and the colonizer exists because of the colonized); (2) There are common elements of exploitation—political, economic, and racial exploitation.

The difference between colonialism and internal colonialism is the external–internal relationship between the colonizer and colonized, which either includes a "minority rule over majority" or "majority rule over minority" system. With colonialism, emphasis is placed on the external–internal relationship of a minority colonizer moving in, controlling, and exploiting the majority colonized. Internal colonialism exists where a minority, indigenous or transplanted, is subjugated and exploited by the dominant majority colonizer.

Another difference between colonialism and internal colonialism is the use of force or violence. Colonization often begins with the use of forced upon involuntary entry.[11] According to Bennett, the colonizer establishes domination over the colonized through violence, "mystification, administration, and coercion."[12] With internal colonialism, the show of force is not necessary because the system of dominance is already in place. After colonization has been established by force, it is the threat or the potential use of force, legislative and judicial powers, cultural repression, and the miseducation of the colonized that institutionalizes and maintains the colonial situation.[13] Therefore, violence is more fundamental in colonialism than in internal colonialism; a *threat* of violence is mainly used with internal colonialism or the fact that the internal colonizers have at their disposal some means of enforcing their system of dominance.

The term *internal colonialism* will be used to describe the structural arrangements of PWIs and the experiences of Black athletes. The college and university campuses function as a smaller power structure, within a greater power structure, with their own system of administration, law enforcement or security guards, and so on. The way these institutions are structured must be considered when examining the adverse experiences, including low academic success, which Black athletes encounter. The internal colonial model will best capture the campus environments because of the unique relationship Black athletes have with PWIs. We will now outline the components of the internal colonial model, which will be used to gain a better understanding of this relationship and analyze Black athletes' experiences at PWIs.

Components of Internal Colonialism

To expand further on internal colonialism and to develop a thorough framework for examining the situation of Black athletes, the following components of internal colonialism will be addressed: the relationship between the colonizer and the colonized, the economic motives of this relationship, the function of race, and the political aspects associated with this arrangement. The first component to discuss is the relationship between the colonizer and the colonized. It is a unique situation and the foundation upon which the system is established.

The Colonizer and the Colonized

Memmi labels the mutual dependence between the colonizer and colonized as the colonial relationship.[14] This relationship binds the colonizer and the colonized together and is essential to the colonial situation. The colonial situation stresses the structural interdependence of the metropolis and the colony and serves as a setting for an analysis of the interdependence of the colonizer and the colonized.[15] Similarly, the internal colonial setting also stresses the structural interdependence between the colonizer and the colonized.

Within the internal colonial situation, the colonizer brings the colonized into existence; by initiating the relationship of mutual interdependence. The colonizer is illegitimately privileged because of usurpation, that is, the colonizer's property and privileges are directly and illegitimately based on the exploitation and pauperization of the colonized.[16] Internal colonialism is made to appear legitimate through illegitimate activity and behavior. Memmi further describes this relationship when he states:

He [the colonizer] finds himself on one side of a scale, the other side of which bears the colonized man. If his living conditions are high, it is because those of the colonized are low; if he can benefit from plentiful and undemanding labor and servants, it is because the colonized can be exploited at will and are not protected by the laws of the colony; if he can easily obtain administrative positions, it is because they are reserved for him and the colonized are excluded from them; the more freely he breathes, the more the colonized are choked.[17]

Conversely, the colonized is viewed as a savage heathen who must be civilized by the colonizer. Memmi also states that, "It is the colonized that is a wicked and backward person with thievish and sadistic instinct....He is hardly ever considered in a positive light unless it benefits the colonizer (e.g., the colonized are good workers)."[18] Basically, the colonized are dehumanized by the colonizer, have no freedom in defining their status, and can only react to the actions of the colonizer. Thus, the colonial situation, from the colonizer's perspective, is an extreme benefit for the evolution and moral development of the colonized.

The relationship between the colonizer and the colonized does not merely exist physically as the oppressor and the oppressed. On the contrary, at the psychological level, the colonizer must believe that his/her position is legitimate while the colonized must accept his/her position. Memmi states that:

> The bond between the colonizer and the colonized is thus destructive and creative. It destroys and re-creates the two partners of colonization into colonizer and colonized. One is disfigured into an oppressor, a partial, unpatriotic and treacherous being, worrying only about his privileges and their defense; the other, into an oppressed creature, whose development is broken and who compromises by his defeat. Just as the colonizer is tempted to accept his part, the colonized is forced to accept being colonized.[19]

★   ★   ★

In the case of Black athletes and PWIs, a similar internal colonial relationship of interdependence exists. Desegregation affected HBCUs' ability to grow and develop athletic infrastructures that nurture and utilize Black athletic talent at the same commercial level as their peer PWIs. Therefore, desegregation was pivotal in assisting the structural interdependence between PWIs and Black athleticism. To expound further, the intercollegiate athletic departments heavily depend on Black athletic talent to generate revenue for their multimillion dollar athletic budgets. Consequently, the majority of elite Black football and basketball players depend on these athletic departments to purchase their athletic talent, for the opportunity to utilize and perfect their athletic skills, with hopes of obtaining a degree and/or a career as professional athletes. There are a few interscholastic basketball players who are bypassing this dependence and need for intercollegiate athletics and opting to compete in international leagues (this topic will be discussed in a later chapter). However, with the current configuration, there is interdependence between the athletes and institutions that bind them into a relationship of mutual interdependence that is initiated during the recruiting process.[20]

Theoretically, this relationship begins during the recruiting phase or what I refer to as the courting or dating process. This process begins the initial stages of developing this relationship and solidifying some sense of mutual dependence, while concurrently detailing the benefits. For example, the recruiting sales pitch is generally, "if you commit to ABC University, you will get a great education and the chance to play in a very competitive conference"; and some programs are taking it to the next level and are indirectly suggesting that they will equip them for the next level. Furthermore, the courting process often involves at least one trip to the university that is used to enhance this relationship, which often further confuses Black athletes about their actual position in this internal colonial situation. From the women involved in this process, the festive events (parties), to the coddling of parents, mixed messages are being disseminated about what exactly is important: academics or athletics. It is one of the most unrealistic experiences a young impressionable athlete can have in making a decision about their athletic and educational future.

Once upon a time, this recruiting and dating process began during the junior and senior years of high school. Now, this process is starting earlier where kids who show athletic prowess in peewee leagues are being tracked, tagged, and labeled as potential recruits. For example, top six graders are being evaluated and rated on their basketball prowess, and they are receiving information expressing interest in their abilities from institutions with premiere basketball programs.[21] Some are being asked to relocate from their families to other school districts to play in an interscholastic athletic system that will prescreen, train, and equip them with the necessary athletic skills that will ensure a smooth transition into intercollegiate athletics. Finally, this relationship is made official and nationally publicized during National Signing Days. This is the time when seniors officially sign letters of intent to play for the college of their choice. National Signing Days have become televised spectacles, which involve local celebrations across this country.

The relationship between the colonizer and the colonized determines their parameters and contacts and ultimately sets the stage for the colonial situation. It will be examined again in later chapters because it is significant and undergirds other components in the internal colonial model. Why this relationship is established and how it is maintained will be addressed when the following components are discussed: economics, politics, and racism.

Economics

Economics is the main purpose or function in the internal colonial situation. There is no other reason for the relationship to exist between the colonizer and the colonized except for the economic motives of the colonizer. Historically, colonialism existed for the sole purpose of enriching the lives of the colonizers. Colonialism, according to Kwame Nkrumah, is "the policy by which a foreign power binds territories to herself by political ties with the primary object of promoting her own economic advantage."[22] Furthermore, Carmichael and Hamilton give an example of how colonization in Africa, was used to obtain raw materials and natural resources that were finished and sold at markets to benefit the "mother country."[23] Consequently, in North and South America, the Caribbean, Asia, and Africa, slavery was an internal colonial institution that was used to increase the economic status of the slave master—the colonizer.[24] Thus, the internal colonial situation is a mechanism that dispossesses the colonized of their material resources and/or it is a means of obtaining cheap labor, where the colonizer benefits by exploiting colonized people's physicality.

The other side of economics in an internal colonial situation is the dependency of the colonized on the colonizer.[25] The internal colonial situation breeds economic success and security for the colonizer, but for the colonized only economic dependency. An example of this is described by Kenneth Clarke when he demonstrated how economics plays a role in the internal colonial situation of the ghetto:

> The ghetto feeds upon itself: it does not produce goods or contribute to the prosperity of the city. It has few large businesses.... In general, a ghetto does not produce goods of lasting worth. Its products are used up and replaced like the unproductive lives of so many of its people.
>
> Even though the White community has tried to keep the Negro confined in ghetto pockets, the White businessman has not stayed out of the ghetto. A ghetto, too, offers opportunity for profit, and in a competitive society profit is to be made where it can.[26]

Therefore, not only are the colonized exploited economically but they also become economically dependent on the colonizer. Here again, the relationship between the colonized and the colonizer is illustrated and the mutual interdependence between the two is evident. We will see that this condition is applicable to the experiences of Black athletes. They are economically dependent on these institutions to fulfill their athletic and academic goals because the Black communities they grew up in cannot fulfill these goals (i.e., besides the historically Black colleges and universities, Black communities have yet to create institutions sufficient in taking full advantage of the athletic talents it nurtures).

Now, regarding the governance and decision-making process in the colonial situation, the political component will be discussed.

Politics

Politics in internal colonialism is the means by which the colonizer rules over the colonized. Generally, political decisions for the colonized are made directly by the colonizer. However, a process of indirect rule or "captive leaders" is also used in the internal colonial situation.[27] Within the internal colonial system of slavery in the United States, slave laws and codes were legislated and enforced to govern this institution. Thus, slaves were politically powerless in making decisions about their lives and livelihood. These decisions were both directly and indirectly made for the slaves by the slave masters (e.g., when to work, when to stop working, where to live, when to eat, etc.). Slaves had no voice in their destinies; their very lives were at the discretion of the slave masters.

The process of indirect rule has been a useful tool in the politics of the internal colonial situation. Basically, indirect rule is a system where the dominant group rules the subordinate with leaders from the subordinate group; these leaders answer to the leaders of the dominant group. It was first recognized in colonial Africa and later in the United States. Kilson defined indirect rule as:

> The method of local colonial administration through the agency of Chiefs who exercise executive authority. It was applied in one form or another throughout British colonial Africa and was, from the standpoint of the metropolitan power's budget, a form of colonialism-on-the-cheap.[28]

In the United States during the 1960s, Carmichael and Hamilton stated that, "The White power structure rules the Black community through local Black leaders who are responsive to the White leaders."[29] In other words, the internal colonial situation's political system creates "token Black leadership." Black leaders are often handpicked by the White power structure and placed in positions where the White establishment can indirectly rule the Black masses. Therefore, these Black leaders are merely puppets and the puppeteer is the White establishment. In this scenario, the puppet is powerless and can move only at the will of the puppeteer. This is the condition of indirect rule in the internal colonial situation.

Another description of indirect rule is the process of co-optation. This process occurs when Black leaders start out as strong advocates for the race but later become co-opted by the White establishment; this co-optation is accomplished because the Black leaders are in economic need of the White establishment. In addition, Carmichael and Hamilton provide an example of co-optation:

> Before Congressman William O. Dawson (a Black congressman from the predominantly Black First Congressional District of Southside Chicago) was co-opted by the White machine, he was an outspoken champion of the race. Afterward, he became a tool of the downtown White democratic power structure: the Black community no longer had an effective representative who would articulate and fight to relieve their grievances. Mr. Dawson became assimilated.[30]

A final comment about indirect rule and co-optation is the distance it places between the Black leaders and the Black masses. In internal colonialism, a gap develops between the leadership and the masses where the identity between the two becomes abstract and the legitimacy of the leaders is questioned by the masses.[31] An example of this is offered by Nkrumah:

> In wide areas of East Africa, where there was no developed system of local government which could be used, headmen, or "warrant" chiefs were appointed, usually from noble families. They were so closely tied up with the colonial power that many Africans thought chiefs were an invention of the British.[32]

Another example is the overseer in the slave system. The plantation overseer or drivers were sometimes slaves who were handpicked or co-opted by slave masters into "leadership" positions. They were used to indirectly rule and manage slaves and ensure productivity.

In conclusion, polity within the internal colonial situation strongly supports the internal colonial establishment: its economic motives and maintenance of the colonizers' superiority over the colonized. The maintenance of the internal colonial power structure and their ability to rule is accomplished through direct and indirect rulership.

Racism

Another component of the colonial situation is racism. Bennett states that, "Racism is a political ideology of racial supremacy supported by or even mandated by the focal institutions of a society."[33] Moreover, Blauner defines racism as:

> A principle of social domination by which a group seen as inferior or different in terms of alleged biological characteristics is exploited, controlled, and oppressed socially and psychically by a superordinate group.[34]

History documents how because of their alleged biological characteristics people of color throughout the world have been subjected to racism by White people. Skin color has been an important marker for identifying people on a group basis. Thus, people are distinguished phenotypically from other people and it is further assumed that people who look different behave differently and are different intellectually and physically. Many times these differences have been framed as some pathology or to mean that these groups are deficient and inferior, both intellectually and biologically.

Other ethnic groups, such as the Jews and the Italians, because of their White skin, have been able to integrate more easily into the White society than have Blacks; especially in the United States. People of color, especially Blacks, have not had this success because they are easily identified everywhere and at any time by their outward appearance. Within the internal colonial situation, not only are Blacks slaves to the ideas others have but they are prisoners of their own bodies.[35] Therefore, the color of skin is a distinguishing factor that regulates racism within the internal colonial situation.

Race and racism within the internal colonial situation are based on more than just the misconception of physical appearances. They are concerned as well with the concerted determination of a White ruling class to keep non-White people and their resources exploitable. Therefore, racism is institutionalized to accomplish this task. Carmichael and Hamilton contend that the colonial relationship between Black people in the United States and the larger (White) society is maintained by institutional racism.[36]

Unlike the personal or individual racism that exists in the colonial situation, where there is an individual act of violence (physical or psychological) against a person because of his/her race, institutional racism involves a pattern of abstract and diffused social practices maintained by the White community against the non-White community. Institutional racism is a group structure that consists of covert acts that receive far less public denunciation than the overt acts of individual racism.[37]

Carmichael and Hamilton summarized both individual and institutional racism by stating that:

Institutional racism relies on the active and pervasive operation of anti-Black attitudes and practices. A sense of superior group position prevails: Whites are "better" than Blacks; therefore, Blacks should be subordinated to Whites. This is a racist attitude and it permeates society on both the individual and institutional level, covertly and overtly.

"Respectable" individuals can absolve themselves from individual blame: they would never plant a bomb in a church; they would never stone a Black family. But they continue to support political officials and institutions that would and do perpetuate institutionally racist policies. Thus acts of overt, individual racism may not typify the society, but institutional racism does—with the support of covert, individual attitudes of racism.[38]

Before we discuss two additional components of the internal colonial model, let me briefly summarize the components of internal colonialism. The relationship of interdependence between the colonized and the colonizer creates an interdependence, where identities are interwoven. The existence of this relationship is due to either the resources possessed by the colonized and desired by the colonizer, and/or because the colonized are a cheap source of labor. The colonized is economically exploited by the colonizer and becomes economically dependent on the colonizer. Again, economics has been considered the main motive for the colonial situation, thus, the existence of this relationship. The next component was politics. Politically, decisions affecting the colonized are made by the colonizer. This is accomplished through direct or indirect rule. Finally, racism was shown to be a catalyst in the maintenance of internal colonialism. Not only is racism practiced on the individual level but it is also an institutional practice that works to subjugate and keep non-Whites and their resources exploitable.

The last sections of this chapter will address two additional components that will complement the internal colonial model: social and cultural components. These components will be explained in the context of the oscillating migrant laborers. The Black communities Black athletes originate from are obviously different from the social and cultural structures of PWIs—the internal colonial settings. This view of Black athletes as oscillating migrant laborers will help further emphasize the dynamics of other components in the internal colonial model as well as add two additional components—social and cultural—to the internal colonial model.

Black Athletes and the Pattern of Oscillating
Migrant Laborers

A dramatic scene in the movie *The Program* shows a Black football player, Alvin Mack, giving his mother a door-knocker for a Christmas present, and telling her that he will buy her the house for the knocker when he becomes a professional football player. Unfortunately, an injury ended his collegiate career and the chance of him buying the house for his mother. Two important points to make regarding Mack's experience and desire is that he saw athletics as a means to a better life and apparently it was a lifestyle that his immediate family or community could not provide. Thus, he had to migrate to Eastern State University to sell his athletic talents, fulfill his dreams, and make good on the promise he made to his mother.

The opportunities of becoming socially mobile and providing for family are common goals for many Black athletes. A college education is one way Black athletes can assist their families and communities. Another opportunity for providing assistance would be to make it to the pros. The economically challenging conditions a significant percentage of Black athletes come from in some ways force them to use their athletic talents in hopes of improving their immediate conditions and the conditions of their families. Because most Black athletes must travel to colleges and universities to use their athletic abilities in exchange for an athletic scholarship (wages) and possibly an education, their relationship with these universities and colleges are similar to the rotation oscillating migrant laborers do between their residence and work locations. This section intends to situate the experiences of Black athletes with the pattern of oscillating migrant laborers to illustrate how this rotation between two distinctively different (socially and culturally) locations can contribute to some of the negative experiences (racial isolation, low graduation rates, exploitation, etc.) Black athletes encounter at PWIs. This process of migration further exacerbates the experiences of Black student athletes at these institutions.

It is important to note that research examining Black athletes at PWIs has taken into consideration the different structural positions they occupy in relation to their counterparts. There are studies that include the stereotypical belief regarding their intellectual inferiority and athletic superiority; the differences in their demographic and academic background; overall college life experiences, mental health issues, and social support, and there are studies that illustrate how the academic performance of Black athletes is lower than that of White athletes once they are on campus.[39] These studies allude to the social and cultural differences Black athletes encounter when they migrate to PWIs.

Oscillating Migrant Laborers

Oscillating migrant laborers are laborers who rotate for various periods of time from a work site residence to a family residence that have two distinct cultural and social settings.[40] Wilson explains that:

> Oscillating migration occurs when men's [*sic*] homes are so far from their work that they cannot commute daily and can not see their families weekly, monthly, yearly or even less frequently.[41]

Wilson further states that during the colonial period around the late 1800s in Kimberley, South Africa:

> The first diggers were oscillating migrants in that they came to the diamond fields for a limited period of time before returning home to Damaraland, Swaziland, the Transkei or wherever they had left their families.[42]

This pattern of oscillating migration was also established in the gold mines on the Witwaterand in South Africa.[43]

According to Stichter:

> As the colonial economy developed, forced and other indirect non-market pressures vastly increased the numbers who participated, voluntarily or involuntarily, in migrant labor.[44]

Taxation (e.g., Hut tax) was one obligation that involuntarily transformed many African people into oscillating migrant laborers.[45] To provide for their families and fulfill different obligations set forth by colonial rule, African people oscillated from their villages to work locations to sell their labor. Philpott describes this as the pattern for migrant laborers where, "migration is perceived as a temporary state, mainly to gain money, which will ultimately result in a return to the home society."[46]

Oscillating migrant laborers enter these work locations fully prepared for labor, that is, their communities have supplied the costs of reproduction for this labor. Therefore, the work location is only responsible to the able working body. The community again assumes responsibility for laborers that are injured and too old to work. The dominant features that make up the pattern for oscillating migrant laborers are: the rotation between work site and home site, the notion of trying to better financial conditions (pay taxes, buy food and clothes) back at home, and the fact that this labor is cheap, that is, the villages assume the greater responsibility for the life of the laborer (bearing the cost of nurturing the skills) but not the benefits.

Using this pattern will highlight the cultural and social challenges Black athletes encounter at predominantly White institutions. Both Stichter and Wilson explained that oscillating migrant laborers rotate from work sites to home residences that have different cultural and social settings. Predominantly White Division I institutions provide a similar situation for Black athletes in that they also experience the rotation between different social and cultural settings. They rotate from their communities' cultural and social settings to those settings of colleges and universities for various periods of time throughout the year to use their athletic talents to receive a scholarship (form wages) with hopes of obtaining an education, and thus a greater chance to assist their families.

For example, after viewing a football team roster of a predominantly White National Collegiate Athletic Association (NCAA) Division I Midwestern university with a 2.4 percent Black enrollment in a state with a Black population of 2.3 percent there were 29 Black athletes on the roster (34 percent of the team) of which 2 were from the state this university was located in, 6 were from other Midwestern states (Ohio, Missouri, and Illinois), 12 were from Southern states (Texas and Florida), 4 were from West Coast states (California mainly), and 5 were from East Coast states (New York and New Jersey); based on their hometown information, all were from urban environments vastly different from the city that housed this institution. Based on the media guides of the teams this institution competed against, this is a typical pattern for these PWIs. This practice is common and the list of predominantly White NCAA Division I institutions (also including Division II and III as they become more commercialized) that have a "pipeline" to the athletic labor pool in Black communities is extensive.

Finally, according to Cicourel, oscillating migrant laborers' experiences are organized around two cultures: their home sites, which include family and friends of similar social and cultural origins; and the work sites that involve social and cultural expression different and unfamiliar to them.[47] Adler and Adler suggest that racial and socioeconomic barriers "leave Black athletes with little in common, culturally, with other students."[48] Therefore, both oscillating migrant laborers and Black athletes operate in this system of dualism best captured by Du Bois's notion of "double consciousness" where there exists a "peculiar sensation... two souls, two thoughts, two unreconciled strivings, two warring ideas in one dark body."[49]

Many Black athletes oscillate to these campuses trying to improve their economic conditions. They face challenges when they arrive at these institutions, similar to those faced by migrant laborers entering different cultural and social settings. Like Alvin Mack, they seek to enrich their lives and the lives of their family through athletic achievement that affords them the opportunity to play professional sports. Their route, especially in the case with football, will require migration to different social and cultural settings that will present socialization and acculturation challenges; at least until these PWIs become more inclusive in their structural configurations.

In summary, the interworking of the components of the internal colonial model creates unique experiences of Black student athletes. From the time of the initial contact between the PWIs and Black student athlete, to the purpose of their presence at these institutions, to finally how the relationship is maintained, we will see how this model can be effective in providing an alternative perspective to the experiences of Black student athletes at PWIs. Table 2.1 further summarizes the components of internal colonialism, highlighting the specific functions of each component.

To conclude, relevant to this discussion is this: the pervasive assumption about Black athletes' intellectual abilities is a racist postulation that requires sufficient attention. This scientific racism contributes to the ideological underpinning of the relationship between the colonized and colonizer, and thus, the internal colonial arrangement—the New Plantation. It is the ideology of the intellectually inferior and physically superior Black athlete that cultivates opposing looks of adulation and "amused contempt and pity."[50]

Table 2.1 Components of the internal colonial model

Components	Dynamics/Functions
Colonizer and the Colonized Relationship	Initiated by the colonizer; mutual interdependence emerges where the colonized and colonizer are bound together through the internal colonial situation. The colonizer's privileges are directly and illegitimately based on the exploitation and pauperization of the colonized.
Economics	The main purpose for internal colonialism is to enrich the lives of the colonizer. The economic success and security of the colonizer exists because of the economic exploitation of the colonized.
Politics	Political decisions for the colonized are made by the colonizer. This process has been maximized by indirect rule. Indirect rule is a system where the colonizer rules the colonized with leaders of the colonized group.
Racism (Individual and Institutional)	Racial (biological) characteristics (skin color, specifically) have been ways that the colonizer identifies, controls, and exploits the colonized. The ability to integrate or assimilate on the part of the colonized is hindered because of their racial differences. Thus, the colonizer is able to maintain this system of exploitation.
Social	Colonized are not a permanent resident, therefore they do not identify with the colonizer's social setting. Colonizer socially isolates the colonized in segregated housing and communities.
Cultural	The colonized are removed from their cultural context. It is suppressed or exterminated by the colonizer in the internal colonial situation.

Source: Albert Memmi, *The Colonizer and the Colonized* (Boston: Beacon Press, 1965); Franz Fanon, *The Wretched of the Earth* (New York: Grove Press, 1963); Franz Fanon, *Black Skin, White Masks* (New York: Grove Weidenfeld, 1967); Stokely Carmichael and Charles V. Hamilton, *Black Power: The Politics of Liberation in America* (New York: Random House, 1967); Robert Blauner, "Internal Colonialism and Ghetto Revolt." *Social Problems* 16, no. 4 (1969).

CHAPTER THREE

Intellectually Inferior and Physically Superior: Racist Ideologies and the Black Athlete

> An ideology, once having taken root in a concrete context, can develop a life of its own and spread to encompass different individuals and groups in different situations that are far removed from the original context in which the ideology developed.
> —Anton L. Allahar, *When Black First Became Worth Less*[1]

A nation's ideology[2] is embedded in its social conventions. These dominant ideas, whether they are about race, gender, class, sexual orientation, and so on, shape the prevailing social order, or the collective consciousness, and ultimately set the course for group and individual behavioral patterns and social interaction. We can contend then that we are both products and consumers of our environment. We are products in that we represent and replicate the ideologies we ingest as consumers. Consequently, behavioral patterns and how we interact with "others" who are different from us is formulated by the knowledge we have consumed and constructed from ideological schemes.

Simply stated, White supremacy is an ideological system that asserts the superiority of Whites over people of color. White skin privilege and the possessive investment in Whiteness are residual benefits and effects of White supremacy.[3] Two prevailing mental constructions that denote White skin privilege and a possessive investment in Whiteness are the historical beliefs about the physical superiority (as it relates to primitive abilities) and the intellectual inferiority of Blacks. It has justified the mistreatment and exploitation of Black people throughout the world: the colonization of African nations, the brutality of slavery, the system of sharecropping, ghettoization, etc, and as I hope to explain, it has been pervasive in the relationship between Black athletes and predominantly White National Collegiate Athletic Association (NCAA) institutions (will be referred to PWIs).[4]

At various times in the United States, institutions have insulated this mental construction to justify patterns of racial inequality, for example, the legal system, religious denominations, and education. Thus, the ideology of the intellectual inferiority (especially) of Blacks has traveled through the annals of U.S. history sustained by legal decisions, theological doctrines, and scientific research; surfacing at times to sustain White skin privilege, supplement the possessive investment in Whiteness, and reinforce this nations' ideology.

An example of the notion of Black intellectual inferiority occurred in October 2007 when eminent biologist and chancellor of Cold Springs Harbor Laboratory on Long Island, James D. Watson, asserted that people of African descent are less intelligent than Whites. The enormity in the impact of this statement is due to the credentials Watson has accumulated and the status he holds in the scientific community, for example, he shares the 1962 Nobel Prize for discovering the double helix structure of DNA; he is the former director of the Human Genome Project, and he has written and lectured extensively on the topic of DNA. Thus, Watson fuels the ideological assumptions and prolongs a nation's belief and adherence to this ideology.

Another example of the persistence of this belief resurfaced in 1994 in *The Bell Curve* authored by Richard Herrnstein and Charles Murray.[5] A major conclusion drawn by Herrnstein and Murray is that:

> Inequality of endowments, including intelligence, is a reality. Trying to pretend that inequality does not really exist has led to disaster. Trying to eradicate inequality with artificially manufactured outcomes has led to disaster. It is time for America once again to try living with inequality, as life is lived: understanding that each human being has strengths and weaknesses, qualities we admire and qualities we do not admire, competencies and incompetencies, assets and debits; that the success of each human life is not measured externally but internally; that all of the rewards we can confer on each other, the most precious is a place as a valued fellow citizen.[6]

This "inequality of endowments" is a euphemism that specifically alludes to dominant historical beliefs about Blacks' intellectual inferiority. This chapter will not attempt to debate this assumption but present how it is pervasive in the structural arrangements and certain institutional practices toward Black athletes. Thus, the intellectual inferiority of Blacks extends beyond an ideology, as a set of dominant ideas, and materializes into institutional practices that Black athletes encounter at PWIs.

★ ★ ★

The role of the mass media (print and electronic including television, radio, magazines, and newspapers) fluctuates within the spectrum of being a lens to celebrate cultural diversity to reinforcing dominant ideologies. The latter has dominated the mass media's portrayal of Blacks to mass audiences.[7] More specifically, the mass media's representation of Blacks, in general, which assists in constructing our understanding of Black athletes, specifically, has given us a limited view of their experiences on predominantly White campuses. It is a perspective that often fuels the racial ideology that Black athletes are intellectually inferior but physically superior because they are specifically recruited for their athletic ability and tolerated as students, or again looked upon in amused contempt. Thus, from signing day to the time they are drafted or their eligibility runs out, the main focus is on their athletic prowess and their academic endeavors, when it is mentioned publicly, it is often their deficiencies that are highlighted (low graduation rates, poor SAT/ACT scores, etc.). There are occasions when Black athletes' academic achievements are highlighted in the media, but it is presented as a freak of nature, an anomaly.

This presentation is a limited view of Black athletes, which positions them as intellectually disadvantaged beings and the institutions of higher learning as the advantaged or superior partner in this relationship. Labeling Black athletes as intellectually inferior is also a limited way of analyzing Black athletes' experiences at predominantly White NCAA Division I institutions (PWIs). Descriptive studies that emphasize the dismal graduation rates, low test (SAT/ACT) scores, and limited academic preparation (such as high school GPAs) prior to entering college are indirect ways of reinforcing the intellectual inferiority of Black athletes ideology; especially when institutional responsibility is rarely mentioned.

Again, this labeling positions these institutions as flawless and without shortcomings. It does not take into consideration the history of Blacks in America, where obstacles existed that have disadvantaged us from educational achievement. We cannot ignore that the cultural bias that is inherent in the SAT/ACT, educational curricula, and how the educational settings provide an advantage to those privileged to the cultural mores similar to the architects of these tests, curricula, and so on, or to those who have reached certain levels of acculturation. Can we overlook the fact that the construction of various aptitude tests are from a certain cultural perspective? Furthermore, relegating Blacks to be intellectually inferior discredits the notion that Blacks have not had access to a Eurocentric education until the late 1800s, and that it was not until the mid-1960s that Blacks received what some might consider "equal" opportunity. In other words, we cannot forget *Plessy v. Ferguson*[8] and believe that *Brown v. Board of Education*[9] made all things equal regarding educational achievement.

Access to equal education remains a quest for many, especially when we examine the U.S. landscape and see gaping disparities in facilities, technological equipment, curricula materials, and etc., between urban, rural, and suburban public schools. The "re-segregation" of public schools must be considered when judging educational achievement levels. Jonathan Kozol's, *Savage Inequalities: Children in America's Schools* captures these disparities and discrepancies that exist in the educating of America's youth.[10] Kozol's account calls into question whether *Brown v. Board of Education* actually put an end to *Plessy v. Ferguson.*

Scientific racism[11] is another reason contributing to the lack of access. For example, this ideology positions Blacks on the lowest rung of the evolutionary ladder, where they are intellectually and emotionally inferior and lack the necessities of surviving in a competitive society. Some of the proponents of this ideology included renowned scholars, scientists, educators, and eugenicists, for example, Sir Francis Galton, August Comte, Lewis Henry Morgan, Samuel George Morton, Herbert Spencer, Arthur Jensen, William B. Shockley, etc. History clearly documents the lifeline of the ideological assumption of Black intellectual inferiority and how policies were created because of it and to support it.[12]

Despite the efforts of W. E. B. Du Bois, Franz Boas, and others, in refuting scientific racist assumptions, this ideology prevails in disguised forms and stereotypical images that have created resistance to Blacks' collective progress. For example, the disproportionate representation of Blacks as athletes compared to students feeds into historical practices where the physicality of the Black body has been valued over the mind.[13] Within this institutional arrangement, Blacks are seen as natural athletes (this also implies that no or very little work is needed to perform as superior athletes); and the only reason they are on these campuses is to play sports. Where Black and athlete have been seen as synonymous, adding student to this description creates a dual identity: the intellectually inferior individual who is not expected to perform as a student and the athletically superior individual who must perform as an athlete.

Although all Black students at PWI may have the Black experience of being racially profiled to be athletes, on numerous accounts, I have had Black male students who do not participate in college sports inform me of how they are consistently racially profiled as an athlete. Personally, even as a graduate student, there were various times when I was racially profiled as an athlete. Some of the Black males I have communicated with have expressed how they have encountered negative experiences such as negative perceptions from faculty members or stereotyped by members of the student body, while others have played the "athlete" card to cash in on social privileges afforded to athletes in a college community.

Within this athletic/academic configuration, oftentimes, when trying to start a conversation, White students, faculty, and staff will make this obvious by innocently and sometimes ignorantly asking, "What sport do you play" or "do you run track, or, you play football, right?" The latter question is the one that amazes me the most because not only have they asked the question but they have assumed an answer as well. This illustrates to me that not only do they make the assumption that you play sports but they have some preconceived notion, whether by race or body type, as to what sport you are supposed to play or played. As scientific racism filters through ways and means of the relationship between Black athletes and PWI, the desire for Black athletes to be accepted and valued on the merits of their intellectual skills instead of their physical prowess is the goal; or at least be able to narrow the gap between their identities of being students and athletes.

Therefore, it is appropriate to look beneath the surface into this complex situation between Black athletes and Division I NCAA institutions where institutional arrangements consistently position Black athletes as intellectually inferior and physically superior. These arrangements have positioned Black athletes in a peculiar situation of duality. W. E. B. Du Bois gives additional insight into this experience of duality when he states in *The Soul of Black Folks*:

> After the Egyptian and the Indian, the Greek and Roman, the Teuton and Mongolian, the Negro is a sort of seventh son, born with a veil, and gifted with second sight in this American World, a world which yields him no true self-consciousness, but only lets him see himself through the revelation of the other world. It is a peculiar sensation this double consciousness, this sense of always looking at one's self through eyes of others, of measuring one's soul by the tape of a world that looks on in amused contempt and pity. One ever feels his twoness, an American, a Negro; two souls, two thoughts, two unreconciled strivings, two warring ideals in one dark body, whose dogged strength alone keeps it from being torn asunder.
>
> The history of the American Negro is the history of this strife, this longing to attain self-conscious manhood, to merge his double self into a better and truer self. In this merging, he wishes neither of the old selves to be lost. He would not Africanize America, for America has too much to teach the world and Africa. He would not bleach his Negro soul in a flood of White Americanism, for he knows that Negro blood has a message for the world. He simply wishes to make it possible for a man to be both Negro and an American, without being cursed and spit upon by his fellows, without having the doors of opportunity closed roughly in his face.[14]

This conceptual framework by Du Bois provides a context that speaks to the issues of Black self-assessment, identity conflict, the racial implication of exclusion because of this "Negro" identity, and the desire to be both and accepted equally. This statement by Du Bois is analogous to the conditions of Black men and women who strive to be both athletes and students at PWI. Being students and athletes at PWI presents a dichotomy; they are "two warring ideals in one dark body." Black athletes, today, are not immune to the historical treatment of their ancestors. Though the treatment may seem better and they may have more privileges and access to more opportunities, the superior physicality of the Black body is an ideology that has been hard to de-institutionalize.

The Physicality of the Black Body

Part of the double consciousness Black athletes have encountered, which has contributed toward the myth of intellectual inferiority and physical superiority, stems from historical images research agendas have used in mainly characterizing Blacks by our physical attributes. We have been labeled as subhuman, legally defined as three-fifths human, represented in the mass media as savage brutes and primates, and disproportionately imprisoned as menaces to society.

Several theories have been employed to support the belief in the inferiority of people of color in general, and Blacks specifically. For example, the Teutonic Origins theory and Social Darwinian theory have contributed to the belief of not only the inferiority of non-White people, but also the superiority of Whites. In the 1600s, Francois Bernier created a hierarchy of physically distinct human beings, ranking Europeans at the top and Africans at the bottom.[15] Furthermore, during the seventeenth and eighteenth centuries, the notion of a "Chain of Being" emerged and became dominant among European intellectuals.[16] The "Chain of Being" started out as a characterization of beings, and was transformed by Carolus Linnaeus (Carl Linnaeus) into a science during the 1730s. Carolus Linnaeus was a Swedish botanist, physician and zoologist, one of the eighteenth century's great naturalists who many called the father of taxonomy. His initial work did not classify the variation between kinds of men, but more so, the arrangement and classification of all living creatures. According to Winthrop D. Jordan in *The White Man's Burden: Historical Origins of Racism in the United States*:

> The Chain of Being, as usually conceived, commenced with inanimate things and ranged upwards through the lowliest forms of life, through the more intelligent animals until it reached man himself; from man it continued upward through the myriad ranks of heavenly creatures until it reached its pinnacle in God.[17]

Apes were considered the first link in the evolution of man; Africans, in this Chain of Being, were considered two links above the apes: one link above orangutans, and several links below Europeans; the European being the link directly below heavenly creatures. This hierarchy not only legitimated chattel slavery in America, but as Jordan suggests:

> It led to a mode of thinking about the basest members of society as primarily and merely physical creatures. It was especially the day-to-day business of commercial slavery, which placed a premium on

the Negro's purely physical qualities. New slaves off the ships were described as "well-fleshed," "strong-limbed," "lusty," "sickly," "robust," "healthy," "scrawny," "unblemished".... The everyday buying and selling and deeding of slaves underscored the fact that Negroes, just like horses, were walking pieces of property.[18]

With slavery, the doctrine of Black inferiority began to take a different shape. It metamorphosed into a dichotomy: intellectually inferiority remained, which adhered to the Chain of Being; and physical superiority began to emerge but only in the context of undeveloped primate or brute strength that required domesticating to make it ideal for the physical demands of slavery and profitable for this institution's maintenance and expansion. This physical superiority remained in the context of the sub-human classification of Blacks. Thus, Blacks were physically superior in their ability to do manual labor, which later emerged as an experiential factor that became one of the explanations for the disproportionate representation and dominance in certain sports. Allegedly, the institution of slavery provided the development of physical abilities that were ultimately transformed into sport performance. According to Jose Parry and Noel Parry:

> Slavery was quintessentially manual labour and represented the model of developed black physique operating under White orders and direction. After slavery, blacks, as members of the manual working class, were caught up in the traditional Western disparagement of manual work. Within the perverted logic of an amalgam of the pseudo-science of eugenics and popular racism, there emerged the extreme notion of the black race as peculiarly fitted for manual labour and, by extension, physical achievement in sport.[19]

The Black body continues to be characterized by its physical attributes, especially in sports. The increased number of Blacks participating in college and professional sports and their success in sports, to a degree, legitimates scientific racists' argument about the physicality of the Black body, and supports the idea that Blacks are superior physically. Explanations for Blacks' success in sports vary from the experiential factors to genetics. Dr. Jay Coakley, distinguished sports sociologist, reviewed the genetic explanations for Blacks success in sports and summarized them into three categories:

1. The bodies of Blacks are proportioned differently than those of Whites. They have longer legs and arms, shorter trunks, less body fat, more slender hips, more tendon and less muscle, a different heel structure, wider calf bones, more slender calf muscles, greater arm circumference, and more of the muscle fibers needed for speed and power and fewer of those needed for endurance.

2. The bodies of Blacks function differently from the bodies of Whites. They mature more rapidly, their lung capacity is lower, they are more likely to have hyperextensibility, that is, to be "double-jointed," they dissipate heat more efficiently, that is they sweat more, they tend to become chilled more easily in cold weather, and they have superior rhythmic abilities.

3. Blacks have a greater psychological capacity to relax and stay physically loose under pressure. They are able to maintain relaxation under stress and remain limber or loose despite the amount of tension.[20]

Some of these genetic assumptions have been revisited by Roger Bannister, a retired neurologist. He suggests that Black athletes have some natural physical advantages over White athletes, specifically sprinters.[21]

Other attempts to explain Blacks' success in sports, in terms of sheer physical ability, were revisited back in the 1989 NBC telecast of "Black Athletes: Fact and Fiction," and has resurfaced in the work of Jon Entine's, *Taboo: Why Blacks Dominate Sports and Why We Are Afraid to Talk about it.* The "Black Athlete: Fact and Fiction" telecast employed geneticists, anthropologists, physiologists, and other researchers to prove that Blacks are innately physically superior. Entine's account is additional evidence that seeks to draw the conclusion that Blacks do have a genetic physical advantage, thus an athletic advantage.

Furthermore, the program reported on tests that measured and compared Black and White athletes' fast-twitch muscle fibers, enzymes, and biochemical levels. The scientists concluded that Black athletes are dominating sports, in general, and basketball, football, and sprinting events in track, in particular, because they possess a higher proportion of fast-twitch muscle fibers and superior enzyme and biochemical levels than Whites. These fast-twitch muscle fibers are supposedly inherent; therefore, Blacks are predisposed to being physically superior.

Another test administered by one of the scientists in this program contrasted the leaping abilities of Black and White college basketball players. Computerized equipment collected data on these players' leaping abilities, which resulted in the following conclusions: jumping ability is genetic; the Black players were better jumpers than the Whites; thus, the "White man's disease" (lack of jumping ability) does exist. The question that surfaced repeatedly in my mind while watching this broadcast is, "How black do you have to be in order to cash in on the gene for fast-twitch muscle fibers or to inherit the jumping gene?" Apparently, miscegenation took place in my ancestral lineage and prevented me from benefitting from these "genetic" predispositions.

Only at the end did this documentary provide an alternative to the notion that Black athletes are physically superior. Dr. Harry Edwards, noted sociologist, presented an opposing view presented during this broadcast suggesting that the physical superiority of Black athletes has evolved through environmental factors and socialization, that is, there is more accessibility to physical expressions (basketball courts, playgrounds, etc.) than intellectual expressions (libraries, museums, etc.) in Black communities.

Crediting Blacks with superior physical ability works to degrade Blacks and minimize our contributions to the growth of this country. This practice has not only justified slavery but also other forms of brutality. For example, D. W. Griffith's, *Birth of a Nation*, (based on Thomas Dixon's, *The Clansman*) took advantage of this belief that Blacks were brutes who were unable to assimilate into American society. Therefore, the terrorist tactics of the Ku Klux Klan were justified and labeled as restoring order to the Southern states.

In the United States, over-emphasizing the physicality of the Black body implies that the Black mind is intellectually inferior. This is a belief that fits well with the assertion of some scholars that Blacks genetically inherited their intellectual inferiority.[22] For example, Galton's theory to support eugenics expressed the belief that intelligence was inherited. Blacks and other minority groups were considered intellectually inferior, thus, eugenics could improve human evolution. This line of inquiry supports the ideals of Blacks as subhumans: again, brute beast—all brawn and no brains.

Furthermore, in conjunction with the belief of Blacks' physical superiority is the Western culture's consignment of premium value to the intellectual or cognitive skills rather than to physical abilities. Noncognitive abilities or physical tasks, such as manual labor, are positioned lower in regards to cognitive and technical skills, such as computer programming, when we examine the economic expenditures and the values placed on each skill. Many of this country's institutions, especially our educational institutions, give precedence to mental abilities over physical abilities. What has ultimately emerged from this inequity in valuing the cognitive over the noncognitive is the ideology of the dumb jock. The "dumb jock" ideology plagues many talented athletes, and for Black athletes, the issue is exacerbated. Dr. Harry Edwards explains that the Black "dumb jock" tragedy affects Black athletes because:

> They must contend, of course, with the connotations and social reverberations of the traditional "dumb jock" caricature; they are burdened also with the insidiously racist implications of the myth of "innate black athletic superiority," and the more blatantly racist stereotype of the "dumb Negro" condemned by racial heritage to intellectual inferiority.[23]

Two proponents who expound this dualist philosophical notion are Jimmy "the Greek" Snyder and Al Campanis. Snyder has stated on national television that Blacks are dominating sports because they are innately physically superior due to breeding practices during slavery. Campanis has also commented on national television that Blacks do not have the intellectual capability to manage a professional team, yet they are physically superior. In other words, both take a dualist approach in explaining the athletic success of Blacks and lack of success in achieving managerial positions in professional sports; from a Western philosophical approach, both Snyder and Campanis proclaim Blacks' physical proficiencies and intellectual deficiencies. It seems an impossible accomplishment for many Whites to hold the possibility that Blacks can be both intellectually and physically equal. Why must we be deficient in one or the other category?

When the notions of Blacks' athletic superiority are coupled with the belief in intellectual inferiority of Blacks, it becomes apparent that Black athletes are not likely to be taken seriously as students. The questions then become, "Are NCAA Division I universities and colleges mainly concerned with how the Black body performs athletically?" and "Do they care about the minds of these students and their academic success?"

Regardless of the academic rules instituted for entrance and eligibility, the cases of universities manipulating these rules to acquire that blue-chip athlete are well documented in the popular press. It is also of little surprise that Black athletes are heavily recruited or mainly recruited, because of their athletic abilities, and token interest, if any, is given to their academic abilities or capabilities. Yet these athletes are penalized (put on academic probation, often with athletic participation suspended) for not performing well academically. Furthermore, it should not be surprising but the highly competitive seasons of these athletes often force them to place academics at a lower priority than athletics. I have witnessed many Black athletes during their active seasons neglect class, class assignments, and projects for the sake of athletics (this was not restricted only to Black athletes, but many White student athletes as well). In my 8 a.m. classes, I have witnessed athletes laboring to try to catch-up on their sleep, which was interrupted by an early morning workout. Unfortunately, I placed a premium on their intellectual abilities and demanded that they stay awake, and informed their teammates to help keep their drowsy teammates attentive.

We have examples at predominantly White NCAA Division I institutions of how the physicality of the Black body has been esteemed over the minds of Black athletes, thus supporting the ideology that Blacks are intellectually inferior but physically superior. These examples illustrate how this ideology has contributed to the development of professional athletes who were illiterate as students (e.g., Dexter Manley, Lloyd Daniels, etc.), or Black athletes with no future in professional sports and limited future in the workforce due to unemployable skills (e.g., Kevin Ross, Fred Buttler, etc.).[24]

I am not insinuating that this illiteracy is mainly the fault of these colleges and universities but it is an example of the continual educational neglect that started prior to their college experiences, and is perpetuated throughout their stay at these institutions. "Social passing," because of athletic abilities and potential, is an unfortunate privilege afforded to many athletes, in general, by junior high and high school teachers and administrators across this country. The temporary glory and short-term benefits of this practice have proven to be detrimental to many Black athletes, specifically. When professional sports is not the end result, the lack of education plays a key role in their ability to be gainfully employed, and diminishes their chances of becoming productive public citizens in their respective communities.

It is rather ironic that Black athletes at PWIs have been cast in this mold of reinforcing historical beliefs, especially given the academic and athletic excellence demonstrated by many of their predecessors. The Black community has produced scholar-athletes who excelled in both academics and athletics during the late 1800s and early 1900s, for example, Moses Fleetwood Walker, Paul Robeson, William Henry Lewis, Fritz Pollard, William Tecumseh, George Jewett, William Arthur Johnson, and many others. They competed at prestigious Northern and Ivy-League schools under racially hostile times, but these athletes graduated with honors and pursued graduate and professional schools; others went on to professional careers as attorneys, educators, and so on; while some participated in professional sports.[25] These Black athletes prevailed against the odds, dominant stereotypes, and physical abuse in their respective sports. I seldom wonder if the unfortunate disconnect between current Black athletes and academic and athletic exploits of their predecessors contributes to keeping them exploitable, or has the shift in their priorities changed so drastically that they are unconsciously fulfilling scientific racist beliefs.

One paradigm shift that has taken place to cause a shift in priorities is where the increase in commercialization of intercollegiate sport has required an increased demand for premium Black athletic talent. Therefore, the focus and priorities have shifted from scholar athletes to commercial athletes, where academics have been given a lower priority in the lives of Black athletes, specifically, and, in general, all athletes in revenue-generating sports, where athletic excellence is required to meet multimillion dollar budget demands. Some of the Black athletes caught in this paradigm shift have benefited athletically by going on and having a successful career in professional sports, while others have been left wanting athletically and academically exploited.

The relationship between Black athletes and PWIs has produced some classic cases, which have reinforced the ideology of the physical superior but intellectually inferior Black athlete. For example, Dexter Manley, former Washington Redskins superstar, is a product of the two warring ideals: a victim of a system that neglected him academically, but exploited him athletically. He graduated from Yates High School in Houston, Texas and attended Oklahoma State for four years as an athlete, not a student. He left Oklahoma State a functional illiterate and had to learn how to read and write while playing professional football. He attended The Lab School of Washington with the determination to improve his reading and writing skills—his life. Manley testified before the U.S. Senate explaining his controversial position as a Black athlete on a college campus. I question whether his bout with drug abuse was a cover-up and a cry for help or was he simply a victim of the negative elements associated with the professional sport culture? In a statement to Tom Friend, Manley expresses the power football had over his life:

> "I'm still living that dream, living that dream," he said. "I missed the life. I grew up, couldn't read or write, so football gave me my personality. Once football was over, I had nothing to live for. Didn't matter if I died."[26]

Fred Buttler is another unfortunate case who was exploited because of his athletic abilities and neglected academically. Buttler was an outstanding high school football player who passed through high school with a C+ average without opening a book. He received a football scholarship from El Camino Junior College despite his third-grade reading level. However, Buttler survived by taking vocational and physical education courses. El Camino Junior College had two outstanding years with Buttler as a cornerback. Thereafter, California State University at Los Angeles recruited Buttler for his athletic superiority, and despite his academic shortcomings, they managed to keep him eligible to compete. However, when Buttler's eligibility ran out, so did the support he received from the faculty and staff. He had no degree and no opportunity for professional football.

Kevin Ross's experience is similar to both Dexter Manley's and Fred Buttler's experiences. Ross graduated from high school in Kansas City, Kansas, similar to Manley, as a functional illiterate. He was recruited by Creighton University. However, Ross scored 9 out of a possible 36 points on the ACT, where the average score for freshmen entering Creighton University was a 23. Although he was denied admission by the university, the athletic department was able to reverse their decision and have Ross admitted as a special admit. Ross played four years of collegiate basketball at Creighton University, similar to Buttler, majoring in eligibility. After his eligibility ran out, he had no offers to play professional basketball, and he lacked the educational skills equivalent to attending four years at a university. Ross enrolled at Westside Preparatory School in Chicago where he took remedial education courses for a year with grade school children. Later Ross sued Creighton for exploiting him as an athlete and allowing him to pass academically while knowing he was illiterate. The case was settled out of court with Ross awarded $30,000 from Creighton.[27]

Finally, another highly publicized example of academic neglect and athletic exploitation that supports the notion of the dumb jock happened with Lloyd Daniels, also known as "Swee' Pea." In, *Swee' Pea and Other Playground Legends: Tales of Drug, Violence, and Basketball*, John Valenti and Ron Neclerio depict the turbulent life of Daniels from the playgrounds of New York City to the Continental Basketball Association.[28] In junior high school, school administrators and teachers assured Daniels that as long as he played well and showed up to school he would receive a passing grade. Lloyd Daniels attended five high schools without receiving a diploma. Despite this academic negligence, Daniels was heavily recruited by major colleges and universities for his athletic abilities. He enrolled at the University of Nevada-Las Vegas (UNLV) where he supposedly made the dean's list before being arrested in a raid of a Las Vegas crack house. He never played a game for UNLV.

There are many other unfortunate situations where major colleges and universities mainly recruit Black athletes to play sports and hopefully stay eligible for four years. With this arrangement, the academic lives of Black athletes are insignificant to many of these intercollegiate athletic programs. Through their athletic participation, Black athletes have been given the charge of creating and maintaining an athletic tradition, as well as, bringing fortune and fame to the school and community while hoping to receive an education in return. Unfortunately, this has been an unbalanced exchange with the Black athletes benefiting far less than the schools.

These cases illustrate the contradictions many Blacks experience in being athletes and students; especially when their athletic abilities are the sole reason they are on these predominantly White college and university campuses. This practice of recruiting Black athletes solely for their athletic talents fuels the idea that Black athletes are intellectually inferior but physically superior.

Is scientific racism as the source of this contradiction an inherent in the relationship between Black athletes and PWI? Are Black athletes "seriously" expected by the campus community (coaches, student-body, administrators, and faculty) to be more than athletes? Or, are Black athletes naive in thinking that they will be considered as legitimate college students? Are Black communities unknowingly supporting this idea of intellectual inferiority and physical superiority by consistently funneling Black youth in the area of sport because of their desire to see them "make it big"? Are the Black communities that bear the burden of developing Black athletic skills co-conspirators in the academic neglect and athletic exploitation of Black athletes?

The answers to these questions will probably vary depending on the person being questioned. However, part of the contradiction stems from our historical experiences in this country. History shows us that our sole purpose for being in this country was for physical labor. We are still looked upon, described, and discussed in regard to our physicality. Did the description of three-fifths human undoubtedly imply that the two-fifths missing related to our intellectual abilities? Basically speaking, since our journey in this country and despite the magnitude of our contributions, we have not been taken seriously as a people with intellectual skills. In other words, intelligent Black athletes are still seen as an anomaly or a novelty.

I was amazed how my college basketball coaches (White) would make spectacles out of Black athletes who performed well academically. Their behavior toward them was probably innocent. However, personally, it made me feel as though I was a freak of nature, a mistake to be both talented athletically and intellectually. Those of us who performed well academically were often highlighted as if we were accomplishing something impossible, or we were doing the unexpected, that is, displaying both physical and intellectual excellence.

Consequently, it is a sad commentary but a necessary dialogue that must address how Black communities have aided in supporting this idea of intellectually inferior and physically superior, especially among Black males. There is a stigma that consistently plagues young Black males who show intellectual promise as opposed to athletic prowess. The research of Dr. John Ogbu and others have demonstrated how young Black males and Black youth, in general, are classified as nerds, bookworms, or "acting White," when they show intellectual potential.[29] There is also the dilemma that Black males who exhibit intellectual potential are classified as effeminate or sissies. The reality of this demonstrates the priorities some have in Black communities. An element of the population in Black communities have unfortunately emphasized the physical development over the intellectual development, which creates a distorted and imbalanced value system around physical and intellectual abilities, as well as, socialization patterns that channel Black males into a limited career path—sport. This is not to say that educational achievement is not valued in Black communities or that the climate in Black communities is anti-intellectual, on the contrary. As stated in the introduction, there has always been a premium placed on education among a large percentage of members in Black communities. However, a prevailing current pulls some toward the belief of Black physical superiority; believing that Black males, specifically, are naturally endowed to be physically superior and should dominate in athletic competition. This has indirectly given misguided allegiance to the ideology that Blacks are intellectually inferior but physically superior.

I have mixed emotions when watching the Black athletic excellence demonstrated in the high school, collegiate, and professional sports. It is good to see a sense of unity in the community providing support, encouraging Black atheletes to be their best, and sometimes demanding athletic excellence, especially among our young Black males. It is rewarding to see Black youth physical expression, where the combination of gross and fine motor skills work in coordination while executing artistic movement against an opponent. However, I have apprehension because of the negative piece to this equation.

For example, for young Black males, competing in athletics is one thing, but when their athletic prowess defines their masculinity, it is a more complex reality. In my community, the young Black males who did not participate in athletic activities were considered "soft"—punks or effeminate. Sport participation allowed me to have some sense of power and the expression of that power over an opponent. Whether it was being able to make a "power move" on a player (i.e., dominating and easily scoring over a defensive player), administering a bone-crushing hit in football, or throwing a batter out in baseball, each provided me with the opportunity to momentarily possess and express power. Sport, then, was a context to express dominance; giving us an opportunity to become men—to be a man (manly) and not a boy. Because we (young and old Black males) have been called and categorized as boys for so long in this country, we have sought various avenues to overthrow this description. One of the ways has been through our sport participation.

Today, this effort to prove our manhood plays out in various forms of rap music and in various styles of sport performances, especially in basketball. The intimidating stare, the in-your-face dunks, or the hardcore messages in rap music are ways for some men to demonstrate power and control. Alternatively, these behavioral manifestations are forms of coping; forms of cool pose.[30] This outward display of masculinity is an unfortunate necessity because America continues to psychologically effeminate Black males, while simultaneously profiting off their physicality.

As for the ideology of the physical superiority and the intellectual inferiority of Black athletes, our desire to use athleticism as the major path for expressing power and control and demonstrating our masculinity inadvertently fuels this belief. It is perpetuated when these institutions mainly recruit Black males for their physicality, exploit it, and fail in providing a quality educational experience for them. As stated earlier, I do not intend to excuse Black athletes from their responsibilities of obtaining an education, but to provide awareness of the challenges they must face in order to succeed at these educational institutions.

This exploitation and miseducation illustrate the continual dehumanization of Blacks by institutions in this society. The dehumanization of Black athletes takes place when these institutions value Blacks more as athletes than as students, especially when output (athletic performance) does not equal input (educational opportunities). This is evident when according to a study of NCAA Division I PWI and HBCUs by the American Institute of Research found that only 31 percent of the Black athletes reported that their coaches encouraged good grades.[31] This is important because coaches have a lot of influence in the lives of student athletes. Because of this influence, coaches have the power to demand academic excellence from student athletes or encourage them to prioritize academics over athletics. One of the trends, which I hope begins to take precedence, is in having coaches' salaries and bonuses connected more to academic progress and graduation than to winning championships and bowl games. Because coaches are hired to win games and get to bowl games and win NCAA championships, this trend will experience considerable inertia.

Yet, in the relationship between Black athletes and PWI, there are those who are resisting academic neglect and refusing to buy into the scientific racist ideologies. An example of where athletics has priority over academics happened at Ohio State University when tailback Robert Smith quit the team because the head and assistant-head coaches, on at least three occasions, pressured him to miss class to attend practice or team meetings.[32] Smith claimed that his physical well-being was of little concern and his education was of less concern to these coaches. It is alarming too but these coaches were doing their job given the context they have to work in and the fact that their livelihood is connected to winning. Therefore, the "Smith-types" are very rare and practically nonexistent.

The risk of being vocal and proactive are often detrimental to the overall well-being of Black athletes; especially if they are seeking to obtain quality playing time and have hopes of making it to the next level. For example, at a Midwestern university, I had frequent discussions with a Black male athlete who knew that he was a threat to the (football) staff—coaches and trainers—because he did not allow them to think for him. He made decisions about not playing with a bruised hamstring, even though the trainers and coaches felt he should play. When it came to academics, he also made his own decisions in reference to his class schedule and the major he desired. Both of these situations, which may seem minor, can cause problems between the player and the administrative (academic support units) and coaching staffs. He was labeled a rebel and "uncoachable" because he made the decisions about himself for himself.

Black athletes are expected to perform superbly in athletics and benefit the PWI they attend. They are not expected to be vocal and proactive in making decisions about their academic future. Although the majoring in eligibility is diminishing slowly, Black athletes have limited educational opportunities in regards to the following: the opportunity to make decisions about degree objectives; and the opportunity to participate in various student organizations (including fraternities) and other campus activities. Many Black athletes I have worked with did not have the time to participate in many extracurricular activities outside of their respective sports. Either their coaches discouraged it or the rigid time structures did not afford them the opportunity to participate. Yes, time demands contribute to some of these limitations, but perception of the intellectually abilities plays a key role in the degree objectives.

The degree programs that Black athletes major in and the classes they take are often chosen for them in order to keep them eligible—majoring in eligibility. The degree programs we witness during televised games are not all programs of interest to many Black athletes. Often times these programs have low or no entrance requirements and limited career opportunities; therefore, Black athletes, specifically, and athletes in revenue-generating sports in general, are clustered into these programs. This next section will examine academic clustering because it works to reinforce the ideology that Black athletes are intellectually inferior but physically superior, which again, has been inherent in the relationship between Black athletes and

PWI, because of preconceived ideas some academic support staff members have about Black athletes.

★ ★ ★

Academic Clustering

Academic clustering among athletes dates back to the turn of the century.[33] *Academic clustering* is best defined as "the grouping or clustering of a disproportionate percentage of athletes into selected majors when compared to the overall university percentage in the same major."[34]

According to Dr. Jay Coakley, academic clustering is evident in specific courses and majors, where athletes in revenue-generating sports, specifically, are overrepresented.[35]

Every televised collegiate sports broadcast provides the public with a snapshot of academic clustering. When athletes are introduced, the following information is generally given: position, height, weight, hometown, and "academic major." If you are not grossly inebriated during these broadcasts, you could notice an interesting pattern of academic clustering. I argue in this section that this practice is part of the structural arrangements that contribute to the ideology of intellectually inferior but physically superior Black athletes. The basic premise is that Black athletes, specifically, and a minority of White athletes in revenue-generating sports, are clustered into majors due to perceived levels of intelligence and as a means to better manage their eligibility. In most cases, the majors, in and of themselves, are legitimate majors that have become holding patterns for athletic departments, and in my personal experience, these majors were not the choice of these athletes but were chosen by default for them. Also, I believe the faculty teaching in these majors are qualified to teach, perform research, and render service for their respective institutions. Therefore, the focus will be more on why athletes, in general, and Black athletes specifically, are over-represented in certain majors.

It is also important to note at the onset that academic clustering is not only associated with intercollegiate athletics. Several areas academic clustering has been noted in are the areas of gifted children, freshmen English composition students, children with behavior disorders, and children challenged with autism.[36] However, the focus of this section will address patterns of academic clustering associated with intercollegiate athletics. The decision for this practice is warranted, because whether it is the athlete or the counselors, the underlying motive speaks to structural arrangements and athletic demands of revenue-generating intercollegiate sports.

To further expound, a perfect example of how this decision is made for the athlete was captured in the *Ann Arbor News* when Rueben Riley, an offensive lineman for the Michigan Wolverines, stated that: "I came into Michigan full of optimism, saying I'm going to do business."[37] Unfortunately, as the article informs:

> Riley finished his Michigan career after the 2006 season; he didn't have his business degree. Instead, he sought a bachelor in general studies, a degree program ignored by Michigan undergraduates on the whole, yet embraced by the school's athletes, especially football players.[38]

Where athletes are clustered, varies from institution to institution. However, the question again is why they are clustered? Rueben Riley is an archetype for many athletes entering universities with specific academic aspirations. Yet, when these aspirations are met with the reality and the demands of competing in major college sports, academic clustering has been a remedy. Riley's experience also highlights incongruence in reality and the perceptions of degree rigor, which again is remedied by academic clustering.

Another example receiving national attention was documented in the *USA Today*, where several athletes expressed disappointment in programs they majored in and graduated with while competing in athletics.[39] A study by *USA Today* surveyed 142 schools (120 Football Bowl Subdivision, FBS, and 22 Division I schools with major men's or women's basketball teams and made these findings:

> 83% of the schools (118 of 142) had at least one team in which at least 25% of the juniors and seniors majored in the same thing. For example, seven of the 19 players on Stanford's baseball team majored in sociology; 34% of the teams (222 of 654) had at least one such cluster of student-athletes; more than half of the clusters are what some analysts refer to as "extreme," in which at least 40% of athletes on a team are in the same major (125 of 235); and all seven of the juniors and seniors on Texas-El Paso's men's basketball team majored in multidisciplinary studies.[40]

Steven Cline, a former defensive lineman for Kansas State University, was one of the athletes who expressed disappointment in majoring in social sciences. According to Cline, his goal in life was to become a veterinarian; however, poor performance in a biology course led advisors to encourage him to consider another major—"an easier path."[41] Marty Tadman, a former Boise State safety and Drew Radovich, a former Southern California offensive lineman both echoed Cline's sentiments of majoring in eligibility instead of pursuing academic careers of interest: Tadman was corralled into communication and Radovich into sociology. Cline best captures their experiences when he states that "Now I look back and say, 'Well, what did I really go to college for? Crap classes you won't use the rest of your life?' Social science is really nothing specific....I was majoring in football."[42]

Majoring in a sport is unfortunately the end result many athletes (both Black and White, male and female) are accomplishing given the demands of athletics. It is these demands that often prevent athletes from pursuing more rigorous academic majors, but, as I have witnessed, for Black athletes, they have been steered away from these majors based on assumptions about their intellectual abilities.

Academic clustering has also received media attention in *The Chronicle of Higher Education*. They noticed that 40 percent of male basketball and football players were enrolled in a less rigorous major called "general studies."[43] A survey by Welch Suggs for, *The Chronicle of Higher Education*, suggests that athletes in intercollegiate athletics are majoring in programs that, "give them plenty of time for practices, weight lifting, and everything else it takes to be a Division I athlete."[44] Unfortunately, these studies have not addressed the issue of race in their examination of academic clustering. The next section will provide an example of academic clustering among athletes detailing race and potential earning salaries of majors.

★   ★   ★

To address academic clustering in certain majors among White and Black football players in intercollegiate athletics over a 20-year period, a major Southern university starting in 1981 and ending in 2001 was examined. Since the average athlete graduates in 5 years, this 20-year period was divided into 5-year increments. Therefore, data was collected from the following years: 1981, 1986, 1991, 1996, and 2001. This study collected data from the following sources: media guides, University Fact Book—Institute of Research & Planning, Academic and Athletic Department Personnel, *Wall Street Journal* (Career Journal), and the *Occupational Outlook Handbook*.

The university where data was collected is located in the Southeast region of the United States and currently has a student body population of around 31,288 students. It offers the following degrees: 19 baccalaureate degrees in 164 major fields, 24 masters degrees in 127 fields, 24 educational specialists degrees, and 4 doctoral degrees in 96 areas in law, pharmacy, and veterinary medicine. This university consists of the following schools and colleges: Arts and Sciences, Law, Agricultural and Environmental Sciences, Pharmacy, Forest Resources, Education, Business, Journalism and Mass Communication, Family and Consumer Sciences, Veterinary Medicine, Social Work, Environment and Design, Graduate School, and Public and International Affairs. This institution is fairly typical in racial demographics, in regard to aspirant PWIs that compete in Division I athletics: 77 percent of the overall student body population is White, 7 percent of the student body population is Black, and the remaining 16 percent consist of ethnic minorities identifying themselves as Hispanic, multiracial, Asian/Pacific Islanders, and Native Americans.

Regarding athletics, the university is a member of the NCAA Division I Southeastern Conference. It offers 9 men's varsity athletics and 11 women's varsity athletics. Further gender demographics of scholarship athletes illustrate that women comprise roughly 40 percent scholarship athletes and men 60 percent. The racial demographics for scholarship athletes are as follows: Black and White males represent 25 percent and 32 percent, respectively, and Black and White females represent 6 percent and 31 percent; Hispanic and nonresident alien males represent 1 percent and 1 percent, respectively, and Hispanic and nonresident alien females represent 1 percent and 3 percent.

To provide an example of the caliber of this athletic department based on revenue, revenue and expenses for the 2006–2007 year were as follows: total revenues were $75,937,460 and total expenses were $61,583,869.[45] During the 2006–2007 year, football generated $59,516,939. Black athletes made up 68 percent of the football team, and during the years examined for academic clustering, the percentage of Black football players ranged from 50 percent to 68 percent.

As stated earlier, the historical patterns of academic clustering among athletes at the collegiate level have been documented in mainstream media and in scholarly research. The focus of this section examines the patterns of clustering among athletes (specifically male athletes) in intercollegiate athletics in the revenue-generating sport of football. More specifically, the major premise is to see the types of academic majors Black athletes on the university football team are majoring in and graduating with compared to their White teammates.

Over the 20-year period, according to the data Black and White athletes have majored in a variety of academic majors. The only major patterns of clustering that were obvious were in 1986, 1991, 1996, and 2001 in the academic majors of Arts and Sciences, Education, and Consumer Economics. In 1986, there were a high percentage of Black and White athletes, 24 percent and 22 percent respectively, majoring in Arts and Sciences[46] (see table 3.1). This equates to 50 percent of Black athletes and 44 percent of the White athletes majoring in Arts and Sciences.

Besides 1986, there were three years that showed a high percentage of Black athletes in the majors of Arts and Sciences, Consumer Economics, and Education: 1991, 1996, and 2001 respectively (see table 3.1). In Arts and Sciences, 26 percent of Black athletes on the team and 47 percent of the Black athletes in 1991, 14 percent of Black athletes on the team and 21 percent of the Black athletes in 1996, and 25 percent of Black athletes on the team and 44 percent of the Black athletes in 2001 majored in these fields. For Consumer Economics, 23 percent of Black athletes on the team and 34 percent of the Black athletes in 1996 majored in this field. For Education, 16 percent of Black athletes on the team and 25 percent of the Black athletes in 2001 majored in this field. To enroll in these three majors, there were no GPA requirements; therefore, students only needed to complete the university score.

Table 3.1 Football roster by majors and race

Major	Number of Black Athletes				Number of White Athletes				GPA Entry Requirements	2001[a] Earning Salary (Median) ($)
	1986	1991	1996	2001	1986	1991	1996	2001		
Arts and Sciences	16	21	11	19	15	0	2	4	Core	28,000
Accounting	0	0	1	0	0	0	0	0	2.6	N/A
Animal Health	0	0	1	0	0	0	0	0	2.7	N/A
Consumer Economics	0	0	18	0	0	0	3	0	Core	N/A
Industrial Arts	5	1	0	0	0	1	0	0	2.5	N/A
Distributive Education	3	1	0	0	3	1	0	0	2.0	N/A
Education	1	1	2	12	0	2	3	7	Core	31,000
Business Education	5	1	1	0	2	1	0	0	2.0	N/A
Biology	0	0	0	0	1	1	1	0	Core	N/A
Sociology	0	0	3	0	0	1	0	0	Core	N/A
Family and Consumer Sciences	0	0	1	3	0	0	0	0	Core	29,000
Math Education	0	0	0	1	0	0	1	0	2.5	27,989
Studio Art	0	0	0	0	0	0	1	0	2.5	N/A
Graphic Art	0	1	0	0	0	0	0	0	2.5	N/A
General Business	0	1	0	2	0	7	6	4	2.4	27,500
Sports Studies	0	0	0	1	0	0	0	4	2.3	21,210
International Business	0	0	0	0	0	0	1	1	2.6	31,963
Housing and Consumer Economics	0	0	1	2	0	0	0	0	Core	20,000
Landscape Architecture	0	0	1	0	0	1	0	0	Core	N/A
Journalism	0	0	0	1	0	0	0	1	2.5	18,930
Business	0	0	0	0	0	1	0	0	2.6	N/A
Pre-Forestry	0	0	0	0	0	0	1	0	2.5	N/A
Recreation and Leisure Studies	1	0	1	0	0	0	1	0	2.0	N/A
Child and Family Development	0	0	4	1	0	0	0	0	2.75	22,330
Speech Communications	0	3	1	0	1	2	1	1	2.0	30,850
Exercise Science	0	0	0	0	0	2	0	0	2.75	N/A
Criminal Justice	0	1	0	0	0	1	0	0	2.5	N/A
Pre-Law	0	0	1	0	0	0	0	0	N/A	N/A
Health and Physical Education	0	0	0	1	0	0	1	0	2.3	26,893
Pre-Medicine	0	1	0	0	0	0	0	1	N/A	N/A
Microbiology	0	0	1	0	0	0	0	1	Formal Application	29,235
Turf Grass Management	0	0	0	0	0	0	0	1	Core	31,500
Marketing	0	0	0	0	2	0	0	0	2.6	N/A
Psychology	0	0	0	1	0	0	0	0	Core	21,900

Continued

Table 3.1   Continued

Major	Number of Black Athletes				Number of White Athletes				GPA Entry Requirements	2001[a] Earning Salary (Median) ($)
	1986	1991	1996	2001	1986	1991	1996	2001		
Marketing Education	0	1	0	0	0	0	0	0	2.0	N/A
Agriculture Economics	0	1	0	0	0	0	0	0	Core	N/A
Agriculture	0	1	0	0	1	0	0	0	2.5	N/A
Agricultural Engineering	0	0	1	1	0	0	0	0	2.5	38,068
Management	0	1	0	0	0	0	1	1	2.6	27,840
Math	0	0	0	0	1	0	0	0	Core	N/A
Finance	0	1	0	0	1	1	0	0	2.6	N/A
Real Estate	0	1	0	0	0	0	1	0	2.6	N/A
Management Information Systems	0	0	1	0	0	0	1	0	2.6	N/A
Social Work	1	2	1	0	0	0	0	0	2.5	N/A
Economics	0	3	0	2	1	2	0	1	2.6	21,000
Art	0	0	0	0	0	1	0	0	2.5	N/A
Geography	0	1	0	0	0	0	0	0	Core	N/A
English	0	0	1	0	0	1	0	0	Core	N/A
Biological Engineer	0	0	1	0	0	0	0	0	2.5	N/A
Political Science	0	0	0	1	0	2	0	0	Core	24,500
Risk Management	0	1	0	0	1	0	0	0	2.6	N/A
Horticulture	0	0	0	0	0	1	0	0	2.5	N/A
History	0	0	0	0	0	0	1	0	Core	N/A

[a]Median potential earning salary is only provided for students majoring in respective fields and graduating in 2001.

Source: Data compiled using university's athletic department media guides.

These four years showed patterns of academic clustering, where one of the years also illustrated a pattern of racial clustering. The only year where there was limited academic clustering was in 1981. In the majors of business and business education, 35 percent of the team majored in these programs: 22 percent were Black athletes, 48 percent were White athletes.

The only year that potential earning salary could be collected was 2001 (see table 3.1). This category showed that, on average, White athletes have the potential to earn $27,221, while Blacks had the potential to earn $24,770, a difference of $2,451. This category may not seem to be a lot until the racial makeup of the team and starters are taking into consideration: Blacks made up 61 percent of the team and 82 percent of the starters were Black (100 percent of the defense is Black and 64 percent of the offense is Black). When considering revenue generated for that year, $12,218,614 (34 percent of total athletic revenue) and $11.4 million is generated by football in the local community, the category of potential earning salary illustrates that Black athletes, though they are the majority of the team and starters, are potentially earning less in comparison to their peers.

★   ★   ★

In summary, the purpose of this section highlights patterns of academic clustering among Black and White athletes in intercollegiate athletics. Academic clustering at this institution became more evident in the later years examined in this study. A higher percentage of academic clustering and racial clustering of athletes in certain majors was present. Also, the potential earning power of White athletes was greater than that for Black athletes.

In conclusion, this chapter presented the ideology that asserts that Blacks are intellectually inferior but physically superior. The pervasiveness of this belief has been sustained by legal decisions, religious doctrine, and scientific research; each one working as propaganda that has operated in legally alienating and religiously demonizing Black people, and systematically theorizing about the lives of Black people. Also, to maintain the stability of this belief, various U.S. institutions have worked at varying times to promote its legitimacy. For example, the institution of religion worked in justifying Blacks' inferiority, thus the colonization of African nations; in the United States, the legal system justified slavery and relegated Blacks to being three-fifths human; and with the likes of the "Bell Curve" hypothesis, members in the institution of higher education have worked to not only diagnose Blacks as intellectually inferior but to also propose that it is inherent.

In sports, the dumb jock belief has functioned to cast a veil over athletes in general, and Black athletes specifically. The dumb jock belief is a means of typecasting and racial profiling that, once internalized, reveals the power that works to set parameters and socially control Black athletes. As mentioned earlier, several athletes have fallen victim to this belief, for example, Dexter Manley and Kevin Ross. Furthermore, this belief has been used to explain the high percentage of Black athletes occupying revenue-generating collegiate sports, and also used to justify their low graduation rates. The idea of the dumb jock has created a level of tolerance and a neglect in responsibilities that has resulted in an unequal exchange between athletic expenditure and education obtainment. With the increase in commercialization of intercollegiate athletics, an even greater gap is created in this exchange.

This practice resembles historical patterns where Blacks have been exploited physically and oppressed mentally; whether during slavery, post–slavery (sharecropping system), or being restricted to entry-level menial task jobs. Blacks have experienced an unequal compensation for the demands placed on their physical abilities, talents, and skills. Intercollegiate athletics proves to be another area where Blacks' physicality, talents, and skills are being under-compensated. Once again, the relationship between the colonized and the colonizer proves profitable to the colonizer.

To provide further insight into this imbalance in the exchange, the next chapter will examine the main reason the colonizer oppresses the colonized—for economic gain.

CHAPTER FOUR
*Operating in the "Black" Financially:
On the Back of the Black Athletic Body*

Slavery rested on the principle of property in man—of one man's appropriation of another's person as well as of the fruits of his labor. By definition and in essence it was a system of class rule, in which some people lived off the labor of others.
—Eugene D. Genovese, *Roll Jordan Roll:
The World the Slaves Made*

Racism expands and contracts within the restrictions established by economic incentives.... The Negro, it is sometimes argued, came into existence and remain inferior so that whites might secure a cheap source of labor.
—Sidney M. Willhelm, *Who Needs the Negro?*

We are now, as were our forebears when they were brought to the New World, objects of barter for those who, while profiting from our existence, deny our humanity.
—Derrick Bell, *Faces at the Bottom of the Well:
The Permanence of Racism*

Capital accumulation is the main purpose for the existence of the internal colonial situation and a significant component in the new plantation model. Historically, colonialism existed for the sole purpose of enriching the lives of the colonizers. In Africa, colonization used free or cheap labor to obtain raw materials and natural resources that were mined, finished, and sold to benefit various European nations. In North and South America, the Caribbean, and Asia it was the internal colonial institution that co-opted the labor and natural resources, which ultimately was used to increase the economic status of the slave masters—the colonizers.[1] Basically, slavery in the plantation system benefited the colonizer and provided them with cheap labor by exploiting the physicality of Black people.

As mentioned in chapter 2, the other side of economics in an internal colonial situation is the dependency of the colonized on the colonizer. The internal colonial situation breeds economic success and security for the colonizer and economic dependency between the colonizer and the colonized. A relationship emerges where the colonized's existence and sustenance is dependent on their connection to the colonizer and the colonizer's economic gain and security is dependent on the colonized. Born out of this arrangement is a mutual dependency, where both parties' purpose determines each's existence, that is, without the motive of economic gain, the colonizer would not need the colonized, nor would there be a need for the colonial situation.

Here again, the relationship between the colonized and the colonizer is illustrated and the mutual dependence between the two is evident. The internal colonial situation of predominantly White National Collegiate Athletic Association (NCAA) Division I institutions (PWIs) present a similar dynamic for Black athletes, where interdependence exists: Black male athletes, specifically, sell their athletic labor in return for an athletic scholarship while these institutions profit generously in return. The exploitation of the Black body is not new to Blacks' experiences in this country for it has consistently provided revenue for the U.S. economy.

The Black Male Body

According to David Eltis,

> The trans-Atlantic slave trade was the largest long-distance coerced movement of people in history and, prior to the mid-nineteenth century, formed the major demographic well-spring for the re-peopling of the Americas following the collapse of the Amerindian population.[2]

It was the trans-Atlantic slave trade that transported the Black body to U.S. plantations for the sole purpose of generating revenue. The Black body was purely a commodity and a natural resource for capital accumulation and expansion for slave ship owners.[3] According to Marcus Rediker in, *The Slave Ship: A Human History*:

> The [slave] ship was thus central to a profound, interrelated set of economic changes essential to the rise of capitalism: the seizure of new lands, the expropriation of millions of people and their redeployment in growing market-oriented sectors of the economy; the mining of gold and silver, the cultivating of tobacco and sugar; the concomitant rise of long-distance commerce; and finally a planned accumulation of wealth and capital beyond anything the world had ever witnessed.[4]

The value of slaves as property also speaks volumes to the premium placed on the Black body. According to David Brion Davis in, *Inhuman Bondage: The Rise and Fall of Slavery in the New World*:

> The slaves' value came to an estimated $3.5 billion in 1806 dollars. That would be about $68.4 billion in 2003 dollars. But a more revealing figure is the fact that the nation's gross national product in 1860 was only about 20 percent above the values of slaves, which means that as a share of today's gross national product, the slaves' value would come to an estimated $9.75 trillion.[5]

We can conclude, based on the redeployment of the Black body, its use in building nations, and its worth in how invaluable it was to the United States, specifically, and Europe, in general. Thus, as a commodity and a source of "unfree" labor during slavery, the Black body helped significantly in contributing to the economic foundation and prosperity of this country and others. Unfortunately, in regards to receiving returns on the labor rendered by the Black body, there has been a grave discrepancy. Even with the minimum subsistence provided by slave owners to insure the productivity of their property, it did not equate to the output or (physical labor) and revenue generated by the Black body.

Since slavery and the post–slavery sharecropping system, this country's need for the Black body has been called into question. The thesis of Professor Willhelm's controversial assessment and indictment of America's racist history, *"Who Needs the Negro,"* contends that technological advancements, in the form of automation, have reduced the need for the Black body, thus, it has transitioned "from the economics of exploitation to economics of uselessness."[6] To further express this nation's attitude toward Blacks, specifically, and the ultimate fate of racist practices, Willhelm poses the question, "Why discriminate when you can eliminate?"[7] Or, as I propose, instead of eliminating, why not (re)create institutions that can undo the economics of uselessness.

Despite Willhelm's disparaging challenge, there are pockets within America that consistently have need of the Black male body, for example, the prison industrial complex remains a profitable economic investment for private investors,[8] and as for the thesis of the new plantation, the intercollegiate athletic industrial complex has emerged as a profitable economic investment that places a demand on Black athletic talent. First, I will provide a brief overview to illustrate how the prison industrial complex has benefited from the exploitation of the criminalized Black body.

Prison Industrial Complex and the Black Body

Once viewed by some as an institution for rehabilitation, the prison system has functioned as an institution that has benefited from Black male labor and presence. For example, in *Worse than Slavery: Parchman Farm and the Ordeal of Jim Crow Justice*, David Oshinsky informs of the profitable system of convict leasing and prison labor.[9] Oshinsky asserts that:

> By the early 1900s, the great bulk of Mississippi's convicted felons had been delivered to Parchman Farm. According to the state penitentiary report of 1917, blacks comprised about 90 percent of the prison population.[10]

Located in the Yazoo-Mississippi Delta, Parchman Farm, also know as Parchman State Penitentiary, was 20,000 acres of Delta plantation that "contained a sawmill, a brickyard, a slaughterhouse, a vegetable canning plant, and two cotton gins."[11]

Oshinsky also highlights data from Proceedings of the Annual Congress of the Prison Association, 1919 showing that:

> The most profitable prison farming on record thus far is in the State of Mississippi...which received in 1918 a net revenue of $825,000....Given it total of 1200 prisoners—and subtracting invalids, cripples, or incompetents—it made a profit over $800 for each working prisoner.[12]

According to Oshinsky,

> Between 1904 and 1970, the prison [Parchman] had housed between 1,800 and 2,500 inmates—the ideal number for a plantation of that size. Between 1970 and 1995, that figure more than tripled, to 6,500 with thousands more expected down the line. Parchman's budget rose to almost $60 million a year.[13]

During the writing of Oshinsky's account, the racial demographics of Parchman's was 70 percent Black, which it had been since the 1930s.[14]

Similarly, another example of the labor exploitation of the Black body is documented by Douglas Blackmon in *Slavery by Another Name: The Re-Enslavement of Black People in America from the Civil War to World War II*. According to Blackmon, from the Civil War until World War II, hundreds of thousands of Black males, specifically, were imprisoned arbitrarily, charged exorbitant fines, required to pay for their own arrests, and when they could not pay (in the majority of the cases), they were forced to work in labor camps.[15] Blackmon documents how Blacks in the Southern states of Alabama, Mississippi, Louisiana, Georgia, Florida, Texas, and North and South Carolina were leased to corporations like U.S. Steel, local farmers and entrepreneurs, lumber camps, and etc., as a source of inexpensive labor. Blackmon's account further purports that revenue generated from this system of neo-slavery equaled tens of millions of dollars that was deposited into the treasuries of these Southern states.

Currently, the prison industrial complex persists as another source of economic exploitation of the Black male body. This fact does not repudiate the criminal activity of many incarcerated Black males but calls to question the disproportionate representation of Black males in prison and the sentencing they receive, which resembles similar practices documented in the aforementioned study by Blackmon. Furthermore, the Sentencing Project,[16] a nonprofit research and advocacy group, has bought attention to the disparity in sentencing of Black males since the "war on drugs movement."

Data from the Sentencing Project illustrates that the United States leads the world in incarceration with 2.1 million people currently in the nation's prisons or jails. Although Blacks make up 12.3 percent of the U.S. population, among the prison population they make up 43.7 percent of the prison population. Consequently, one in eight college-age Black males are either in jail or prison in the United States. At the current rate, predictions indicate that one in three Black males will spend at least a year of their life in prison. In addition, spending for the prison industrial complex in 2007 was $43.9 billion, and in 2008, it is predicted to be over $52 billion.[17] It is also important to note that the privatization of prisons is a $2 billion-a-year industry. According to the Bureau of Justice Statistics and the Sentencing Project, the average annual cost to incarcerate an inmate in a state prison is from $22,650 to $25,000. The business and trend of building more prisons is gaining considerable momentum, especially when reading scores of second, third, and fourth graders are used to predict how many prison beds will be needed to house future inmates.

The prison industrial complex is one example of the exploitability of the Black male body. Before examining the intercollegiate athletics, I will provide a brief outline of the economic arrangements of the plantation system, which require a need for the Black body. The plantation system will provide a historical context and a comparative example of how the Black body has been exploited for labor and, as I intend to illustrate, how within intercollegiate athletics, it continues to be valued as a tool to further capitalist expansion.

Economic Analogy of the Plantation System and Intercollegiate Athletics

Throughout the history of slavery, regardless of its place in the world, it has consisted of unique economic and social arrangements. The "traditional interpretation" of the system of slavery, in the United States specifically, has been contested by several scholars to be unprofitable to the majority of slave owners.[18] According to Eugene D. Genovese, these arguments centered on the following:

A low level of capital accumulation, the planter's propensity to consume luxuries, a shortage of liquid capital aggravated by the steady drain of funds out of the region, the low productivity of slave labor, the need to concentrate on a few staples, the anti-industrial, anti-urban ideology of the dominant planters, the reduction of Southern banking, industry, and commerce to the position of auxiliaries of the plantation economy.[19]

However, Robert Fogel and Stanley L. Engerman assert that slave plantations were vital labor systems that were highly profitable, extremely efficient, and generated more output than "free farms" or farms operated by freedmen.[20] Furthermore, Roger L. Ransom and Richard Sutch suggest that:

American slavery had been a viable economic institution because the value of the slave's labor exceeded the value of the provisions they consumed. The southern slaveowner had been expropriating the entire product of the slaves' labor and in return provided only the food, shelter, and clothing necessary to keep the slaves healthy and hardworking.[21]

Finally, Alfred H. Conrad and John R. Meyer using an economic approach instead of an accounting approach concluded that slavery was profitable to the South, especially in the Cotton Belt region.[22]

Regarding crop production and slave labor, several agricultural crops in Brazil, Spanish America, British and French Caribbean, and the United States, produced the need for slave labor and the Atlantic slave trade. Sugar, indigo, tobacco, and cotton were the major slave crops, of which, sugar or "White Gold" created the greatest demand for slave labor.[23] During the 1700s the majority of the slaves imported during the Atlantic slave trade were shipped to the sugarcane plantations in the Caribbean, Mexico, and Brazil. Yet in the United States, rice and indigo were major sources of riches for South Carolina's planters. But according to Lawrence Goldstone in *Dark Bargain: Slavery, Profits, and the Struggle for the Constitution*:

For a time, indigo complemented and briefly outstripped rice as a source of riches for the planters, but rice was king. And the engine for both crops was slaves.[24]

Goldstone further notes that:

Rice only began to be profitable when an army of blacks was imported from Africa and the planters switched from dry land planting to damming the freshwater swamps that dotted the land near the coast. Rawlins Lowndes knew from whence he spoke when he declared, "Without negroes, this state is one of the most contemptible in the Union...that whilst there remained one acre of swampland in South Carolina, he should raise his voice against restricting the importation of negroes. Negroes were our wealth, our only natural resource."[25]

Rediker further asserts that:

By the abolition of slavery, roughly 3.3 million slaves were working in the Atlantic "plantation complex."... Their production was staggering. In 1807 alone, Britain imported for domestic consumption 297.9 million pounds of sugar and 3.77 million gallons of rum, all of it slave-produced, as well as 16.4 million pounds of tobacco and 72.74 million pounds of cotton, almost all slaved produced. In 1810 the enslaved population of the United States produced 93 million pounds of cotton and most of 84 pounds of tobacco; they were themselves, as property, worth $316 million.[26]

Rediker cites Robin Blackburn's estimates in illustrating the profits gained by the system of "slave-based production of the New World."[27] Blackburn estimates that this production "had cost slaves 2,500,000,000 hours of toil...a gross sum that could not have been much less than £35,000,000."[28] According to Rediker, this was equivalent to "3.3 billion 2007 dollars."[29]

Although cotton was not the main slave crop to drive the Atlantic slave trade, it provides an example of the volume of revenue generated mainly by Black labor. The boom of the cotton industry in the United States extended from the 1790s to 1860. Table 4.1 illustrates the gross revenue generated from cotton by slave labor. It highlights the growth in this industry both in slave numbers, cotton production, and average output per slave. The price of cotton range from $.37 per lb in the early 1800s and fluctuated from a low of $.32 per lb to $.9 per lb during the period of 1818–1860. Taking the price of cotton during the 1860s, which was around $.15 per lb, and the amount of cotton exported, the gross revenue generated equaled $287,805,150. Although the debate on the profitability

Table 4.1 Gross revenue generated from slave labor and cotton production

	1810	1820	1830	1840	1850	1860
Total slaves in the United States	1,103,700	1,538,098	2,009,043	2,487,356	3,296,408	3,950,511
Cotton exported, lbs	88,819,000	127,800,000	298,459,102	743,941,061	1,111,570,370	1,918,701,000
Average export for each lave, lbs	80	83	143	295	337	485

Source: E. N. Elliott, *Cotton Is King and Pro-Slavery Arguments,* 3rd ed. (Augusta, GA: Pritchard, Abbott, and Loomis, 1860); and Lewis Cecil Gray, *History of Agriculture in the Southern United States to 1860,* 2 vols. (Gloucester, MA: Peter Smith, 1958).

of slavery or whether slave owners saw a significant return on their investment in slave labor still exists, the major point of emphasis is that significant amounts of revenue were being generated from slave labor.

Finally, E. N. Elliott, an advocate for slavery, in *Cotton Is King*, makes
an interesting, although questionable comment regarding the status of
slaves and their labor. He states that:

> The person of the slave is not property, no matter what the fictions
> of the law may say; but the right to his labor is property, and may be
> transferred like any other property.[30]

It is questionable because slaves were both property and their labor was
property. Therefore, the benefit of slavery was at least twofold: profiting to
the slave trader and the plantation owner. This comment is a more accu-
rate assessment of the modern-day Black athlete competing in revenue-
generating intercollegiate sports. They are not necessarily property of the
institutions they compete at, but as we will examine in the next section,
their athletic labor is property and profitable to these institutions.

★ ★ ★

As we examine the structure of intercollegiate athletics, a similar conclusion can be drawn where the athlete is not necessarily the property of
the institutions, but its the rights to athletes' labor and the profit off of
their labor that makes the plantation model appropriate in examining the
experiences of Black male athletes. Within the current new plantation
model of intercollegiate athletics, the NCAA and its member institutions
not only profit off of the labor of athletes, in general, and Black athletes,
specifically, they also profit off of their images.[31] For example, the sale
of sports jerseys and championship T-shirts generates an estimated $6–7
million a year for the NCAA.

Furthermore, regarding the multiple streams of revenue in intercollegiate athletics, a debate about its profitability exists. Clearly, there are
institutions that function at a deficit year after year, yet there are others
that have operating budgets that have increased significantly in ten years
and some have doubled. Thus, whether the athletic departments and institutions are breaking even or making a profit from the revenue sports of
football and basketball is debatable, because if an athletic department had
a budget of $50 million and it only makes $48 million, it still generated
revenue. More specifically, the point of emphasis is that revenue is being
generated and some members of the athletic department are reaping the
benefits, while others may be operating at a deficit or simply breaking
even. Many of the programs that are operating at a deficit are doing so
because of their drive to keep up with schools that have larger economic
resources (donors, endorsements, corporate sponsors, media rights, etc.).

Therefore, they are simply operating beyond their means in attempts to compete in the athletic arms race.

An overview of the revenue generated by PWIs is outlined in the following tables. These tables are only economic snapshots of the revenue generated in big time college athletics: Table 4.2 illustrates the top NCAA athletic programs based on operating budgets—this table also includes overall expenses and football and basketball revenues and expenses; table 4.3 highlights the universities spending the most on recruiting budgets; table 4.4 illustrates the revenue generated by the 2007–2008 Associated Press Top 10 College Football programs; table 4.5 illustrates the revenue generated by the 2007–2008 Associated Press Top 10 College Basketball programs; Table 4.6 highlights highest paid football coaches; table 4.7 illustrates the highest paid basketball coaches; and finally, tables 4.8 and 4.9 illustrate the largest football stadiums and basketball arenas among NCAA athletic programs. You will notice some common themes regarding teams and conferences represented throughout the data listed within these tables. The main point is to inform of the amount of revenue involved with NCAA intercollegiate athletic programs, and how a significant percentage of revenue is generated by sports with a high percentage of Black male athletes.

Table 4.2 Top 20 teams based on total revenue and expenses

Institutions	Total Revenue ($)	Total Expenses ($)	Football Rev./ Exp. ($)	Basketball Rev./ Exp. ($)
Ohio State	109,382,222	109,197,910	59,142,071/32,538,319	12,898,413/3,987,583
U of Florida	107,781,004	92,111,182	58,904,976/20,691,405	9,064,053/8,134,621
U. of Texas	105,048,632	89,313,533	63,798,068/17,565,006	14,678,656/6,594,163
U. of Tennessee	95,401,868	92,557,525	31,193,706/13,903,184	7,301,964/3,611,347
U. of Michigan	89,079,982	68,292,190	50,982,629/14,750,836	7,536,902/5,299,018
Notre Dame	83,586,903	57,406,114	63,675,034/17,842,288	2,947,106/3,196,599
U. of Wisconsin	82,579,472	81,401,732	34,105,991/19,771,064	14,332,269/5,315,234
U. of Alabama	81,946,464	71,463,235	53,182,806/21,340,593	6,854,107/4,141,759
Auburn University	81,696,758	68,907,966	56,830,516/22,950,759	5,349,714/4,402,168
U of Iowa	80,203,645	70,904,103	45,335,026/28,851,512	10,274,661/5,718,590
LSU	76,499,511	72,232,715	48,141,751/16,408,162	5,261,990/3,202,539
USC (California)	76,383,688	76,383,688	31,705,207/18,699,944	3,747,231/4,149,235
Penn State	76,327,504	71,974,048	44,014,052/14,609,828	5,642,120/3,645,693
U. of Georgia	75,937,460	61,583,869	59,516,939/16,372,291	5,823,995/2,939,396
U. of Nebraska	71,121,812	70,899,239	26,264,849/13,834,134	2,613,353/3,793,663
U. of Oklahoma	69,430,569	69,266,317	37,263,255/18,790,701	5,829,692/4,231,966
Texas A&M	69,413,648	69,413,648	37,123,296/16,619,256	7,303,377/6,258,741
Stanford	65,480,187	63,834,193	12,927,407/12,892,487	6,049,183/3,277,456
U. of Minnesota	64,828,596	64,828,596	17,390,376/8,304,534	9,277,073/3,069,003
UCLA	61,309,668	61,309,668	23,539,593/16,872,615	9,108,587/5,262,775

Source: U.S. Department of Education, http://ope.ed.gov/athletics/ (accessed April 22, 2008).

Table 4.3 Top 10 programs spending the most on recruiting and 10-year increase

Institutions	2006–2007 ($)	2001–2002 ($)	1996–1997 ($)
U. of Tennessee	2,005,700	1,419,400	915,000
U. of Notre Dame	1,758,300	1,014,600	674,000
U. of Florida	1,451,400	1,097,300	665,000
Auburn U.	1,374,900	1,228,900	646,000
Kansas State U.	1,316,700	626,600	359,000
U. of Georgia	1,284,000	1,020,000	605,000
U. of Nebraska	1,275,000	925,300	826,000
U. of Arkansas	1,259,700	749,000	506,000
Duke U.	1,245,300	592,500	378,000
Ohio State U.	1,236,800	691,200	522,000

Source: U.S. Department of Education, http://ope.ed.gov/athletics/ (accessed April 22, 2008); Chronicle of Higher Education, http://chronicle.com/free/v54/i47/47a00102.htm (accessed April 22, 2008).

Table 4.4 Associated Press College football top 25 poll, 2007–2008

University/Team	Revenue Generated by Football ($)	Total Sport Revenue ($)	Stadium Size/Capacity
LSU	48,141,751	76,499,511	92,400
Georgia	59,516,939	75,937,460	92,000
USC	31,705,207	76,383,688	92,746
Missouri	15,284,731	48,634,512	68,349
Ohio State	59,142,071	77,978,797	102,329
West Virginia	25,174,217	32,113,768	60,000
Kansas	11,258,985	65,194,721	50,071
Oklahoma	20,412,787	46,667,284	82,112
Virginia Tech	40,634,499	65,487,381	66,233
Boston College	17,452,269	57,392,077	44,500
Texas	63,798,068	105,048,632	94,113
Tennessee	31,193,706	95,401,868	102,037
Florida	58,904,976	107,781,004	88,548
BYU	10,142,975	32,100,899	64,045
Auburn	56,830,516	81,696,758	87,451
Arizona St.	23,519,742	53,473,276	71,706
Cincinnati	8,162,664	34,172,785	35,097
Michigan	50,982,629	89,079,982	106,201
Hawaii	7,533,652	12,579,190	50,000
Illinois	20,764,472	56,804,174	69,249
Clemson	32,029,237	55,741,548	80,301
Texas Tech	20,827,440	53,561,872	53,000
Oregon	21,495,626	50,489,771	54,000
Wisconsin	34,105,991	82,579,472	80,321
Oregon State	28,299,199	45,409,990	45,674

Source: Poll posted at the end of the 2007–2008 season. Data collected from U.S. Department of Education: http://ope.ed.gov/athletics/ (accessed April 22, 2008).

Table 4.5   Associated Press College basketball top 25 poll, 2007–2008

University/Team	Revenue Generated by basketball ($)	Total Sport Revenue ($)	Stadium Size/Capacity
North Carolina	17,215,199	58,188,501	21,750
Memphis	6,405,720	29,335,795	18,119
UCLA	9,108,587	61,309,668	12,829
Kansas	13,223,255	65,194,721	16,300
Tennessee	7,301,964	95,401,868	21,000
Wisconsin	14,332,269	82,579,472	17,142
Texas	14,678,656	105,048,632	16,755
Georgetown	11,534,863	27,358,934	20,600
Duke	13,410,114	47,507,169	9,314
Stanford	6,049,183	65,480,187	7,392
Butler	1,463,988	10,235,838	10,757
Xavier	9,421,233	18,538,464	10,250
Louisville	23,216,728	54,589,997	18,865
Drake	1,239,978	11,407,671	7,002
Notre Dame	2,947,106	83,586,903	11,418
Connecticut	7,761,834	52,811,643	10,167
Pittsburgh	7,645,937	37,465,582	12,508
Michigan State	13,225,963	73,171,907	14,759
Vanderbilt	6,620,614	39,021,876	14,168
Purdue	9,565,497	56,293,562	14,123
Washington St.	2,830,494	31,928,453	11,566
Clemson	7,395,101	55,741,548	9,749
Davidson	1,320,770	8,626,786	5,700
Gonzaga	3,647,003	13,623,182	6,000
Marquette	13,061,279	21,803,021	19,000

Source: Poll posted at the end of the 2007–2008 season. Data collected from U.S. Department of Education: http://ope.ed.gov/athletics/ (accessed April 23, 2008).

Table 4.6   Top 10 highest paid college football coaches, 2007–2008

Coaches	Institution	Yearly Salary ($)
Bob Stoops	Oklahoma	6,500,000
Charlie Weis	Notre Dame	4,200,000
Pete Carroll	USC	4,000,000
Les Miles	LSU	3,751,000
Nick Saban	Alabama	3,750,000
Jim Tressel	Ohio State	3,500,000
Urban Meyer	Florida	3,400,000
Kirk Ferentz	Iowa	3,400,000
Mack Brown	Texas	2,910,000
Bobby Petrino	Arkansas	2,850,000

Source: Data was collected from the following source: http://www.usatoday.com/sports/college/football/2007-12-04-coaches-pay_N.htm

The sale of media rights is another significant stream of income that generates revenue for many NCAA athletic departments. For example, Michael Smith and John Ourand outline the details of one of the lucrative collegiate media rights deals between ESPN, CBS, and the Southeastern

Table 4.7 Top 10 highest paid college basketball coaches, 2009–2010

Coaches	University	Yearly Salary ($)
John Calipari	Kentucky	3,960,000
Billy Donovan	Florida	3,300,000
Bill Self	Kansas	3,000,000
Thad Matta	Ohio State	2,500,000
Tom Crean	Indiana	2,360,000
Bruce Pearl	Tennessee	2,300,000
Rick Pitino	Louisville	2,250,000
Rick Barnes	Texas	1,800,000
Tom Izzo	Michigan State	1,800,000
Tubby Smith	Minnesota	1,800,000

Source: Data was collected from the following source: http://www.usatoday.com/sports/college/mensbasketball/2007-03-08-coaches-salary-cover_N.htm

Table 4.8 Top 10 largest college stadiums, 2006–2007

Institution	Stadium Name	Capacity
Michigan	Michigan Stadium	107,501
Penn State	Beaver Stadium	107,282
Tennessee	Neyland Stadium	104,079
Ohio State	Ohio Stadium	101,568
UCLA	Rose Bowl	92,542
LSU	Tiger Stadium	92,400
Alabama	Bryant Denny Stadium	92,158
Georgia	Stanford Stadium	92,058
USC	LA Memorial Coliseum	92,000
Florida	Ben Hill Griffin Stadium	88,548

Source: Data was collected from the following source: http://www.nokia sugarbowl.com/Football_Knowledge/Football_Stadium/47054.html

Table 4.9 Ten largest NCAA basketball arenas

Institution	Stadium Name	Capacity
Syracuse	Carrier Dome	33,000
Tennessee	Thompson-Boling Arena	24,535
Kentucky	Rupp Arena	23,500
BYU	Marriott Center	22,700
N. Carolina	Dean Smith Center	21,750
Georgetown	MCI Center	20,674
Seton Hall	Continental Airlines Arena	20,049
Saint Louis	Savvis Center	20,000
Portland State	The Rose Garden	19,980
NC State	RBC Center	19,722

Source: Data was collected from the following source: http://www.infoplease.com/ipsa/A0105720.html

Conference (SEC).[32] According to Smith and Ourand, ESPN will pay the SEC a staggering $2.25 billion over the next 15 years—about $150 million a year—for the conference's TV rights, giving the network all of the SEC's content that was not taken by CBS's 15-year, $55 million a year contract. Furthermore, Smith and Ourand explained that this will provide an average of $205 million a year in media rights beginning in 2009–2010 and running through fiscal 2025. They concluded that the SEC's total payout to its schools in 2007–2008 was $63.6 million after the conference's cut, which was distributed among the 12 universities and each school received about $5.3 million this past fiscal year; however, this revised deal could increase annual revenue to $15 million per school.[33]

Other media deals worth noting are with Host Communication, CBS Collegiate Sports Properties, and ISP Sports and several NCAA institutions. For example, Host Communications has contracts at various rates with the following universities: University of Kentucky, a 10-year contract for $80.5 million, University of Arizona, a 12-year, $80.4 million extension that runs from 2007–2019, and the University of Tennessee, a 10-year deal for $83.4 million, which started July 2007 and continues to June 2017.[34] Both contracts with Host and University of Kentucky and Tennessee include guaranteed revenue: Kentucky is guaranteed $79 million and the University of Tennessee is guaranteed $68 million rights fees and $15.4 million in capital improvements. Additional media rights deals include the following: CBS Collegiate signed a 10 year, $75 million deal with Louisiana State University; ISP Sport has a 10-year $66 million deal with FSU and a 9 year, $51.3 million deal with Auburn University.

Apparel agreements with major athletic shoe corporations are other lucrative streams of revenue for several NCAA athletic programs. Some examples of these agreements include the following: Nike has an 8-year, $28.34 million deal with the University of North Carolina–Chapel Hill; Adidas has an 8-year $60 million deal with University of Michigan, a 10-year $60 million agreement with Notre Dame, a 8-year, $26.67 million agreement with Kansas University, and a 5-year, $19.3 million deal with the University of Tennessee; and Under Armour has a 5-year, $10.5 million agreement with Auburn University, and a 5-year, $17.5 million agreement with the University of Maryland.

Finally, stadium naming rights is another stream of revenue NCAA athletic programs is using to generate revenue. Table 4.10 highlights some of the lucrative deals made between universities and sponsors.

The above examples are a brief overview of the multiple streams of revenue generated by several PWIs athletic programs. It is also important to note that these institutions are able to attract this mainly because of the sports of football and men's basketball, although the revenue benefits all of the varsity sports.

Regarding revenue generated by the NCAA, the CBS contract to broadcast the NCAA Men's Final Four Basketball Tournament is the major source of NCAA revenue. The next section will examine the racial demographics of the NCAA Men's Basketball Tournament and their contributions to the capital accumulation of the NCAA.

Table 4.10   Intercollegiate stadium naming rights agreements

Institution	Sponsor(s)	Price ($)/Term
California State University, Fresno	Save Mart Supermarkets and Pepsi Bottling Group	40 million/20 year
University of Maryland	Comcast	20 million/25 year
Ohio State University	Value City Department Stores	12.5 million/NA[a]
San Diego State University	Cox Communications	12 million/NA[a]
Texas Tech University	United Supermarkets	10 million/20 year

[a]Length of the term undisclosed.

Source: Ari Weinberg, "The Business of Basketball: Biggest College Sports Arena Naming Deals," *Forbes*, http://www.forbes.com/2003/03/24/cx_aw_0320ncaa.html (accessed October 25, 2008).

The NCAA Men's Basketball Tournament: On the Backs of Our Black Brothers

The employment percentages of Black males in revenue-generating sports (football and basketball) at the intercollegiate level and professional football and basketball cannot go without notice. Black males comprised 46.9 percent of NCAA Football Bowl Subdivision (FBS) and 58.9 percent of NCAA Division I basketball during the 2005–2006 season; 65.5 percent of the NFL, and 73 percent of the National Basketball Association (NBA) during the 2005–2006 season.[35] Intercollegiate and professional football and basketball are sports that have consistently employed a high percentage of Black athletes.

The focus of this section is to examine the racial demographics and the different levels of contributions (i.e., games played, games started, points scored, and minutes played) of each racial group for the 64 teams selected to the 2006 Men's NCAA basketball tournament in order to challenge Professor Willhelm's assessment. The reason the focus is on basketball is because 90 percent of the NCAA revenue is generated from the Division I men's basketball tournament. This includes CBS's contract ($6.1 billion over 11-years) that equate to about $545 million per year to televise the tournament. It is calculated that less than 1 percent of the 360,000 student athletes that compete at the NCAA Division I level during this season generate 90 percent of this income.[36] According to Andrew Zimbalist, the 2008 tournament prove even more profitable. He states that:

> Last year, Madness brought in $548 million from TV rights and an additional $40 million from ticket sales and sponsorships, together representing an eye-popping 96% of all NCAA revenue.[37]

When we consider the revenue generated from this tournament, we need to question, what are the racial demographics of the athletic labor class that is generating this revenue and what are the levels of contribution among these racial groups? This section of the chapter intends to examine not only the representation of Black athletes in the NCAA Division I tournament, but also the level of contribution Black athletes make on their respective teams.

To obtain racial demographic information, the NCAA Division I men's basketball bracket was used to examine the teams that comprised the 2006 tournament. Data was compiled to assess the racial demographics for each bracket (Oakland, Atlanta, Minneapolis, and Washington DC)[38] and the overall racial demographics of the tournament. Once the teams were identified, each team's Web site was examined to compile the following data: race of the athlete and season data, which included games played, games started, total minutes, and total points.

Once the data was compiled, descriptive statistics were applied to this data to provide a snapshot of the contributions each racial group made toward their team's success. The purpose for this data was to examine the level of contribution athletes by racial groups made during the year in assisting their team in reaching the tournament.

★   ★   ★

The 2005–2006 NCAA Division I Men's Basketball Tournament was comprised of 64 teams totaling 853 players; an average of 13 athletes per team. The bracket was divided into four sub-brackets with each of the sub-brackets having 16 teams. These 16 teams will ultimately be reduced to 8 teams, which would compete at one of the regional locations (Atlanta GA; Oakland CA; Washington DC; Minneapolis MN). Eventually, one team from each region would make it to the final four, which was housed in Indianapolis, IN.

Table 4.11 illustrates the following: racial demographics of the 16 teams in each regional location; the seasons' total games played, games started, points scored, and minutes played; and the percentages of games played, games started, points scored, and minutes played for each racial group.

★   ★   ★

The number of Black athletes currently participating in the moneymaking collegiate sports of basketball and football are in fact overwhelming compared to their White counterparts and other races. The revenue-generating sports of football and basketball encompass nearly all the financial needs of the NCAA and its member institutions. From just the broadcasting money of the NCAA championships, $453 million was generated, not to mention the money from the regular season, conference championships, and fan support. Comparing college basketball revenue to college football, college football generated $192 million inclusively on all the bowl games combined.[39] Specifically, in college basketball,

Table 4.11 Racial demographic information (Season totals)

Race	Number of Athletes	Games Played	Games Started	Minutes Played	Points Scores
Atlanta GA Bracket					
African American	119	3,257	1,736	71,202	25,196
	(57)	(63.7)	(65.9)	(66.8)	(66.6)
White	80	1,593	808	30,677	10,975
	(38.3)	(31.1)	(30.7)	(28.8)	(29)
International (European Descendent)	7	206	69	3,697	1,248
	(3.3)	(4)	(2.6)	(3.5)	(3.3)
International (African Descendent)	3	59	22	1,017	404
	(1.4)	(1.2)	(0.8)	(1)	(1.1)
Oakland CA Bracket					
African American	123	3,430	1,762	71,124	25,674
	(58)	(64)	(68)	(67)	(68)
White	76	1,632	738	29,510	10,706
	(36)	(31)	(28)	(28)	(28)
Asian	1	7	0	9	0
	(0.5)	(0)	(0)	(0)	(0)
International (European Descendent)	2	34	2	323	103
	(0.5)	(1)	(0)	(>1)	(0)
International (African Descendent)	10	221	113	4,511	10,706
	(5)	(4)	(4)	(4)	(4)
Washington DC Bracket					
African American	141	3,667	1,816	75,682	28,174
	(64)	(68)	(70)	(72)	(74)
White	72	1,460	663	25,463	8,551
	(33)	(27)	(26)	(24)	(23)
Hispanic	2	40	1	434	106
	(0.7)	(1)	(0)	(0)	(0)
International (Hispanic)	1	32	32	834	290
	(0.3)	(1)	(1)	(1)	(1)
International (European Descendent)	2	36	16	299	68
	(0.7)	(1)	(1)	(1)	(0)
International (African Descendent)	3	82	62	1,666	639
	(1.3)	(2)	(2)	(2)	(2)
Minneapolis MN Bracket					
African American	119	3,191	1,651	69,409	25,288
	(57)	(61)	(63)	(66)	(67)
White	74	1,661	823	29,768	10,385
	(35)	(31)	(32)	(28)	(27)
Hispanic	2	39	0	369	156
	(1)	(1)	(0)	(1)	(1)
International (European Descendent)	7	171	109	3,649	1,517
	(3)	(3)	(4)	(3)	(4)
International (African Descendent)	8	213	28	2,405	560
	(4)	(4)	(1)	(2)	(1)

Note: Percentages are given in parentheses.
Source: Data compiled using respective universities' athletic department media guides and NCAA Tournament media guides.

nearly all of the NCAA revenue is incurred during the months of March and April with the basketball championships. Again, of the 90 percent income generated from two months out of the year, less than 1 percent of the total student athletes create this surplus. Of this one percent, more than half were Black athletes and their contributions far exceeded their representation.

Black athletes played, started, and scored more than two and a half times as much as White athletes; and comparatively speaking against all the other racial groups. The representation of the White, Hispanic, European, and Asian athletes pale in comparison to the Black athletes during the NCAA basketball season and championships. For the entire season, Black athletes were on the floor 64.4 percent of the time, started 66.6 percent of the games played, played a total of 68.1 percent of all the minutes combined, and scored a staggering 68.7 percent of all the points of the largest revenue-generating activity collegiate sports has to offer.

The distribution of the races of athletes participating in the four regions of the NCAA tournament (Atlanta, Minneapolis, Oakland, and Washington DC) was categorically similar, but the East Coast regional (Washington DC) displayed the highest percentages of Black athlete participants. The most consistent statistic was participation of athletes, where Blacks consisted of 57–63 percent, with the most being in Washington DC. The brackets in Tabel 4.11 show overwhelming statistic regarding the total points scored by race and region wherein the distribution varied between 67 and 74 percent, and the highest totals were in the Washington DC bracket once again. The lowest percentages of the representation of Black athletes occurred in the Oakland bracket. The

Table 4.12 NCAA tournament summary: Total games, points, and minutes by race

Race	Number of Athletes	Games Played	Games Started	Minutes Played	Points Scored
African American	502 (59)	13,545	6,965	287,417	104,332
		(64.4)	(66.6)	(68.1)	(68.7)
White	302 (35)	6,246	3,032	115,418	40,617
		(30.1)	(64.4)	(27.3)	(26.8)
Asian	1	7	0	9	0
	(0.05)	(0.1)	(29)	(0)	(0)
Hispanic	4	79	1	803	262
	(0.5)	(0.4)	(0)	(0.2)	(0.2)
International	1	32	32	834	290
(Hispanic)	(0.05)	(0.2)	(0)	(0.2)	(0.2)
International	18	447	195	7,968	2,936
(European Descendent)	(2)	(2.1)	(1.8)	(1.9)	(1.9)
International	24	575	225	9,599	3,287
(African Descendent)	(3)	(2.7)	(2.3)	(2.3)	(2.2)

Note: Percentages are given in parentheses.

Source: Data compiled using respective universities' athletic department media guides and NCAA Tournament media guides.

percentages of Black athletes are higher on the East Coast as compared to the West Coast, and the statistics show this to be true with an increase in representation and productivity of Black athletes in the East.

The teams, when announced and placed within the four regions, have the capability of playing anywhere in the country. However, the top teams in each region are consistently placed in the bracket closest to their school, and in recent years the NCAA tournament selection committee selects the teams and places and tries to keep each team closer to home to reinforce the "student-athlete" mentality of college sports, so as to ensure a minimal amount of time missed from school.

Overall, Blacks represented 59 percent of the total athletes playing in the NCAA Men's Basketball Tournament during the 2005–2006 season, 67 percent of all the games started, 68 percent of all the minutes played, and scored an astonishing 69 percent of all the points may have to pursue semiprofessional or professional basketball as opposed to staying in school to receive their fair dues (see table 4.12).

★　★　★

The results of this data may appear to be obvious when one examines the overall percentages of Black athletes represented in NCAA men's basketball; however, the goal was to illustrate the important role Black male athletes are to these institutions, especially with an enormous TV contract on the line. The economic gains of this tournament speak volumes to these institutions' need for Black athletic talent. Their labor is undeniably needed to sustain the profit-driven motives of these institutions. Furthermore, with the NBA enforcement of an age limit, a situation develops where Black athletes are dependent upon these institutions because they now become the only purchasers of this talent—a monopsony. A similar pattern is also replicated in the racial demographics of the 2007–2008 NCAA Men's Basketball tournament: African American 59 percent (526), Whites 32 percent (287), and International 9 percent (47–34 Black, 14 White).

This practice can easily extend to intercollegiate football and the lucrative bowl games that culminate the season. Table 4.13 provides a snapshot of the racial demographics that make up the 2008 Bowl Championship Series, conference and team payouts, attendance, and Neilson ratings. It is interesting to note, regarding over-representation of athletes competing in BCS games, 51 percent are Black athletes, 38 percent are White athletes, 3 percent are Hispanic athletes, 6 percent are Asian/Pacific Islander, and 2 percent of the athletes are classified as other. It is also interesting to note that the BCS games paid out around $170 million to the ten teams or respective conferences, while non-BCS bowl games paid out about $80 million to the 56 teams or respective conferences that competed in those bowl games. 2009 Bowl Championship Series,

Table 4.13 Bowl Championship Series information, 2008

	Black	White	Hispanic	Asian/PI	Other
Allstate BCS National Championship					
LSU 38	41 (67)	20 (33)	0		0
Ohio State 24	45 (42)	50 (47)	3 (3)		9 (8)

- Louisiana Superdome (72,000 Capacity); 2008 Attendance: 79,651
- 2008 Payout per Conference: $17 million
- 2008 Nielsen Rating: 14.4

Rose Bowl					
Southern Cal (USC) 49	41 (53)	27 (35)	3 (4)	4 (5)	2 (3)
Illinois 17	66 (61)	39 (36)	0	0	3(3)

- The Rose Bowl (91,000 Capacity); 2008 Attendance: 93,923
- 2008 Projected Payout per Team: $17 million
- 2008 Nielsen Rating: 11.11

Tostitos Fiesta Bowl					
West Virginia 48	40 (44)	50 (54)	2 (2)		
Oklahoma 28	61 (57)	40 (38)	5 (5)		

- University of Phoenix Stadium (73,000 Capacity); 2008 Attendance: 70,016
- 2009 Projected Payout per Team: $17 million
- 2008 Nielsen Rating: 7.7

FedEx Orange Bowl					
Kansas 24	46 (48)	42 (44)	6 (6)	0	2 (2)
VA Tech 21	71 (63)	39 (34)	2 (2)	1 (1)	0

- Dolphin Stadium (76,500 Capacity); 2008 Attendance: 74,111
- 2008 Projected Payout per Team: $17 million
- 2008 Nielsen Rating: 7.4

Allstate Sugar Bowl					
Georgia 41	52 (63)	29 (35)	2 (2)	0	0
Hawaii 10	20 (18)	25 (22)	5 (4)	57 (51)	6 (5)

- Louisiana Superdome (72,000 Capacity); 2008 Attendance: 74,383
- 2008 Payout Per Conference: $17 million
- 2008 Nielsen Rating: 7.9

Source: Data collected from university athletic team media guides and the following Web site: Bowl Championship Series on MSN, "BCS Bowl Facts," http://www.bcsfootball.org/bcsfb/facts (accessed October 28, 2008).
Note: Percentages are given in parentheses.

illustrated in Table 4.14, present a similar pattern of representation and revenue generated.

★   ★   ★

It should not take a long stretch of the imagination to see how Black male athletes contribute significantly to the athletic labor class; thus, to the

Table 4.14   Bowl Championship Series information, 2009

	Black	*White*	*Hispanic*	*Asian/PI*	*Other*
FedEx BCS National Championship					
Florida 24	70 (57.9)	45 (37.2)	2 (1.7)		1 (0.8)
Oklahoma 14	60 (59.4)	37 (36.6)	0		4 (4.0)
• Dolphin Stadium (72,230 Capacity); 2009 Attendance: 78,468					
• 2009 Payout per Conference: $17.5 million					
• 2009 Nielsen Rating: 17.0/27					
Rose Bowl					
Southern Cal (USC) 38	53 (49.1)	47 (43.5)	1 (0.9)	7 (6.5)	
Penn State 24	31 (29.8)	71 (68.3)		1 (1.0)	1 (1.0)
• The Rose Bowl (91,000 Capacity); 2008 Attendance: 93,923					
• 2008 Projected Payout per Team: $17 million					
• 2008 Nielsen Rating: 11.11					
Tostitos Fiesta Bowl					
Texas 24	51 (49.0)	50 (48.1)	3 (2.9)		
Ohio State 21	44 (39.3)	63 (56.3)	1 (0.9)	1 (0.9)	3 (2.7)
• University of Phoenix Stadium (73,000 Capacity); 2008 Attendance: 70,016					
• 2009 Projected Payout per Team: $17.5 million					
• 2008 Nielsen Rating: 17.0/27					
FedEx Orange Bowl					
VA Tech 20	66 (54.5)	52 (43.0)	2 (1.7)	1 (0.8)	
Cincinnati 7	40 (51.3)	38 (48.7)			
• Dolphin Stadium (76,500 Capacity); 2008 Attendance: 74,111					
• 2009 Projected Payout per Team: $17.5 million					
• 2008 Nielsen Rating: 7.4					
Allstate Sugar Bowl					
Utah 31	34 (32.7)	46 (44.2)		23 (22.1)	1 (1.0)
Alabama 17	61 (58.1)	44 (41.9)			
• Louisiana Superdome (72,000 Capacity); 2008 Attendance: 74,383					
• 2008 Payout Per Conference: $17 million					
• 2008 Nielsen Rating: 7.9					

Note: Percentages are given in parentheses.
Source: Data collected from university athletic team media guides and the following Web site: Bowl Championship Series on MSN, "BCS Bowl Facts," http://www.bcsfootball.org/bcsfb/facts (accessed February 20, 2008); "Fox Earns 17.0 Overnight For BCS National Championship Game" http://www.sportsbusinessdaily.com/article/126777 (accessed March 2, 2009); "FedEx. BCS National Championship Game January 8, 2009: Postgame Notes," http://www.gatorzone.com/football/stats/notes/post/20090108200000.pdf (accessed March 2, 2009).

overall bottom-line of the revenue generated. Their presence as starters and their representation on the top football and basketball programs in the country speak volumes to PWIs' need for Black male athletes.

Within this current economic configuration, another area to consider is the contribution Black male athletes are making toward "Title IX sports"[40]: those sports that are added to meet gender equity requirements, which undoubtedly are played mostly by White women (e.g., rifle, golf, equestrian, rowing, bowling, and lacrosse). According to Welch Suggs:

Only 2.7 percent of women receiving scholarships to play all other sports at predominantly white colleges in Division I are black. Yet those are precisely the sports—golf, lacrosse, and soccer, as well as rowing—that colleges have been adding to comply with Title IX.[41]

Therefore, since Title IX has provided very limited opportunity for Black females but additional opportunities for White women to compete and Black male athletes make up the greater percentage of the revenue-generating sports that contribute to athletic departments' revenue, and thus their ability to support these additional sports, a re-occurring historical relationship between the White female and Black male has been resurrected. I refer to this contribution and connection as the "Driving Miss Daisy" syndrome.

The Black male-White female relationship in the United States has a storied history. Although intimate relationships between Black males and White females were forbidden by the system of White supremacy and legislated by lynching mobs during slavery and post–slavery periods, these relationships occurred and were managed through clandestine engagements. During these historical periods, the social order prescribed more palatable and professional arrangements for White females and Black males in the form of master/servant relationships, where Black males served the needs of Whites, in general, and White women; this service was in the role of carriage drivers, house servants, chauffeurs, and so on. Though the laws against miscegenation are buried in the annals of U.S. history, the role of Black males serving the needs of White women continues to prevail in our society.

Driving Miss Daisy, the Pulitzer Prize-winning play by Alfred Uhry, captures a 25-year relationship between a wealthy, White strong-willed Southern matron (Miss Daisy) and her Black chauffeur (Hoke) during the racially charged 1950s and '60s. The Hollywood version of this play cost $7.5 million to produce in movie form and earned $93.6 million at the box office. It went on to capture three Academy Awards for best actress (Jessica Tandy), best screenplay adaptation (Uhry himself), and best film of 1990.

The essence of this movie reiterates the master (Miss Daisy)—servant (Hoke) relationship. At her disposal, although initially reluctant, Hoke endures the degradation and verbal abuse from Miss Daisy, yet served her faithfully. Although Hoke was compensated economically, his responsibility as chauffeur/caretaker was his internal colony, and it relegated his potential in a racially structured society and oppressed his ability for self-expression. Although he was a man, he was perceived to be less than a man—invisible, simply a cog in the machinery of the Jim Crow South. Hoke's visible presence as a man was only in theory, mere imagery, in the minds of White Southerners. In the social reality of this era, Hoke was deemed a boy and a personified disposable instrument made accessible for the comforts and privileges of the White establishment; regardless of its benevolence. Therefore, pushed to the limits of invisibility, Hoke is provoked to cry out and proclaim to Miss Daisy, *"I ain't some back of the neck you look at while you goin wherever you got to go. I am a man."* Yet, a man racially assigned and relegated to the position of service—driving Miss Daisy.

The institutional arrangements of NCAA Division I athletics present a similar Miss Daisy-Hoke relationship, where Black male athletes are invisible as men but strategic in bearing the burden of generating revenue for athletic departments across the United States. Disguised under the auspices of gender equity requirements in college athletics, where once again the benefactors have mainly been White women, Black males find themselves locked in this perpetual relationship of servicing the needs of the White establishment, in general, and White women, specifically.

Conclusion

At the 2006 NCAA centennial convention, the association's president, Myles Brand, State of the Association Address entitled, *"The Principles of Intercollegiate Athletics"* outlined three key principles that constitute the collegiate model:

1. Those who participate in intercollegiate athletics are to be students attending a university or college.
2. Intercollegiate athletics contests are to be fair, conducted with integrity, and the safety and well-being of those who participate are paramount.
3. Intercollegiate athletics is to be wholly embedded in universities and colleges.[42]

As a final "major issue," within the context of the three principles, he spoke of how the intercollegiate athletic enterprise mirrors the financial structure of the larger university. Therefore, as "not-for-profit" entities, they are in the business of generating revenue; however, the revenue is to be redistributed to meet "the institution's mission and strategic direction."[43] Brand goes on to emphasize the need to, "end the ambivalence and do the best job we can in developing revenue for our athletic departments."[44] Brand's goal for the association and its institutional members is to increase commercial activity with ethical practices and as long as "it is done so in a way that fully respects the underlying principles of the university."[45] He notes that this is achievable within the amateur nature of intercollegiate athletics because, " 'Amateur' defines the participants, not the enterprise."[46] He ends this address with the following statement: "Let's celebrate the student-athlete!"[47]

In celebrating the athlete, the tone of his address, however, appeared to inevitably increase the demand placed on their lives. Increasing commercial activity cannot be achieved without demands being placed on the commodity that drives this enterprise—the athlete. One controversial issue that consistently emerges in the context of increasing commercial activity is ownership of an athlete's identity. Brand stated that the sale of broadcast rights and logo licensing is "mandated by the business plan" to increase commercial activity.[48] Thus, this mandated business plan to increase commercial activity will ultimately fall on the backs of Black male athletes to fund this plan and this commercial motive.

Therefore, to answer Sidney Willhelm's question, "Who needs the Negro?," the internal colonial situation of NCAA Division I Intercollegiate Athletics needs the Black athlete. Capital accumulation was clearly the motive for the plantation system, and it can be argued that it is also the preeminent motive for NCAA member institutions. Currently, the sports that are the most profitable are the sports of football and basketball, and the unfortunate twist is that Black male athletes make up the larger percentage of these teams. Thus, the New Plantation economic motives situates Black male athletes as necessary entities in generating revenue for athletic departments at many PWIs. Once again, the Black body proves to be necessary for the capitalist exploitation and expansion of various American industries. The intercollegiate athletic industrial complex proves to be one of these industries that are thriving on the backs of Black male athletes.

CHAPTER FIVE

The Black Athlete's Racialized Experiences and the Predominantly White Intercollegiate Institution

"Dirty nigger!" Or simply, "Look, a Negro!"
I came into the world imbued with the will to find a meaning in things, my spirit filled with the desire to attain to the source of the world, and then I found that I was an object in the midst of other objects.

—Franz Fanon, *Black Skin, White Masks*

Introduction

Growing up Black in the South privileges one with insight into issues involving race and race relations. My early experience with race relations began in my small hometown, where hypersegregation prevailed in communities, schools, churches, recreational centers, etc. Blacks' contact with Whites was very limited, except for school and work. Although there were Blacks whose economic status would classify them as middle to upper class, relatively speaking, their race relegated them to always being subordinate in their interaction with the White citizens in this community. It was not until the desegregation of the school system that the interaction between racial groups increased, but not necessarily positively. Our Black skin made us objects by which others, based on predetermined assumptions, perceived our worth and structured interracial interaction.

After leaving the South, racial objectification was experienced in different ways. Encountering Whites who either had no or very limited contact with Blacks always presented interesting phenomena. The feelings and looks of discomfort, bewilderment, suspicion, skepticism, etc., were quite evident during these engagements. I will never forget a First Lieutenant in my military unit who grew-up in upper peninsula of Michigan expressing the fact that he had never seen a Black person in person until he went to college. This was not surprising because I vividly remember several occasions in northern Midwest cities during the early nineties where I was the first encounter Whites had with Blacks. I remember the embarrassment parents experienced trying to silence "little Johnny" for blurting out in complete amazement, "look mom, there's a Black person." How amusing it must have been for them to see a Black person—live and in person, instead of only the media renditions they received and used to construct their frame of reference about different racial groups.

Despite the pockets within the U.S. population that are completely naïve or blatantly ignorant about race, this country has since developed an acceptance and an admiration for several Blacks that have reached levels of prominence. In politics for example, Colin L. Powell was admired by a majority of the U.S. population from 1998 until 2004. Since 2005, Condoleezza Rice has been considered the most popular member in the Bush administration. During the presidential election, Senator Barack Obama, now President Barack Obama, had a celebrity-like following throughout many parts of the world. For example, in Berlin, it was estimated that he drew a crowd of over 200,000. Clearly, some of this attendance was out of curiosity and skepticism, but it also speaks to his popularity and admiration.

In the media industry, Oprah Winfrey remains the most popular television personality for four of the last five years. Several Black actors and entertainers have emerged to garner honor and admiration across racial lines, for example, Denzel Washington, Halle Barry, and Will Smith.

Furthermore, in the world of sports there are several Black athletes who have been accepted and are admired by a majority within this country and globally. Since the retirement of Michael Jordan, Tiger Woods, Kobe Bryant, and LeBron James are the most popular sports stars; nationally and internationally.

As it relates to race, this country has made tremendous progress given the fact of its horrible history of slavery, racial segregation, and terrorist acts of lynching. I must draw caution to the abbreviated list of Blacks who have transcended racial barriers and evolved to be accepted and admired by the masses. I understand the argument of cultural critics and scholars that profess the end of racism, especially with the Democratic Party's nomination of a Black male and the election of the United States' first Black president, or those who proclaim the insignificance of race. I would love to believe the following statement by William J. Wilson, as it pertains to economic rewards that:

> Race relations in America have undergone fundamental changes in recent years, so much so that now the life chances of individual

blacks have more to do with their economic class position than with their day-to-day encounters with whites.[1]

I do not think class trumps race in the majority of communities in this country. Therefore, the statement made by W. E. B. Du Bois that "The problem of the twentieth century is the problem of the color-line" still has relevance in the twenty-first century.[2] For example, during the 2008 elections an AP-Yahoo News poll designed in partnership with Stanford University to survey racial attitudes concluded "that 40 percent of white Americans hold at least a partly negative view toward blacks."[3] Thus, despite the few Blacks who have achieved certain levels of honor and acceptance from multiracial audiences, race is still a factor in day-to-day interaction with Whites and institutions supported by the ideology of White supremacy.

Although race as a biological construct is contested vigorously by both physical and social scientists, the phenotypical expressions produced by genetic variations contribute to perceived differences that have supported the ideology of White supremacy. Skin color has been an identifiable expression that has been a major determinant in decisions regarding race. It has operated as a visual determinant that helps in racially categorizing individuals; even with individuals like President Barack Obama and Tiger Woods where using skin color to determine race is problematic because half of their ancestry lineage is denied existence.

Race as a social construct has significantly contributed to the experiences of Blacks in this country and prescribed roles for us to follow. This country has experienced significant progress in race relations. There are yet social institutions that lag in becoming racially progressive, and as it pertains to these institutions, race still matters in determining our social mobility and our social well-being. It is interesting to note that there are some contradictions about the concept of race. I recall one contradiction being exposed by a White male who expressed how he felt uncomfortable and disjointed at a predominantly White university, and his pressing desire to leave—an "in living" color version of Jamie Kennedy's character from *Malibu's Most Wanted*. In my initial contact with this individual, I noticed a level of ease and comfort in our interaction. There was no White supremacy posturing or expression of racial arrogance. After questioning his place of origin, he explained that he grew up in a predominantly Black community and attended a predominantly Black high school. Ironically, he found himself, as a young White male in a predominantly White setting designed for Whites, discontented because of the "Whiteness"—a case of cognitive dissonance. I found his encounter with having a "Black experience" to be an interesting dilemma in race relations, because if a White male is disgruntled in his own environment, what hope is there for Blacks. History presents us with numerous images and terminology of Blacks with a high preference to identify or to be with the Whites—Toms, Sellouts, Oreos, and so on, but limited versions when the phenomenon is reverse; besides the ones previously mentioned in

od comedies: Jamie Kennedy in *Malibu's Most Wanted* and Steve
ı *Bringing Down the House.*

The prevailing question that remained after our encounter was, "if he
is uncomfortable at this predominantly White university, can he imagine how Blacks in general feel?" I began to contemplate on how Blacks
have developed "thick skins," coping mechanisms, and role-playing tactics to survive in settings where they are the minority, and to question the
institutional arrangements that are persistent in maintaining Blacks in a
minority status.

★　★　★

The presence of the Black athlete at PWIs has provided an assortment of
positive and negative experiences. History bares record of the athletic and
academic achievements of many Black athletes who have matriculated to
and graduated from predominantly White colleges and universities (see
Chapter 1). Consequently, their racial differences have incurred various
forms of racism. This chapter will focus on how race plays a major part in
impacting the experiences of Black athletes in the internal colonial settings of predominantly White National Collegiate Athletic Association
(NCAA) Division I institutions (PWIs).

As previously stated in the historical overview chapter, Black athletes
have encountered various experiences because of their racial heritage.
Thus, racism has presented itself in the form of individual (overt) racism
and institutional (covert) racism. Both forms of racism directly impact
the experiences of Black athletes at PWIs; however, institutional racism will be the major focus of this chapter. This is not to disregard the
overt racist acts that continue to occur at PWIs, because I am reminded
by Black athletes each semester of overt racism they have encountered.
These students experience overt racism in the communities that house
these institutions and on campus by students, faculty, and staff members. This racism includes acts of being called "nigger," being followed
in department stores, treated inferior in classrooms, clustered in certain
majors,[4] and so on. To a certain degree, it is institutional racism that fuels
individual racist practices; especially when there is a gap in cultural and
racial competence and racial representation. In other words, cultural and
racial incompetence plus low racial representation fosters racial insen-
sitivity. Thus, the major premise of this chapter is to illustrate how the
institutional racist practices of PWIs impact the experiences of Black
male athletes.

Institutional Racism—Where Race Does Matter

The prerequisite to racism is the construction of race and the belief
in the racial superiority of one specific racialized group. Race has a

long and varied history in regards to its utility. According to Manning Marable:

> Race is an artificial social construction that was deliberately imposed on various subordinated groups of people at the outset of the expansion of European capitalism into the Western Hemisphere five centuries ago.[5]

In the United States, race as a social construct is based on phenotypical differences, mainly skin color, where white-skinned people are positioned as superior to people of color. This is the fundamental belief undergirding the system of White supremacy. Consequently, race is grounded in ideals of power, privilege, oppression, and exploitation, where White supremacy situates white-skinned people in positions of power and privilege, and as a result, people of color have been oppressed and exploited; oppression and exploitation based on race are forms of racism. We can conclude that White supremacy is the premise of racism.

The validity and reproduction of the system of White supremacy is a result of racism being institutionalized in various social institutions and cultural practices.[6] As previously noted in chapter 2, institutional racism is a viable component to the internal colonial setting. To expound further and to delineate from overt racism, Carmichael and Hamilton's definition of institutional racism best captures its essence in the following statement:

> Racism is both overt and covert. It takes two, closely related forms: individual whites acting against individual blacks, and acts by the total white community against the black community.... The first consists of overt acts by individuals, which cause death, injury or the violent destruction of property. This type can be recorded by television cameras.... The second type is less overt, far more subtle, less identifiable in terms of *specific* individuals committing the acts. But it is no less destructive of human life. The second type originates in the operation of established and respected forces in the society, and thus receives far less public condemnation than the first type.[7]

Carmichael and Hamilton further expose the deceptive nature of institutional racism and distinguish it from individual racism in the following statement:

> When a white terrorist bombs a black church and kill five black children, that is an act of individual racism, widely deplored by most segments of the society. But when in the same city—Birmingham, Alabama—five hundred black babies die each year because of the lack of proper food, shelter and medical facilities, and thousands more are destroyed and maimed physically, emotionally and intellectually because of conditions of poverty and discrimination in the black community, that is a function of institutional racism.[8]

The important conclusion to draw from these statements is that institutional racism is disguised in structural arrangements and institutional practices that present challenges and function in ways that are just as destructive as covert racist acts; ultimately, it negatively impacts the experiences of Black athletes. Because it is camouflaged within the structural arrangements and institutional practices, locating the origin and administrators of this practice is evasive.

Institutional racist practices by PWIs that affect the lives of Black male athletes, specifically, incur both structural and ideological concerns. Structurally, at PWIs, the disproportionately high representation of Black male athletes in revenue-generating sports and low representation of Black males in the student body paints an interesting portrait and propagates mixed messages. On the one hand, it sends the message that these institutions mainly value and reward Black athletic excellence, thus providing them with the opportunities to utilize their athletic talents. However, based on the high representation of Black males as athletes and the low representation of Black males that make up the student body visually suggests that the same tenacity and desire for their intellectual talents remain wanting. Therefore, ideologically and visually, all Black males are initially cast as athletes and are subject to the age-old stereotypical mind of being labeled athletically superior but intellectually inferior. Visibility and hypervisibility are key factors: especially when PWIs are nationally and internationally represented by athletic teams that are predominantly Black. Yet, when visiting the various campuses, Black males are scarcely represented.

Tables 5.1 and 5.2 illustrate the major differences in the representation of Black males and Black male athletes at the 2007–2008 Associated Press College Football and Basketball Top 25 PWIs, and the revenue generated by each sport.

The issue is not in having equal representation, that would be impossible, but to recognize the messages this sends when Black males are well represented in highly visible sports. Recruiting Black males specifically for their athletic ability is an institutional racist practice that reinforces beliefs about Blacks' intellectual capabilities and athletic abilities. It creates unique experiences for Black males who do not participate in varsity team sports, as well as, for Black males who are highly visible as celebrity athletes.

To strictly state that the disproportionate representation of Black males at PWIs is a conscious and concerted institutionally racist practice is an evasive argument to prove. It would be similar to making the claim that the disproportionate representation of Whites in the National Basketball Association (NBA) is a form of institutional racism. However, if, for example, the NBA purposely used Zip Codes as a measure for drafting and signing players to NBA teams and the majority of the White players lived outside those Zip Codes, then this practice could arguably be

Table 5.1   Associated Press College football top 25 poll, 2007–2008

University/Team	Black Males on Football Team (%)	Black Male Undergraduates (%)	Revenue Generated by Football ($)[a]	Total of Athletic Revenue (%)
LSU	52	3.5	48,141,751	63
Georgia	72	2	59,516,939	78
USC	52	2.3	31,705,207	42
Missouri	42	2.2	15,284,731	31
Ohio State	42	2.9	59,142,071	76
West Virginia	48	1.8	25,174,217	78
Kansas	45	1.6	11,258,985	17
Oklahoma	71	1.8	20,412,787	44
Virginia Tech	62	2.6	40,634,499	62
Boston College	42	2.2	17,452,269	30
Texas	57	1.8	63,798,068	61
Tennessee	51	3.5	31,193,706	33
Florida	59	3.6	58,904,976	55
BYU	8	0.2	10,142,975	32
Auburn	50	4.1	56,830,516	70
Arizona St.	49	1.9	23,519,742	44
Cincinnati	47	4	8,162,664	24
Michigan	46	7.1	50,982,629	57
Hawaii	24	0.7	7,533,652	60
Illinois	54	2.7	20,764,472	37
Clemson	56	3.6	32,029,237	57
Texas Tech	39	2.3	20,827,440	39
Oregon	42	1	21,495,626	43
Wisconsin	39	1.2	34,105,991	41
Oregon State	31	0.9	28,299,199	62

[a]Data collected from the following source: U.S. Department of Education: http://ope.ed.gov/athletics/ (accessed June 15, 2008).

Source: This top 25 poll was posted at the end of the 2007–2008 season. Data collected from Universities' Office of Institutional Research, Universities' Factbooks, and Media Guides from the Official University Athletic Departments' Web sites, and The Integrated Postsecondary Education Data System (IPEDS).

considered a form of institutional racism. However, there are questionable means PWIs use to obtain a desired end.

The use of entrance exams, (e.g., the SAT or ACT) has been hotly debated as an institutionally racist practice that exhibits race and class bias and creates a disadvantage for a significant population of racially marginalized groups; especially for Blacks and Latino Americans (which include Mexican Americans and Puerto Ricans) who score the lowest among racial groups (e.g., Native Americans, Asian, White American).[9] These racial groups score the lowest on all three areas of the SAT: critical reading, mathematics, and writing. Regarding class, according to the U.S. Census median earnings in 2007, these racial groups earn considerably less than other racial groups.[10] This creates a perpetual cycle of racial subordination because academic performance and educational attainment is associated with income and income is stratified along racial lines in the

Table 5.2   Associated Press College basketball top 25 poll, 2007–2008

University/Team	Black Males on Basketball Team (%)	Black Male Undergraduates (%)	Revenue Generated by Basketball ($)[a]	Total of Athletic Revenue (%)
North Carolina	59	3.7	17,215,199	30
Memphis	100	10	6,405,720	22
UCLA	50	1.3	9,108,587	15
Kansas	47	1.6	13,223,255	20
Tennessee	65	3.5	7,301,964	8
Wisconsin	27	2.4	14,332,269	17
Texas	50	1.8	14,678,656	14
Georgetown	69	2.9	11,534,863	42
Duke	38	3.7	13,410,114	28
Stanford	50	4.7	6,049,183	9
Butler	36	1	1,463,988	14
Xavier	86	3.5	9,421,233	51
Louisville	65	4.5	23,216,728	43
Drake	35	2.2	1,239,978	11
Notre Dame	36	2	2,947,106	4
Connecticut	92	2.6	7,761,834	15
Pittsburgh	93	2.9	7,645,937	20
Michigan State	40	3	13,225,963	18
Vanderbilt	63	3.3	6,620,614	17
Purdue	50	2.5	9,565,497	17
Washington St.	20	1.1	2,830,494	9
Clemson	67	3.6	7,395,101	13
Davidson	27	3	1,320,770	15
Gonzaga	50	.7	3,647,003	27
Marquette	80	2.1	13,061,279	60

[a] Data collected from the following source: U.S. Department of Education: http://ope.ed.gov/athletics/ (accessed June 15, 2008).
Source: This top 25 poll was posted at the end of the 2007–2008 season. Data collected from Universities' Office of Institutional Research, Universities' Factbooks, and Media Guides from the Official University Athletic Departments' Web sites, and The Integrated Postsecondary Education Data System (IPEDS).

United States.[11] Furthermore, these racial groups have met certain levels of inertia and resistance in the process of assimilation; either due to the skin color or language barriers.

Beyond these tests scores that depict racial and class disparities, one cannot ignore the inception of these tests and the meaning inherent in their use. Consider, for example, Carl Brigham, the man known as "the father of the SAT" and College Board advisor. Brigham's views of racial intellectual superiority placed Americans of Nordic ancestry as superior in intelligence to those of Alpine or Mediterranean ancestry, while immigrants were less intelligent than Native Americans. Finally, at the bottom of Brigham's hierarchal chart of "American" superior intellectual ability were Blacks. He proclaimed that if "the importation of the negro" was not contained, it would lead to the deterioration of American intellectual superiority.[12] Therefore, if the "father of the SAT" adhered to racist ideology, it is not a huge leap to believe that his "brain-child" did not inherit similar ideals of proving the intellectual inferiority of the "negro," specifically, thus, proving the need to reduce their importation and perpetually relegating the "negro" to an inferior status.

The point of significance is that racist measures of perceived intelligence and academic potential can be used to institutionalize racist practices that relegate certain racial groups to a cycle of poverty and a revolving door of lower classism. This undoubtedly is the case when higher education is a process of breaking this cycle, yet, access to higher educational institutions is regulated by standardized tests, which reserves its benefits for those who are able to garner and master the skills of test taking.

Where some Black male athletes have been able to receive special admission despite their SAT/ACT scores and because of their potential to provide athletic labor, these scores have prevented access for other Black males, specifically. Therefore, in the context of PWIs, the low percentages of Black males, who are not varsity sports athletes, demonstrate the success of covert measures that "originates in the operation of established and respected forces in the society," yet have operated to limit their social mobility.[13]

In this context, generalizations abound where the Black male body becomes a signpost for the White gaze to ascribe to all Black males, specifically, and Black students in general, the status of special admits or products of affirmative action. The race and gender of the Black male magnify this gaze, and foster unique experiences at PWIs. Thus, institutional racism situates them into positions that reinforce racist ideologies about athletic prowess and intellectual wanting. This section will examine how the over-representation of Black males as athletes and their visibility in profile sports not only signify institutional racism but also create interesting dynamics for both Black males and Black male athletes at PWIs.

Black Males (Nonathletes) at Predominantly White Institutions

The presence of Black males at PWIs presents a blessing and a burden. Since the 1980s, the war on drugs has created a pipeline that has ushered many Black males from the cradle to prison. As stated in chapter 4 and worth noting again, the rise of the prison industrial complex is a $52 billion-a-year industry and the United States leads the world with 2.1 million people currently in prisons or jails. Blacks make up 12.3 percent of the U.S. population, but 43.7 percent of the prison population. One in eight college-age Black males are either in jail or prison in the United States. Furthermore, at the current rate, predictions indicate that one in three Black males will spend at least a year of their life in prison.[14] Although the rate of Black males entering college has decreased since the 1970s, their presence at these institutions of higher learning is a blessing because it signifies how there are Black men prevailing against the odds, stereotypes, and predictions. Consequently, a significant population of Black males have succumbed to structural pressures (e.g., high unemployment rates, allure of the open drug market in some Black communities, access to substandard education, high school dropout rates, etc.) or interpersonal pressures (e.g., Kawanza Kunjufu's "fourth-grade failure syndrome"[15] or Shelby Steele's "disbelieving anti-self"[16]) that have adversely impacted the experience of Black men, and has forced many young Black males to choose lifestyles that lead to criminal activity and thus a life trapped in the prison industrial complex pipeline. Despite these statistical odds, there are Black males who are choosing higher education as an avenue for social mobility.

The burden ensues when prevailing racial ideologies that are inherent in the institutional arrangements of PWIs and reflect and reinforce larger sociocultural beliefs impact the experiences of Black students, in general. According to Dr. William B. Harvey:

> The nation's colleges and universities exist as a part of, not apart from, the interconnected matrix of organizations and institutions, economic and political forces, values and attitudes that comprise the larger socio-cultural environment. While they have often presented themselves in such a way as to suggest that they functioned with a greater sense of humanitarianism and at a more cerebral level than the general public, where matters of race have been concerned, institutions of higher education have historically manifested discriminatory and prejudicial practices and policies.[17]

Thus, the racial climate and culture of PWIs, instead of being leaders in the pursuit of higher learning, evolving intellectually, and reconciling the commonalities of humanity by deconstructing ideals of race and racial differences and dethroning its usefulness in maintaining the system of White supremacy, condones and at times fosters racist ideologies, which hinders its potential of promoting racial harmony.

Young White students with impressionable minds shaped by racist propaganda during their youth enter the sociocultural settings of academe, which are fortified with racist ideologies, and instead of having their views and beliefs challenged, they are tolerated and further reinforced. Their initial contact with Black males, specifically, is through a veil of racial ignorance that has framed all Black males in their minds to be thugs, gang-bangers, gangsta-rappers, or athletes and prohibits any meaningful interaction. Based on the historical stereotypes about race and gender that has meandered throughout portals of history and survived to plague both the perpetrator and the victim, these minds have already constructed a reality and an identity for Black males. The burden for Black males at PWIs has been to endure these constructed realities and prefabricated identities and reconstruct a meaningful existence while they seek to learn, grow, graduate, and become productive citizens. Race, then is a factor that shapes the experiences of Black males and Black male athletes at PWIs. Again, in this situation, race provides a social marker where parameters emerge to establish boundaries of social interaction. Therefore, race, as a social construct, assists in maintaining power relations between the racial minority and the racial majority.

In dialoguing with Black males (nonvarsity sports athletes), they have expressed how their race and gender have played a major role in their presence at PWIs. A focus group of Black males[18] I met with on a regular basis provided insightful information about what it is like being a Black male at a PWI. One upperclassman described his experience as being a "third class citizen" among the Black student body population, where athletes are number one and members of a Black fraternity ranked second in the hierarchy of popularity. There was consensus among this group that, among the White student population, if you were not an athlete as a Black male your stock was worthless. Another Black male (also an upperclassman) further expressed this fact when he and a friend (another Black male) were invited to a party by a White male student. At the party, in which they represented the minority, they were approached several times and questioned if they were athletes. Each time they responded "no," the White students withdrew immediately in dismay and bewilderment. Eventually, the Black males decided to play the "athletic card" and their popularity reversed tremendously; they drew a small crowd that began to question them on season predictions, status of other team members, etc. The conclusion he drew from this experience informed him of his status as simply a Black male student versus the status of being a Black male athlete. Within this social context, he realized that playing the athlete card afforded them privileges beyond those their nonathlete identity endowed.

In pursuing this issue with the larger group, other Black males (nonathletes) informed me of the dilemmas they face in being racially and athletically profiled and their challenges in not playing or playing the Black male athlete card. Other members of the group expressed never playing the athlete card because they wanted their acceptance to be about who they were as a person and not simply about an athletic identity they were perceived to have. Furthermore, the institutional arrangements that foster a low representation of Black males on campus place Black males who are nonvarsity sport athletes in a position of needing to disassociate themselves from the "Black male athletic identity," especially in the academic context, because of stereotypical beliefs from faculty members and fellow students. Oftentimes, this was accomplished through verbally expressing in class discussions that they were not athletes, or making sure they did not dress in stereotypical athletic garb: university sport paraphernalia, team sweats, etc.

Another theme emerging from one of our discussions involved the question from neighborhood friends and White peers at the institution: "Why this University?" Although academically it is a nationally ranked institution, why a Black male would attend this institution and not be an athlete was questionable; as if the only reason Black males attend this university is to compete athletically. This further highlights the prescribed roles Black males are expected to fulfill at PWIs. One group member reminded me of a White female's comment in a class discussion about how she believed that the only way many Black males were at this PWI was because of their athletic abilities. Based on the high visibility of Black males as athletes in revenue-generating sports, it is not hard to make similar conclusions.

Overall, these Black males' experiences centered on migration issues that required making an adjustment to the PWIs environment. I asked if there was any resentment toward Black male athletes. No, was the group consensus. Many of them knew several Black male athletes personally, and these personal relationships helped them to understand their personal plights as nonathletes and the plight of Black male athletes at this PWI. With this group of Black males, they saw race and gender as common denominators between them and Black male athletes, and those issues involving race and gender prevailed over their differences; in other words, both were subject to having a "Black experiences." They both shared a common dynasty: making it by any means necessary. Unfortunately, with the low graduation rates of Black males (nonvarsity sport athletes), they are benefiting far less in this arrangement.

Black Male Athletes at Predominantly White Institutions

Black male athletes are the "bread-winners" or "workhorses" for PWIs athletic departments across this nation. The level of competition, the commercial appeal, and economic growth of intercollegiate athletics would be drastically different without Black athletic talent. Similar to Nelson George's description of Blacks' influence in the game of basketball from Dr. James Naismith's version,[19] Black males have elevated intercollegiate athletics to its commercial level today. However, in the process they have had to endure the perils of racism in a variety of forms (covert and overt), while assisting in the capitalist expansion of PWIs.

Racism is a product of both White supremacy and racial stratification. And according to Robert Miles, racism is a relation of production.[20] It was an indispensable aspect in the process of capital accumulation during the periods of colonialism and slavery, and it remains indispensable in the process of exploiting the labor of people of color in the process of accumulated capital.

It is hard to be critical of racism when we look at the opportunities NCAA Division I revenue-generating sports of basketball and football have afforded many young Black males. There is evidence that points to the direct social mobility intercollegiate athletics have provided as an avenue into professional sports, or the indirect social mobility experienced by

Black male athletes who have graduated and transitioned into rewarding careers. Therefore, the racism argument is elusive in light of the convincing "rags-to-riches" stories given considerable media attention.

However, it is also hard not to be critical of racism when we look at the percentages of Black male athletes who comprise these teams, and not only that, but the percentage of starters they represent—especially in the top 25 most lucrative programs in the nation. It is hard not to be critical of racism because the return of investment (receiving an education and graduating) is low. Thus, the exploitation of labor is called into question when we compare the "rags-to-riches" stories to the "rags-to-despair" stories; especially when the United States has a storied past of exploiting the Black body for athletic labor with the motive of capitalist expansion.

The migration of Black athletes into this interracial relationship begins during the recruiting process, where contact is initiated by the institution. This denotes the direction of power when it appears that these institutions are at the mercy of these youth until they make a decision on signing day. These young athletes do exhibit some level of power in choosing an institution, but it is limited and within the parameters set by the institutions. Mainly because these institutions, operating collectively under the NCAA umbrella, function as oligopsonies, where, as buyers of athletic talent, they set the tone for the intercollegiate athletic market; especially in the sports of football and basketball. Therefore, young athletes aspiring to play intercollegiate athletes can choose where to play, but the power that determines if they play and how they will play is beyond the scope of their control.

This is slowly being challenged by a few top-ranked high school Black basketball players who are opting to develop their game in the European basketball market; mainly due to the NBA age limit requirement.[21] A case in point is Brandon Jennings, who was labeled the most talented basketball player in the country in 2008. Jennings decided to forego playing for a NCAA member institution and play in Europe. He is currently playing for the Italian League club Pallacanestro Virtus Roma. Jennings is potentially opening an avenue of opportunity that will alter the power intercollegiate athletics have over young Black talent.

Without a doubt, this has created an outcry from college coaches because it threatens the quality of talent in their athletic labor pool. However, a few who have taken this route have been forewarned of the challenges young players will have adjusting and playing in the European League: language barriers, cultural adjustment, distance from family and friends, limited playing time, playing against more mature and dominant players, career-ending injury, and potential lowering of draft stock.[22] This outcry should not be alarming since college coaches are the group who are benefitting the most from this arrangement.

Unfortunately, only a very few young athletes will be able to take advantage of this opportunity. The majority will be at the disposal of intercollegiate athletic industrial complex, where the gate that leads to careers in professional sport narrows significantly, while the gate that leads to academic achievement and graduation is a secondary option that receives little attention until option one has been completely exhausted. Many times, by then, they are scrambling to make sense of the years spent chasing a dream deferred that pursuing a degree and graduating can either be a ray of hope or hope minus its initial appeal.

In addition, the issue of race is obvious for Black male athletes from their initial contact with and eventual arrival at PWIs. It is no secret why they are there. Often racially isolated among other Black teammates, they develop a system of survival beneath their athletic identities. It is the athletic identity[23] that comforts and constrains Black males at PWIs. It provides comfort in regards to self-worth. In a conversation with a Black male athlete, Jason, a junior recruited from South Florida, with a look of elation he expressed, "Doc, you don't know what it feel like to have 80,000-plus fans screaming in excitement; there is nothing like it in the world." From Jason's tone and the way his words complemented the way he looked, I could sense that though he was hundreds of miles from his community and cultural context, the moments on the field with a cheering crowd gave him meaning, a sense of worth. His athletic identity gave him these privileged experiences that enabled him to survive in the broader social environment of a university that was utterly different from his place of origin. For him, the visibility of his race was concealed beneath the cloak of his athletic identity. Thus, athletic identity functions as a cloaking device, concealing one's racial identity; potentially deceiving some of their racial identity.

It was hard to contest with Jason's enthusiasm and provoke him to wake out of this dream state and face reality, because it worked for him. It seemed futile and a disservice to inform him that he was simply a cog in a plantation system that only wanted him for his athletic labor. Why discourage him? He was happy to be at this PWI; content with the roles of supplying athletic labor and parading as a student. He spoke decisively about getting his degree, however, "the League" (NFL) was his immediate and ultimate dream.

Race is also a factor in setting parameters on social interaction and academic development; more so for Black male athletes because of the athletic/labor demands. Race and gender impacts both Black males' and Black male athletes' ability to assimilate into campus culture. Yet, the athletic identity of Black male athletes affords them with greater privileges and a broader social circle than Black males who are nonathletes; this obviously varies with their status on the team (e.g., starter vs. third string) and media exposure. The exploits of Black male athletes are evident when you survey the small following of fans and groupies they manage to develop as their stock (performance, playing time, and exposure) increases from year to year. For members of their fan and groupie entourage, the Black body is not only admired for its athletic prowess and mystique, but it also becomes their ticket for a more meaningful life: economically, socially, and psychologically. Hence, as long as they are playing well, they period-ically transcend race and their Black skin is hidden deeply beneath their athletic identity; enabling them to attract interracial admiration, friend-ship, and intimacy.

A prominent Black athlete at one of the institutions I worked at became too familiar with this reality, when his performance slipped and it ulti-mately impacted the team's overall performance. He became aware of how quickly colorblind adoration can change to color-conscious racial slurs. Consequently, the comfort and privileges athletic identity provides for Black male athletes is unstable and fleeting. In conversations with several Black male athletes, they are aware of fair-weather fans and peers in their respective communities. It has been a source of frustration and stress when their identities as athletes do not transcend their race, and they become targets of racial ignorance. Race seems to have a polarization effect, where White individuals revert to when the reality of Black male athletes humanity is exposed (i.e., as long as they are performing god-like athletic feats, entertaining the masses they transcend racial identity; but once they fall from grace they become, well, just another nigger that needs to go back to Africa).

This speaks to an interesting practice some Whites in this context have managed to master: the compartmentalization of race. This is the ability to either ignore race or tolerate racial difference during times of convenience. The reality of Black male athletes being adored, honored, and cheered while Black males (nonathletes) are ostracized or ignored because they lack the athletic identity, demonstrates the practice of compartmentalizing race.

When coupled with race, Black males' athletic identity is a constraint that confines them to being one-dimensional. It is no secret that there is a majority of the mass audience that cheers them on each week who believe that Black athletes do not deserve to be at these institutions of higher learning, and they believe the only reason Black males are at these institutions is because they can run fast and jump high; and their predic-tion would not be totally inaccurate. Their athletic identity and physical ability can only take them so far within the academic milieu. Therefore, in the academic setting, beyond the glamour of game day, stares of amused contempt haunt Black male athletes.

A Black male athlete and former student in my course expressed his frustration with the stereotypical beliefs about his race, gender, and intel-lectual abilities. He migrated from a high school where he was an aca-demically decorated student. He represented what Dr. C. Keith Harrison has coined as the "Scholar-Baller."[24] He was known in his community for both his academic and athletic prowess. However, at this PWI, despite his academic credentials, his race, gender, and athletic identity constrained him to historical stereotypes and images that sustain the system of White supremacy. He expressed how, at this institution as a Black athlete, he was perceived to be intellectually incapable by his peers and White faculty members. He was a joy to have in class discussions because he created cognitive dissonance for White students who had constructed a reality about him from their limited frame of references and stereotypical beliefs.

★   ★   ★

Similar to their internally colonized predecessors, the Black male athelete too finds that race is ultimately a defining factor. It functions as a social marker within the colonial setting. Thus, the colonized were easily and specifically identified by their race. Their physical and social movement was regulated because of their skin color. It determined their existence and ascribed their identity in the colonial setting. Race binds them to a world constructed by the colonizer, which prescribes their worth and value based on their output or ability to produce.

For the Black male located in the internal colonial settings of PWIs, race functions similarly. According to Stuart Hall, race is a floating signifier; its meaning fluctuates given the context.[25] As Hall further suggests, it "floats in a sea of relational meaning" where the context provides the script. Thus, Black males and Black male athletes share race and gender in common and this commonality occasionally causes them to occupy the same space, however, their experiences vary significantly when athletic identity cloaks the racial identity of Black male athletes. Therefore, a Black male means one thing and a Black male athlete means something different in the context of PWIs. To a certain degree, athletic identity allows Black male athletes to have a different experience and to mean something different to PWIs than Black males who are nonvarsity sport athletes.

Black male athletes are necessary to the economic vitality of the revenue-generating sports of basketball and football at PWIs. Their overrepresentation on these teams situates them as an exploitable labor force who sustains the intercollegiate athletic industrial complex. This overrepresentation also speaks to the premium and demand for their athletic labor and an expected level of output; because Black athletes are always recruited to play or to add depth to a roster. As a necessary element for the athletic labor force, their race then places them within a historical relationship with the exploited Black labor that preceded them on plantation fields. This Black labor was converted into a system of production that sustained the internal colonial system of slavery and slavocracy, which contributed to both Southern and Northern economic development.

In summary, structurally, Black males (athletes and nonvarsity athletes) are visible at PWIs. Although access to PWIs for Blacks, in general, and Black males (nonvarsity athletes), specifically, is limited, Black male athletes are necessary fixtures within the intercollegiate athletic complex. Therefore, ideologically, the structural arrangements reflect and reinforce stereotypical beliefs about intellectual inferiority and physical superiority for Black males. When the most visible representations of Black males at

PWIs are consistently athletes, it supports age-old scientific racist ideals and practices. Upon contact, Black males are immediately racially and athletically profiled. The burden and blessing of being profiled varies in degree of intensity. Yet, navigating this terrain and receiving an education and graduating speak to the fortitude of Black males. In spite of the odds, the low representation, the low expectations, and the low graduation rates (37 percent national average in 2007),[26] Black males who are prevailing is commendable. Yes, the 63 percent who do not graduate from these institutions is a dismal rate and require inquiry, but the 37 percent are a testament of hope and an example of how PWIs are contested terrains where Black males are resisting ideological beliefs.

Race clearly is a factor impacting the experiences of Black students at PWIs. Institutions of higher education should approach this issue both at the structural and ideological levels. Increasing numbers without addressing the culture and the ideologies that prevail in academe is insufficient. It creates a cycle where Blacks are forced to always adjust, attempt to acculturate, and disarm racist ideology, when the institution should set the tone and be the leaders in fostering an inclusive environment: culturally, socially, psychologically, and so on. Beyond the admission policies implemented to increase minority enrollment, the ethos of PWIs must actively embrace racial differences not as a condescending or paternal act, but as a necessity for its relevance in the global market.

CHAPTER SIX

The Sociocultural Environment of Predominantly White NCAA Institutions: The Black Athlete as Oscillating Migrant Laborers

One ever feels his twoness....
> —W. E. B. Du Bois, *The Soul of Black Folks*

The concept of marginality dates back to the works of Robert E. Parks and Everett V. Stonequist. Stonequist suggests that a marginal "man" is an individual who toils between two distinct cultures, often experiencing discontent, alienation, and maladjustment.[1] Parks asserts that:

> One of the consequences of migration is to create a situation in which the same individual—who may or may not be a mixed blood—finds himself striving to live in two diverse cultural groups. The effect is to produce an unstable character—a personality type with characteristic forms of behavior. This is the "marginal man." It is in the mind of the marginal man that the conflicting cultures meet and fuse. It is, therefore, in the mind of the marginal man that the process of civilization is visibly going on, and it is in the mind of the marginal man that the process of civilization may best be studied.[2]

Both Stonequist and Parks inform of the conflict and controversy that exist for marginal people. These are individuals who live multilayered or disjointed lives, or what Viktor Frankl referred to as having experiences of "cultural hibernation."[3] Some researchers suggest that we all experience marginality in some form during our lifetime based on religion, race, ethnicity, and so on; whether open or secret.[4]

The social and cultural disconnect Black athletes experience at PWIs is due in part to the oscillating migrant labor patterns they encounter as a result of the internal colonial relationship. As outlined in the introduction, the oscillating migrant labor patterns produce unique experiences for Black athletes. It presents occurrences of situational marginality where Black athletes contend with their twoness. In order to maximize their athletic abilities, many Black athletes, who are born and raised in communities distinctly different from the ones they find themselves in at the PWIs, tolerate this situational marginality. This chapter will focus on the sociocultural challenges Black athletes encounter on predominantly White National Collegiate Athletic Association (NCAA) Division I institutions (PWIs), which spatially creates a sensation where "one ever feels his twoness."

To summarize, the oscillating migrant laborers' experiences are organized around two cultures: home sites, which include family and friends of similar social and cultural origins; and work sites, which involve social and cultural expression different and unfamiliar to them.[5] These laborers rotate for various periods of time during the year between these two distinctly different cultural and social settings.[6] The major purpose for oscillating migrant laborers' patterns is the forced need to sell their labor and utilize their skills in hopes of improving their financial conditions back at home (pay taxes, buy food and clothes). The fact that this labor is cheap makes it profitable to the buyers of this labor; that is, the villages assume the greater responsibility of the laborer (bearing the cost of nurturing) but not the benefits.

Similarly, Black athletes engage in oscillating migrant labor patterns. They seek to utilize their talents, thus, they sell their athletic labor in hopes of improving their education and eventually their socioeconomic status. Therein lies the blessing and burden of this arrangement: the blessing is the potential for direct or indirect mobility (going to the next level professionally or getting a college degree and becoming gainfully employed); the burden in the extraction of resources from the Black community with no return on their investment. And, an additional burden is the potential risk of not being accepted in either setting, because they have assimilated too far into one (PWIs settings) and too far away for the other (their home community).

★ ★ ★

The *Brown v. the Board of Education of Topeka, Kansas* (1954) decision provided Blacks with greater access to predominantly White public institutions of higher education that were once off-limits and out of reach to Blacks' academic ambitions. The migration of Blacks and other minorities to these institutions has altered the racial demographic and cosmetic configuration of the student body yet the institutional configuration of many of these institutions has remained monocultural. Instead of being environments that embrace and value diversity while fostering mutual acculturation between the institution and students from diverse cultural backgrounds, they have forced assimilation, alternation (or code-switching), or attrition on students of color from different cultural backgrounds.[7]

Forms of capital are also relevant to the patterns of oscillating migrant laborers. According to Pierre Bourdieu, there are several types of capital: economic, social, cultural, and symbolic.[8] Bourdieu gives the following explanations for each form of capital and how it can present itself:

> As economic capital, which immediately and directly convertible into money and may be institutionalized in the form of property rights; as cultural capital, which is convertible, on certain conditions, into economic capital and may be institutionalized in the form of educational qualifications; as social capital, made up of social obligations ("connections"), which is convertible, in certain conditions, into economic capital and may be institutionalized in the form of a title of nobility.[9]

According to Bourdieu, symbolic capital is:

> Capital—in whatever form—in so far as it is represented, i.e., apprehended symbolically, in a relationship of knowledge or, more precisely, of misrecognition and recognition, presupposes the intervention of the habitus, as a socially constituted cognitive capacity.[10]

Because the institutional arrangements of PWIs are structured to service and privilege individuals who have inherited, in most cases, a higher level of capital, in its varying forms, Black students' migration to these institutions and their adjustment to the sociocultural environments of the institutions presents challenges. For example, Torres used cultural capital theory to illustrate how campus life at a college traditionally designed to serve "wealthy white students" is difficult for "non-affluent Blacks."[11] The public institutions of higher education, which house most of the top 25 NCAA Division I athletic programs, similarly are designed to serve and privilege individuals with certain levels of inherited capital and present challenges to Black students, in general, and Black athletes, specifically.

As mentioned in the introduction, scholars have engaged the topic of Black students at predominantly White colleges and universities.[12] For over 30 years, the literature addresses the challenges, highlights the success stories, and details the development of programs to enhance Black students' transition, retention, and graduation from these institutions. There continues to be a need for cultural diversity initiatives and advocates of multiculturalism to seek inclusion within the culture of PWIs, which includes the curricula and power structures of the institutions.

★   ★   ★

It is abundantly clear that there are athletic departments at PWIs that are progressive in recruiting Black male athletes, specifically, for the revenue-generating sports of football and basketball, and there are some that are improving their minority hiring practices in administrative and coaching positions. However, the change is slow, thus, the culture and climate of PWIs athletic departments continues to reflect those of the greater institution.

Cultural diversity is a two-pronged attack that involves changes at the structural level (i.e., the hiring practices, racially diversifying athletic departments—making cosmetic changes) and at the ideological level (i.e., addressing the stereotypical myths that maintain the system of White supremacy and White skin privilege and deny Blacks, specifically, access to key administrative and head coaching positions; for example, the intellectual inferiority myth or the lack of experienced or qualified candidate pool smoke screen). Without these changes at both levels, Black athletes are migrating into departments where they are further politically, socially, and culturally alienated. The structural and ideological arrangements of these departments must move beyond hiring one or two Black administrators in peripheral positions or assistant coaches to recruit and contain the Black athletic talent, yet they have no real "veto" power; these hires are either token concessions, or more likely a means of recruiting and stocking revenue-generating sports with premium Black talent.

Meanwhile, Black athletes' migration is layered: one level is at the institutional level, where they are migrating into campus life and a student body that are vastly different from them culturally and socially; and the next level is the athletic department, where they are migrating into an athletic culture consisting of a smaller group of students and administrators who reflect the racial demographics and sociocultural mores of the larger institution, which again, is immensely different from their social and cultural frames of reference.

This is very much the case for oscillating migrant laborers; they generally enter socioeconomic and cultural settings that are different from their home sites. They also are leaving locations where they are the majority and going to locations were they become the minority. Therefore, because both groups oscillate between two social and cultural settings, they probably experience double consciousness, that is, the peculiar sensation that requires them to maintain two identities.

Because of the oscillating migrant laborers' phenotypic differences, life in hostels or communes (social), and cultural differences, they experience a sense of being different and racial isolation in the culture they migrate into.[13] Their racial differences coupled with moving into different social and cultural environments contributes to Black athletes' experience a sense of being different from other students and racial isolation.[14] The history of the United States reveals how Blacks have always been in an unusual situation, made to feel different and racially isolated; a situation that has been referred to by Ralph Ellison as "invisibility" where Black athletes are "surrounded by mirrors of hard distorted glass."[15] The environments they are in refuse to see them for who they are, only for how fast they can run and how high they can jump. This basically has been the history of Blacks in the United States: during slavery they were seen as something of use value; later, they were seen as brutes and animalistic in nature; today, at these institutions, they are once again seen as property for use value.

To expound, many Black athletes leave communities and schools where they are the majority not really knowing what it feels like to be a minority or the impact of being "out numbered." Several Black athletes have voiced this dilemma to me and expressed the adjustment they have made to cope with this transition. Most have used self-induced racial isolation until a level of comfort and trust is accomplished in this new environment. Others have used this as an excuse not to go to class, where they have to deal with being the only one or two Blacks in class and by default representatives for the race; while others have used it as an excuse not to venture far beyond the athletic culture, where they would have to endure the stares of curious and suspicious onlookers questioning their very presence on campus.

Like clockwork each semester for over 15 years I have witnessed Black athletes and Black students, in general, migrate to PWIs and create enclaves; some because it is normal human behavior to group oneself around similarities, but many have voiced that it is due to the nature of the environment: that is, some perceive it as different and unwelcoming; some suggest it is culturally conservative and "unaccepting"; while some have experienced it as bordering on racially hostile.

I can usually distinguish the Black students (including athletes) who have migrated from a predominantly Black community and high school and those from a predominantly White community and high school. For the former, their interaction is mainly within their race, thus, their social circle is more homogeneous. For the Black athletes in this category, I generally see them in groups of two or three—in the cafeteria, going to class, or to practice. On the other hand, for the latter, they have a greater level of comfort and mobility in the predominantly White university setting, they tend to have greater interracial interaction, and they have at least one White friend.

I have also witnessed two catalysts that determine the level of Black males acculturation (and sometimes assimilation[16]): (1) cultural diversity has been encouraged by parents, family, or high school coaches; or (2) their levels have increased as a result of interracial dating. Marcus was a Black male athlete who fit the description of the first group. Though he grew up in a predominantly Black community, he recognized the significance of being culturally diverse and realized his social capital would increase if he expanded his social circle. For the former, interracial dating has become a common practice, which sometimes produces acculturation for both the Black male and White female.

In addition to these challenges, being in a place where one feels different from others and being racially isolated can stimulate the feeling that Black athletes lack control over their lives, that is, the social, cultural, and racial makeup of the institutions are not necessarily situated to accommodate Blacks in general and Black athletes specifically. Their input into the structural makeup of these institutions is of no value because they are viewed as mere athletes. Their lives are structured so that they are to be given input: told when and where to go and when and where to be. I only wonder if these athletic departments feel that not having control over their lives would jeopardize the potential productivity and profit of their commodity. This basically illustrates what Harry Edwards refers to as institutionalized powerlessness, which when manifested produces this lack of control Black athletes have over their lives and the exploitation of their athletic labor.[17]

Labor exploitation is another similarity that situates Black athletes within the pattern of oscillating migrant laborers. Both groups are trying to maximize their skills and talents to benefit their families and themselves, however, there is nowhere in the Black communities or the villages where Black athletes or oscillating migrant laborers can trade their skills for profit or for their benefit (e.g., there is no place in Black communities where a jump shot, catching a football, or running the fastest 100 meters could turn into a college education and a degree). These skills are of little value to Black athletes if they remain in these communities because there is limited, if any, need or benefit for them. To use these skills and talents, Black athletes and oscillating migrant laborers must relocate to different locations and contract their talents out to these institutions.

These predominantly White NCAA Division I institutions act as a monopsony where they are the only buyers of this service, except in rare cases where there is direct entry from high school into professional sports. They issue out yearly athletic scholarship and in return they benefit in the following ways: sell of media rights, tickets, the sell of licensing products, that is, caps, jackets, T-shirts, and so on. Furthermore, if a team appears in one of the collegiate bowl games or other national tournaments that attract a lot of lucrative sponsors and advertisers, or if the team is a member of a conference that has revenue sharing and one of the teams from the conference makes it to a bowl game or national tournament, the institution benefits either directly or indirectly.

Mike Fish gives two other examples to illustrate the revenue generated at these institutions and how little trickles down to the athletes: at the University of Kentucky, a basketball scholarship is $11,434, the coach's salary package is at $1.95 million, and the basketball program grosses close to $12 million; another example is at the University of Florida where a full scholarship for the football team is $7,070, the coach's salary package is $940,810, and the football program grossed $27.9 million.[18]

Many athletes and spectators of college athletics have been naive in believing that a grant-in-aid equates to the use of their skills and talents. There is the view by several researchers of collegiate sports that the labor output is not equal to the education received or the profits made from commercial ventures, thus economic exploitation exists.[19] D. Stanley

Eitzen and George H. Sage have precisely captured this exploitation when they suggest:

> The businesslike character of big-time college sport is more directly responsible for one additional problem. Young men (and more recently young women) are paid slave wages (room, board, and tuition) to bring honor and dollars to their university.... Thus, there are two questions of morality: 1) the use of athletes to hustle money for the university; 2) the exploitation of the athletes by paying them indecent wages.[20]

In a survey of NCAA Division I, II, and III Black college basketball players, Wilbert Leonard suggests that the exploitation is greater for them than White athletes because:

> Being an athlete had forced more Blacks into taking a less demanding major, cheating academically, taking gut classes, hustling professors for grades, having others write their papers, and taking fewer courses during the term. Blacks felt more pressure to be an athlete first and a student second, felt less confident that they could handle college work, were more likely to have insufficient credits to graduate, were less likely to have been able to meet academic admission requirements without being an athlete, felt more threatened about the consequences of not abiding by the coach's philosophy and felt inadequately rewarded for their efforts.[21]

Similar to the low wages oscillating migrant laborers are paid, Black athletes also receive low wages on the return of their athletic labor in the form of receiving a lesser quality of education due to the limited time they have available for the educational process; the educational process extends beyond going to class every day to socializing with research and study groups, participating with student organizations, and attending campus activities apart from athletics. Allen Sack recognized the imbalance in this exchange and concluded that because of the inadequate education received by the average student athlete it equates to merely the bare necessities to exist on these campuses.[22] This exploitation is compounded for Black athletes because many lack adequate academic preparation needed prior to entering these institutions, and they receive passive academic support at these institutions.

Another similarity that exists between Black athletes and oscillating migrant laborers that again addresses the issue of exploitation is the issue of who bears the cost developing and nurturing the skills and talents that is converted into athletic labor. In both cases, it is the communities and villages where Black athletes and oscillating migrant laborers grow up that bear this cost until the time they are ready to be recruited or relocated to work. They arrive on location, the campus, ready to compete or work. The majority of the training, conditioning, and skills needed are acquired prior to entering the campus. With this athletic preparation, it is still a common practice that Black athletes are recruited to play and not to ride the bench. Basically, if they are on full grant-in-aid, Black athletes are expected to learn the offensive and defensive plays and step in and contribute. Therefore, these institutions, in the case of Black athletes, bear none of the cost of developing and nurturing the skills and talents, but they receive the majority, if not all, the profit of their labor.

The communities must also bear the cost of these athletes when they return injured, no longer able to compete in sports and with very limited or no occupational skills. These athletes can possibly become an unexpected burden to their families and communities if they are unable to complete a degree with "employable opportunities" or acquire some occupational skills.

Conclusion and Ideas for Change

Similarities were identified that exist between Black athletes and oscillating migrant laborers. Both groups experience marginality. For Black athletes, they enter different social and cultural settings from a disadvantaged position, which may contribute to the high attrition and low graduation rates of Black athletes. Both groups experience economic exploitation for their labor and the rotation between communities and work sites to better use their skills and talents. This rotation benefits these institutions because the communities of Black athletes bear the cost of developing and nurturing the skills and talents for athletic labor. Considering Black athletes' conformity to the pattern of oscillating migrant laborers, their experiences can be placed in a broader theoretical and cultural context, thus hopefully reducing the myopic view that is often used in analyzing the experiences of Black athletes and trying to establish programs to meet their needs.

This myopic view has mainly concentrated on Black athletes as being intellectually inferior, therefore, remedial courses, light course loads, as well as the basic skills approach to improve reading, writing, and study skills have been the focus of many programs designed for athletes in general and Black athletes specifically. I do agree with several of the researchers that advocate building stronger academic support systems, freshman ineligibility, *enforcing* the 20 hours per week athletes have to spend on their sport, and investing into the school systems these athletes graduate from to increase future athletes academic preparation.[23] There needs to be social and cultural changes made to the structures of the institutions.

Harries's account of migrant laborers' living conditions in the compounds of Mozambique and South Africa over a period of time began to resemble the various cultures of individuals that populated them, especially through religious, entertainment, and social activities.[24] He did not conclude that making the work location more culturally identifiable made the working conditions more amicable or the exploitation less drastic for oscillating migrant laborers, but in conjunction with the recommendations mentioned earlier, could facilitate more positive experiences for Black athletes at predominantly White NCAA Division I institutions.

These institutions' social and cultural structures must begin to resemble the social and cultural structures of the students that attend them, more specifically Black students. Attention, support, and funding are needed in the area of going beyond the rhetoric of cultural diversity in order to minimize the differences experienced by all students who relocate to these institutions. These campuses as well as the cities where these campuses are located must not only be inviting and accepting for the athletic talents these students have to offer but they must be accommodating of the social and cultural backgrounds of Black athletes. These institutions need to realize their limitations and deficiencies in their relationship with certain populations and be willing to seriously address and correct these limitations and deficiencies.

The multicultural and diversity endeavors occurring at many of these institutions must move beyond the mere celebration of food and cultural apparel during a day or month out of a year. These predominantly White institutions that have access to Black churches and businesses must reach out to them to assist them in the transition and socialization of Black athletes. Those institutions that do not have this luxury must work to become more multicultural in social functions, curriculum, and faculty and staff representation.

Multicultural curriculum must be continually developed to permeate throughout all departments, not just Black Studies departments. Faculty and staff must become more diversified, especially the athletic departments at these institutions. This diversification must differentiate itself from the late 1970s hiring practices of Black coaches and administrators that as Dr. Harry Edwards states, "amounted to little beyond cosmetic transition devoid of any substantive potential for transformation."[25] Basically, the "good ole boy" network that perpetuates this monocultural environment must be destroyed. This networking suggests that you hire individuals of like color, in most cases if possible, but at least individuals who have the same identities, that is, identify with the White culture. The "good ole boy" network has been breeding mediocrity and debilitating many athletes' lives. There needs to be a revolutionary affirmative action at these institutions.

Finally, when it comes to reducing the labor exploitation, the recommendations mentioned above are indirect ways of lessening this experience. Short of paying athletes, there must be greater measures applied to balancing the exchange between athletic participation and college education and degree completion. If these institutions expect four years of the very best running and jumping in the country, then these students should expect the very best educational assistance in the country. This may mean

developing and enforcing more rules to enhance the academic achievement for all athletes.

The deficiencies of these institutions in combination with Black athletes conforming to the pattern of oscillating migrant laborers could be
major contributors to the high attrition and low graduation rates of Black
athletes at predominantly White institutions, as well as the experiences
they have with feeling different from other students, racial isolation, and
the feeling that they lacked control of their lives.

Future research in this area could address how the cities, where these
institutions are located, could assist in changing the social and cultural
settings. Many of these cities generate revenue from having a collegiate
athletic team in their area. Therefore, it would be advantageous for
them to invest in their investment, that is, create an environment that is
productive for Black athletes, not only athletically, but also educationally, culturally, and socially. Many times the hostility experienced off-
campus by Black athletes can have an effect with on-campus experiences.
University administrators and city officials should be aware of the racial
climates that exist in their cities and work toward racially harmonious
communities.

The relocation of Black athletes from their communities to culturally
and socially different ones is a dramatic experience for many of them and
presents challenges of acculturation. The plantation model denotes the
challenges that enshroud Black athletes at PWIs. I admire the Black male
and female athletes who have mastered the marginal experience and navigated this terrain successfully with coping mechanisms like alternation
or code-switching. However, again, acculturation should be a two-way
process where the multiple parties involved should work toward achieving
cultural competence in theory and practice.

One additional comment that sets the stage for the next chapter regarding the political component is the fact that the oscillating migrant labor
patterns of Black athletes contributes to their powerlessness. According
to R. A. Schermerhorn, power against minority groups has been accomplished in three ways: (1) eradication or relocation of a group by a group of
greater power; (2) group of greater power dominates weaker group from
a distant location; (3) and the group of greater power relocates group of
lesser power within a territory where they can maintain control.[26] It is this
last form of power that is accomplished by way of the oscillating migrant
laborer experience; thus, rending Black athletes economically exploited
and political powerless.

CHAPTER SEVEN

Politics and the Black Athletic Experience

In the 1960s, when young African-Americans were asked the question "What do you want?", we frequently replied: "A [B]lack face in a high place."

—Manning Marable, *Beyond Black and White: Transforming African American Politics*

Intercollegiate athletics is admired for its entertainment value and often assumed by many to be apolitical. Frequently, the entertainment value overshadows and dull our senses to the political aspects associated with intercollegiate athletics. The politics of intercollegiate athletics mainly involve the legislative and governing powers of national associations, such as, the National Collegiate Athletic Association (NCAA) or the National Association for Intercollegiate Athletics (NAIA), regional conferences (e.g., Big 10, Atlantic Coast Conferences [ACC], Southeastern Conference [SEC], etc.), and the university administration (e.g., faculty athletic representatives). Purely as legislative bodies, these associations, conferences, and committees generally function in the capacity of developing standards involving the following: recruitment, academic eligibility, rule enforcement, competitive safeguards and medical issues, site selection for championship events, and so on. According to the NCAA, "All of the Association's governing bodies strive to promote student–athlete welfare through legislation and program initiatives."[1]

Although the original purpose of their existence was legislative, they have evolved to be in the business of marketing goods and services and wealth distribution. This is significant to the plight of Black athletes because they make up the largest percentage of the athletic labor force that contributes to the NCAA new business paradigm. Similar to the internal colonial political relations outlined in chapter 2, the colonized political powerlessness was in direct correlation with the colonizer's hegemony. Thus, the colonized were at the political mercy of the colonizer and were totally dependent upon the legislative and governance structure of the plantation, which, as chattel, yielded the colonized no rights.

The politics of intercollegiate athletics that are relevant to this chapter specifically regard the decision makers who create policies, approve legislation, and enforce the policies that govern the lives of college athletes, in general, and Black athletes, specifically. In the case of Black athletes, their political voice is silenced because of the ideology of amateurism, the paternalistic nature of the NCAA and its member institutions[2], and because there is a lack of representation at the leadership level—that is, athletic administrators and coaches. This chapter will examine how the ideology of amateurism and paternalism and the lack of representation in leadership positions consign Black athletes to positions of political powerlessness. It will examine the leadership structures of the NCAA and its member institutions to see how it is a microcosm of the leadership structure of the larger U.S. society.

It is important to note at the onset that increased representation does not equate to having a voice in the decision-making process. Remember colonial rule involves governance where political decisions are made for the colonized without their input and often with the aide of indirect rule. Also, remember that the process of indirect rule is a system where the dominant group rules the subordinate with leaders from the subordinate group; therefore, leaders among the colonized are co-opted by the colonizer and become minions who answer the dominant group.

Furthermore, efforts to create greater representation of Blacks in leadership positions to provide Black athletes with a voice can also create what Manning Marable refers to as "symbolic representation" where, in the case of the Black community, there "is a belief that if an African American receives a prominent appointment to government, the private sector, or the media, then [B]lack people as a group is symbolically empowered."[3] The fallacy to this thesis emerged when, as Marable states,

> A new type of African-American leadership emerged inside the public and private sectors, which lived outside the black community and had little personal contacts with African American.[4]

Therefore, "a Black face in a high place" has not always equaled change in Black communities or for Black people. For example, the election of Justice Clarence Thomas to the Supreme Court represented "a Black face in a high face" yet it also revealed, as Marable suggest, "the inherent contradictions and limitations of simplistic, racial-identity politics."[5] Similarly, other levels of Black leadership in the post–civil rights era chart the disconnectedness some Black leaders have with the lives and interests of Black people. However, authentic racial representation will move beyond symbolic empowerment and produce effective empowerment that transforms the powerless Black athletes into being active and proactive participants in the political process that impacts their lives. Thus, changing the leadership structures by increasing Black representation of the NCAA, university administrators, athletic departments, and athlete governing bodies, does not guarantee a change in political empowerment for Black athletes. Yet, it improves on the current state of affairs where their voice is completely mute.

With that said, developing an understanding of ideological and structural issues that nourish the current political landscape of intercollegiate athletics is paramount to diminishing political powerlessness among Black athletes. The next section will address the ideology of amateurism and paternalism as a means to maintain social control and ownership of means of production, where the revenue generated by athletes' labor and image or identity is controlled by athletic administrators campaigning to have the interest of the athletes at the heart of their decision-making process.

The Ideology of Amateurism and Paternalism

As mentioned in the introduction, according to the NCAA Manual, amateurism, as defined by the NCAA, declares that

> Student-athletes shall be amateurs in an intercollegiate sport, and their participation should be motivated primarily by education and by the physical, mental, and social benefits to be derived. Student participation in intercollegiate athletics is an avocation, and student-athletes should be protected from exploitation by professional and commercial enterprises.[6]

This ideological system has prevailed, undergirds the governance of collegiate athletics, and is a primary means of social control. Under this ideology, athletes' resources (skills and images) are extorted while they are restricted to an antiquated principle, which regulates their behavior and determines their benefits.[7]

Amateurism has also positioned PWIs within a paternal relationship with athletes, where collegiate athletes are provided with security and protection "from exploitation by professional and commercial enterprises." Paternalism has been referred to as the "sweet persuasion" by Mary Jackman.[8] Furthermore, Jackman suggests that

> The father authoritatively dictated all the behaviors and significant life-decisions of his children within a moral framework that credited the father with an assailable understanding of the needs and best interests of his children. They, in turn, accepted implicitly and absolutely the authority of their father—occasional bouts of independence were not unexpected, but never tolerated.[9]

Therefore, the decisions that govern the lives of collegiate athletes are made with an understanding of the needs and best interests of the athlete; thus, this assumes that these institutions know the interests and what is best for athletes. It is important to note that the limits of this analogy pivot on motives: a father's love for his children is his motive for the need to govern the behaviors and decisions of his children; whereas social control and economic exploitation are the motives of PWIs. This is especially evident when one examines the rules instituted and enforced that prevent athletes from benefiting from their talents and images beyond their yearly scholarships, or the rules that are instituted to exhibit complete control over their bodies rendering them powerless in the decision-making process that govern their lives.

A perfect example of NCAA efforts to protect athletes from exploitation by professional and commercial enterprises occurred with Jeremy Bloom. Jeremy Bloom was a collegiate football player for the University of Colorado and a world-class freestyle skier who was declared ineligible by the NCAA for receiving endorsements to offset expenses he incurred while training for the '06 Winter Games in Turin, Italy. For the protection from exploitation by professional and commercial enterprises, the NCAA provides prohibited him from any ownership of his identity, image, the product he produces, or any entrepreneurial ventures he may engage in beyond their respective sports. Therefore, the message the NCAA is sending is that they, and the corporations affiliated with them through sponsorship, endorsements, and outsourcing, are the only ones allowed to profit from the athletic talents and images of athletes.

Another example of the powerlessness is the recent ruling by the NCAA regarding online college football fantasy leagues. In a case that involved Major League Baseball, a lower court ruled that players' names and statistics are public knowledge and free to be used by fantasy leagues was upheld by the U.S. Supreme Court. Implications of this ruling impact the NCAA and have prevented them from challenging CBS Sports use of players' names and statistics.[10] However, the NCAA firmly adheres to their stance that athletes are amateurs and cannot take part in new business enterprises, such as, these online fantasy leagues, which uses their real names and statistics. As Dr. Richard Southall, director of the College Sport Research Institute and assistant professor at the University of North Carolina—Chapel Hill, has expressed that, similar to the sale of player jerseys, this decision by the NCAA further forces athletes to pay for their own image.

Finally, another example of the NCAA paternalistic efforts can be witnessed with it rules regarding sports wagering. Their goal is to preserve the integrity of the game and protect the welfare of athletes and the NCAA brand. Even the acts of "harmless" or "friendly" sports wagering is prohibited by athletes. This can be noted in the judgments rendered in the following "sport wagering" cases:

Eligibility ID-24291; Secondary ID-22795—Student-athlete wagered a maximum of $10 with friends on a professional football game. Institution suspended student-athlete from one regular season game and made student-athlete complete 10 hours of community service. Eligibility reinstated on the condition that student-athlete complete the community service.

Eligibility ID-26367; Secondary ID-25195—Student-athlete wagered $10 on Super Bowl. Institution made student-athlete donate $10 to charity, sit out first contest and one week of practice. Eligibility reinstated based on institution's actions.

Eligibility ID-22633; Secondary ID-20318—Student-athlete made "friendly wager" with a radio host on the outcome of his own game. Bet that if the team won, the radio host would have the student-athlete over for dinner, and if the team lost, the student-athlete would wear the opposing team's jersey on campus. Institution required student-athlete to complete 10 hours of community service. Eligibility reinstated.[11]

It is interesting to note how minor the infractions are, yet how stern the penalties administered by the NCAA or its member institutions in governing and controlling the lives of athletes. The message the NCAA is sending is that the friendly sport wagering of dormitory or office pools is taboo for athletes regardless of its innocence and insignificance.

One way the NCAA has attempted to police itself and supposedly provide athletes with an avenue to give input into the decision-making process is with the creation of student-athlete advisory committee (SAAC). SAAC is a committee consisting of student-athletes assembled to provide insight on the student-athlete experience. The SAAC also offers input on the rules, regulation, and polices that affect student-athletes' lives on NCAA member institution campuses.[12] The mission of SAAC is "to enhance the total student-athlete experience by promoting opportunity, protecting student-athlete welfare and fostering a positive student-athlete image."[13] A summary of its objectives are as follow:

Generate a student-athlete voice within the NCAA structure; solicit student-athlete response to proposed NCAA legislation; recommend potential NCAA legislation; review, react and comment to the governance structure on legislation, activities and subjects of interest; actively participate in the administrative process of athletics programs and the NCAA; and promote a positive student-athlete image.[14]

At the national or division level, the SAAC is comprised of one student from each conference that makes up each of the NCAA Divisions. SAAC members are selected by athletic administrators that comprise the Division I Leadership and Legislative Councils, formerly the Division I Management Council, from a pool of three nominees from each conference, and they serve a two-year term.[15] Furthermore, according to the SAAC guidelines:

The Division I SAAC reports directly to the Division I Management Council and two SAAC members participate in each meeting of the

Management Council as nonvoting members. It is through these two mechanisms that NCAA Division I student-athletes offer input and assist in shaping the proposed legislation by which their division is governed.[16]

SAAC is numerically structured accordingly: Division I has 31, Division II has 25, and Division III has 23 for a total of 79 students that comprise the SAAC. It is interesting to note that during the 2006–2007 years, approximately 402,793 students participated in NCAA sports;[17] thus, 78 students are to provide a voice for over 400,000 students. Furthermore, the racial demographics of Division I SAAC members are worth noting; of the 31 students SAAC members, 6 are Black: 2 are at Historically Black Colleges and Universities (HBCUs) and 4 are at PWIs.

There is also SAAC at the campus and conference levels that assist in providing a voice for athletes. At the campus level, the focus of SAAC is much more parochial and involves the following functions:

> Promote communication between athletics administration and student-athletes; disseminate information; provide feedback and insight into athletics department issues; generate a student-athlete voice within the campus athletics department formulation of policies; build a sense of community within the athletics program involving all athletics teams; solicit student-athlete responses to proposed conference and NCAA legislation; organize community service efforts; create a vehicle for student-athlete representation on campus-wide committees (e.g., student government); and promote a positive student-athlete image on campus.[18]

SAAC's functions at the campus level resembles the method of indirect rule, especially as it relates to promoting communication between athletics administration and student-athletes; disseminating information; providing feedback and insight into athletics department issues, and promoting a positive student-athlete image on campus. These functions create a facade of political interaction, while masking their ability to socially control the lives of athletes.

Although this is a noble attempt in providing athletes with a voice in the legislative process that impact their lives, I cannot help but be critical of the construction of SAAC because it creates another layer in the bureaucratic hierarchy of intercollegiate athletic governance. I also question it because the political power of the members is unfortunately determined by the councils that select them. Thus, the criterion for selection regulates the partisanship of the nominees and ultimately the members who are selected. In other words, radical agendas are marginalized because the process of selection neutralizes the voices of the members.

Both Black male and female athletes have expressed to me their disgruntlement when voicing their concerns and complaints through this committee. A summation of their responses suggest that it lacks leverage in dealing with weighty matters involving coaching changes, the loss of scholarship due to coaching changes, scholarship distribution, racial issues, budget allocation for their respective sports (especially regarding women's nonrevenue-generating sports), and so on. For them, this committee serves as window dressing enticing some to feel that student athletes have a voice in the athletic governance process. It is basically a form of political camouflage to give the appearance that the welfare of student athletes is paramount.

The ideology of amateurism and the paternalistic nature of PWIs in seeking to protect the athlete from commercial exploitation fosters a culture of political powerlessness. The voice that SAAC provides on behalf of athletes is questionable because it is constructed for them yet members are selected for them by NCAA councils. Oppression can never be removed nor can a voice of the oppressed speak from the position of authenticity when the oppressor decides what to hear and determine who will speak on behalf of the oppressed.

Speaking more specifically to political powerlessness of Black athletes at PWIs, the representation of Blacks in leadership positions must be taken into consideration. Again, there is no guarantee that an increased representation of Blacks in leadership positions will equate to Black athletes having a political voice at the legislative tables within intercollegiate athletics. Yet, the intercollegiate athletic landscape is demanding progressive changes to the racial demographics of administrative positions in intercollegiate athletic departments.

Race and Representation in Intercollegiate Athletic Leadership Positions: The Black Athletic Administrators and Coaches Dilemma

Having a voice and being represented in levels of leadership has the potential of diffusing powerlessness experienced by underserved populations. The inspiration produced with the election of President Barack Obama is an example of how having representation in leadership position is important—both for symbolic and literal empowerment. I remember walking through the airport the day after the election and seeing a confidence and assurance that this election had spawned in Blacks in general, and Black males specifically. I will never forget the comments and facial expressions of a Black male security officer: his verbal comment was simply, "It sure feels good," as his facial expression told a story of excitement and relief of the possibility of finally having a voice or having someone that has had similar racial and gendered experiences in the highest office in the nation and one of the most powerful positions in the world. The psychological uplift from this election, though it may be short-lived, is strategic in inspiring millions into believing they can be heard, that they can make a difference, and that change is possible.

In the context of sports, the late Gene Upshaw, executive director of the National Football League Players Association, expressed his reasoning in encouraging owners to hire more Black coaches in the National Football League (NFL). His rationale was twofold: it is the right thing to do given the racial demographics of the league and that in the age of free agency there is the potential for Black players to show more loyalty to Black head coaches.[19] Upshaw asserts that Black players who have played for Black coaches on average:

> talk about how much they love playing for those guys [Black coaches]. The main reason is because they are good head coaches, but another reason is because black players feel a sense of loyalty to them because they are black coaches.[20]

I do not want to be presumptuous in believing that having a Black coach will automatically create positive experiences for Black athletes, because clearly this is impossible given the cultural heterogeneity that exists among Black people. In other words, there are White coaches who may be just as qualified in relating to Black athletes and fostering a positive environment and sporting experiences. However, Upshaw's insightful comments have fallen upon deaf ears when we examine the presence of Black coaches in the NFL and intercollegiate athletics; especially in the sport of football.

The infectious presence of racism is apparent when examining the racial representation of Blacks in intercollegiate head football coaching positions, specifically, and in administrative leadership positions, in general. Comments from Terry Bowden further expound on the controversy involved in hiring Black head football coaches:

> A profession that so desperately seeks a level playing field offers nothing close to one for the black athlete who aspires to rise to the pinnacle of the college coaching profession. Plainly and simply, folks, this is discrimination. More precisely this is one of the last and greatest bastions of discrimination within all of American sports. In college football, we are winning games, building programs and making millions of dollars with the sweat and blood of African-American athletes. I should know. In the last dozen years, my family alone has made more than $30 million as Division I-A head football coaches. At least once a day, I get asked, "When are you getting back into coaching?" Heck, schools don't need to hire me. They need to hire from the untapped talent that exists within the pool of black assistant coaches. It really isn't that hard to understand why big-time college football is in this embarrassing situation. Quite simply, the 117 Division I-A schools are white. They have a large majority of white students, with 95 percent of the schools with white presidents and 89 percent with white athletics directors. They also have a whole lot of white alumni

who aren't afraid to let their opinions be known; especially the fact that they don't want a black head football coach....Many presidents won't hire black coaches because they are worried about how alumni and donors will react.[21]

Bowden's comments are profound in the sense that he exposes institutional racist practices that have prevented Blacks from moving into major colleges' head coaching positions. He also exposes the fact that Blacks are welcomed as long as they are running fast and jumping high for the institutions, but they are unwelcome in positions of authority and leadership. Finally, his comments allude to the fact that it is not about qualifications as much as it is about racial preference and White skin privilege.

We have examined the racial demographics of athletes in the revenue-generating sports of football and basketball at some of the nation's top intercollegiate athletic programs, but how do they fare in relation to the hiring of Black administrators and coaches?

Specific racial demographic information speaks clearly to the under-representation of Blacks in intercollegiate athletic administrative and coaching positions in relation to the percentage of Black athletes that make up revenue-generating sports. Tables 7.1–7.4 provide a snapshot of 2005–2006 racial demographic information of Black administrators, Black head coaches, Black assistant coaches, and the percentage of Black athletes at NCAA Division I Institutions.[22]

Regarding the number of Black head coaches in both the Football Bowl Subdivision (FBS) and the Football Championship Subdivision (FCS), a drastic decrease occurred in 2008. According to the 2008 Black Coaches and Administrators (BCA) Football Hiring Report Card, only

Table 7.1 Percentage of Black administrators at PWI NCAA Division I institutions, 2005–2006

Position	
Athletic Directors	5.5
Associate Athletic Directors	8.3
Assistant Athletic Directors	8.7
Senior Woman Administrators	10.6
Academic Advisors	23.5
Overall	9.1

Table 7.2 Percentage of Black head coaches at PWI NCAA Division I institutions, 2005–2006

Men's Teams	7.4
Women's Teams	6.6
Men's Revenue Sports	17.1
Women's Revenue Sports	12.1

Table 7.3 Percentage of Black assistant coaches
at PWI NCAA Division I institutions, 2005–2006

Men's Teams	17.5
Women's Teams	13.2
Men's Revenue Sports	26.9
Women's Revenue Sports	31.8

Table 7.4 Black student athletes at PWI NCAA Division I
institutions, 2005–2006

Total Athletes	76,953
Black Athletes	15,552 (20.2)
Total Athletes in Revenue Sports	22,183
Total Black Athletes in Revenue Sports	11,279 (50.8)

Note: Percentages are given in parentheses.

four coaches of color were hired during the 31 vacancies during the 2007–2008 season.[23] Consequently, BCA report that:

> The 2008 season began with eight coaches of color, six of whom were African-American. With the recent firings of Coach Ty Willingham and Coach Ron Prince, there are now only four African-Americans, a Latino and a Pacific Islander as head football coaches in the FBS.[24]

Furthermore, regarding diversity among campus and conference leaders for NCAA Division IA Institutions in 2007, the Institute for Diversity and Ethics in Sport at the University of Central Florida reported that Whites represented "93.3 percent of the presidents, 86.7 percent of the athletics directors, 93.5 percent of the faculty athletics reps [representatives], and 100 percent of the conference commissioners."[25] Of the 120 NCAA Division IA Institutions surveyed, there were only five (4.2 percent) African-American men (Bowling Green University, University of Houston, Middle Tennessee State University, Washington State University, and Ohio University) that were presidents, and no African-American women.[26] Regarding Faculty Athletic Representatives, there were only four (3.4 percent) represented at these institutions.

The report further highlights the racial demographics among faculty at the 120 NCAA Division IA Institutions survey and concluded that "Excluding non-resident aliens who were faculty, whites hold 83.3 percent of the faculty positions at those schools while a mere 3.5 percent of the faculty were African-American.[27]

Finally, at the NCAA Headquarters a similar pattern resulting in a lack of representation exists. Table 7.5 provides the racial demographics of leadership at the NCAA Headquarters. The NCAA Headquarters represents the seat of power that governs all three divisions of intercollegiate athletics. The individuals in these leadership positions are the decision

Table 7.5 Racial demographics at the NCAA headquarters, 2007

Position	White (%)	Black (%)
Vice Presidents/Chief of Staffs	82.4	17.6
Chief Aides/Directors	77.4	14.5
NCAA Administrators	78.4	18.4
NCAA Support Staff	80	16.5

Source: Richard E. Lapchick, "Think beyond the Competition: 2006–07 Racial and Gender Report Card," http://www.tidesport.org/RGRC/2007/2006-07_RGRC.pdf (accessed October 15, 2007).

makers who provide legislation and establish policies that impact the lives of over 400,000 athletes. As stated earlier, its governance structure has evolved from simply having an advisory responsibility to be in the business of marketing goods and services and wealth distribution.

The data in the above tables paint a disturbing picture of the structure of leadership in charge of intercollegiate athletics. It is important to note that the NCAA has had one Black president in its history: James Frank of Lincoln University (Missouri) was elected as the NCAA first Black president in 1981. Beyond Frank's tenure as president and the token representation of Blacks peppered throughout the ranks of leadership, the leadership structure of intercollegiate athletics resembles the PWIs' administrative structure and the broader U.S. political system of governance and administrative control. Simply stated, the discrepancy exists when there is a high percentage of Whites in leadership positions who are governing and benefitting financially off the athletic labor of Black males.

Once again, the control over the Black male's body and profiting off its physical expenditure is in the hands of White males. As the most powerful commodity that generates the revenue that drives the top intercollegiate programs in the nation, Black males are also the most powerless in regards to political voice and representation.

★   ★   ★

The struggle for Black emancipation from colonial rule was and is in part a struggle for the right to have a voice in the democratic process. It was and continues to be a struggle to define ourselves, determine our destinies, and have control over the fruits of our labor. Initially defined in the U.S. Constitution as three-fifths human, Blacks were denied access in the political process; thus, not allowed to vote. It was legislation such as Fourteenth Amendment to the U.S. Constitution which superseded the ruling that Blacks were three-fifths human, and the Fifteenth Amendment to the U.S. Constitution that prohibited citizens from being denied voting privileges based on their race, which gave us a voice in the political process. In addition, the "African American" civil rights movement and the Black Power Movement were both monumental in their efforts to end racial discrimination and segregation in public facilities and in government services (e.g., education and public transportation), and sought economic empowerment and self-sufficiency within Black communities. Both also made efforts to diminish the predominantly White political control that ruled at the local, state, and national levels; thus, the motto of "a [B]lack face in a high place" explains elements of the motivation behind the movements. History proclaims the many monumental efforts made by individuals whose lives were sacrificial offerings surrendered so that Blacks, specifically, can have a political voice and representation in the leadership structure that governs this nation.

The inertia we are witnessing in the racialized leadership structures of the universities and intercollegiate athletic departments is a contradiction to the diversity initiatives these institutions purport and a shameful reminder of colonial rule that clearly sought to commodify and control the Black body and the labor and products it produced.

There are organizations worth noting that are putting forth efforts to address the powerlessness of collegiate athletes, specifically, and increase the number of Black coaches in intercollegiate athletics, in general: one is the National College Players Association (NCPA), formerly named the Collegiate Athletes Coalition (CAC), and another is the Black Coaches Association (BCA). The NCPA is striving to increase the rights of athletes and reduce their powerlessness by providing them with a voice to address NCAA policies that impact their lives. The NCPA has outlined ten goals they seek to achieve in order to accomplish their mission to "provide the means for college athletes to voice their concerns and change NCAA rules."[28] The impact of the NCPA was noted in its support of the *White v. NCAA* lawsuit settlement, which resulted in the NCAA making $445 million available to athletes through the Student–Athlete Opportunity Fund (SAOF) over the next six years and to offset expenses related to medical insurance premiums, parking fees, travel expenses home, and clothes.[29]

On the other hand, the BCA is lobbying the NCAA to institute an "Eddie Robinson Rule" similar to the Rooney Rule, which was created in 2003 and requires NFL teams to interview at least one minority candidate for head coaching positions that are vacant. At the time, Commissioner Paul Tagliabue informed NFL teams who do not interview a minority candidate for head coaching position that they would be subject to fines of $500,000 or more. In 2003, the Detroit Lions were the first recipient to receive a fine of $200,000 for not interviewing a minority for the vacant head coach position created by the firing of Marty Mornhinweg.

Another effort by the BCA is examining the hiring practices of Division IA and IAA head football coaches and rating their performance using a Hiring Report Card.[30] The BCA also publishes a hiring report card regarding NCAA Division I women's head basketball coaches.[31] The goal of reporting the hiring practices of these institutions is threefold: to provide insight into the hiring process, expose glaring discrepancies, and acknowledge efforts of improving racial diversity.

The NCPA and the BCA are two examples of associations attempting to improve the voice of athletes in general and increase minority representation in leadership positions, specifically. As with any system of oppression, a shift in political power does not only rely on external forces applying pressure or with concessions from the ruling class, but in the words of Frederick Douglas:

> Power concedes nothing without a demand. It never did and it never will. Find out just what any people will quietly submit to and you have found out the exact measure of injustice and wrong which will be imposed upon them, and these will continue till they are resisted with either words, or blows, or with both. The limits of tyrants are prescribed by the endurance of those whom they oppress....Men may not get all they pay for in this world, but they must certainly pay for all they get. If we ever get free from the oppressions and wrongs heaped upon us, we must pay for their removal.[32]

★   ★   ★

This chapter sought to outline the political challenges of Black athletes at PWIs. These challenges include the ideology of amateurism and paternalism and PWIs' elusive tactics of being altruistic yet annulling the political voice of Black athletes. Another challenge regards the lack of representation in leadership positions. Whether it is with the SAAC, in athletic administration, or in the ranks of coaching, the presence of Blacks are disproportionately represented; thus lessening the chance of Black athletes having a representative to be a voice in the decision-making process. Again, representation does not necessarily equate to having a political voice, especially when Black leadership has been co-opted by the White establishment. Therefore, the struggle for representation and a political voice must be an informed and a conscious struggle; not merely one that seeks cosmetic changes where Black faces controlled by the White establishment are put in high places. History has documented how this has been detrimental to social progress and the democratization of the political process.

The disconnect and the gap between the colonizer and the colonized who are politically oppressed is vast. Narrowing this gap will require altering the status quo, embracing diversity, relinquishing control, and empowering the disempowered. The time is far spent where Black bodies are exploited physically to accumulate capital for institutions that render them powerless and deprive them of their rights of making informed decisions about their lives. Too often, the reality of their political impotence is clouded amidst the recruiting sale's pitch, the glamour and hype of "game day," and the illusion that they will become professional athletes. The latter is the most devastating in regards to socially controlling and manipulating athletes and keeping them in submission and politically powerless.

Efforts to reform intercollegiate athletics must take into consideration the political powerlessness of Black athletes and athletes in general. Chapter 9 will address athletic reform and the challenges in providing quality educational opportunities for the internally colonized Black athlete.

In the next chapter, we will examine how interscholastic programs are practically breeding grounds that are replicating the behaviors of intercollegiate athletics and creating delusions of grandeur for young Black males who are seeking to be the next multimillion dollar athlete showcased on ESPN Top Ten Highlights or on MTV Cribs.

CHAPTER EIGHT

Friday Night Lights: A Dream Deferred or Delusions of Grandeur

High school athletics have become the latest entree on the American sports menu, served up to help satisfy the voracious appetite of the fan. As a result, scholastic athletes are on the verge of becoming as important to the billion-dollar sports industry as their college brothers and sisters—and just as vulnerable to big-time exploitation.

—Gerald Eskenazi, *New York Times*[1]

H. G. Bissinger's, *Friday Night Light's: A Town, a Team, a Dream*, provides tremendous insight into the interworkings of high school football in the state of Texas.[2] Although his primary focus detailed the 1988 season of the Permian Panthers, a high school football team in Odessa, Texas, it captured a culture of high school football that is replicable throughout the United States. It also grasps the issues of how a town and a team's love for football create misguided priorities that privilege athletics over academics. Furthermore, it highlights the sores of racism that fester beneath the glamour of the lights on every Friday night during the fall football seasons.

Bissinger's analysis provides a critical examination of the preeminence high school football has in the lives of communities like Odessa, Texas, throughout the United States. He informs on how the town of Odessa, supported and even idealized high school football to the point of obsession. During the fall of each year, the community businesses actually function around the football schedule in order to attend games. Friday night football was a staple in this community and it gave meaning to the lives of Odessa, Texas residence.

Another interesting feature of Bissinger's account of interscholastic football in Odessa, Texas, is the culture of high school football, specifically, and sports, in general. Football is and has been an American passion and a favorite pastime. It is important to note that the culture of football places a premium on masculinity, and for many young boys, it is a rite of passage into manhood. It is a training ground for masculine development, where the ideals of masculinity are branded into the psyche of young boys who endure and make the team. There is no crying in this testosterone-driven emotionally conservative environment. Emotions are only allowed to be expressed during celebratory moments or in moments of defeat and only if the defeat is significant: championship-type competitions. Teams are a type of fraternity, a group of unarmed mercenaries who develop a brotherly bond that often lasts a lifetime. On and off-the-field, they are expected to take care of one another, even sometimes when race or class segregates a community, team dynamics sometimes affords them the opportunity to transcend these differences to achieve a common goal and reach a specific destiny. According to Elliott J. Gorn and Warren J. Goldstein:

> It [football] built camaraderie among men who were expected to take up leadership positions in their communities. The intense emotional identification fostered by football bound men to one another and to their class long after their gridiron days had passed. The shared experience of violence made these bonds especially strong. The risk of serious injury run by each player, the degree to which he depended on his fellows to protect him, the relief at surviving danger, and the sense of having gone through something together that others could not share gave football players the feeling of being special, distinct, and worthy. Such feelings are also perhaps the defining characteristic of the bonds between combat veterans of military units.[3]

It is the culture of football that creates a unique experience for its participants. Beyond the positive traits and characteristics of training leaders, instilling hard-work ethics, fostering teamwork, and so on, there are negative aspects of this culture that have garnered national media attention, for example, the objectification of women, hazing,[4] the abuse of illegal and prescription drugs, and anti-intellectualism.

It is this culture that cultivates dreams of playing at the intercollegiate and possibly the professional levels. For many young Black males, who desire to excel beyond the economic and social limitations of their family and community, football, specifically, and sports, in general, become a way out; an avenue to a better life. They are bombarded with images of athletes, like themselves, who started in similar socioeconomic conditions and become representatives of the "rags to riches" model.

I would be hard-pressed in writing about the experiences of Black athletes in the intercollegiate setting and not highlighting their experiences at the interscholastic levels. This chapter will examine how the increased commercialization of interscholastic sports, specifically football, is impacting lives and communities and creating breeding grounds for dreams deferred and delusions of grandeur. This chapter will also examine the role interscholastic football plays in the lives of Black males in a small Southern town. It is an unfortunate reality for these Black males, but their delusions of grandeur are concealed within every dream deferred. Black male athletes will be at the center of this analysis, because they are currently filtering through these interscholastic programs and supplying the labor for many of the nationally ranked intercollegiate programs in this nation.

Interscholastic Sports and Athletic Capitalism

A growing trend in the United States is athletic capitalism in interscholastic sports, which is a result of increased commercialization. Simply stated, the design of interscholastic sports is expanding more to accumulate capital rather than to supplement the educational experiences of the student. Consequently, this expansion is at the risk of exploiting the athletes. The transition has shifted sports from being a cultural practice that is a means of building character and socializing youth in developing American cultural values (e.g., discipline, hard work ethic, patriotism, etc.)[5] to being a product for capital accumulation and consumption. In other words, the increased commercialization of interscholastic sports in the United States has shifted its primary focus from character development to a commercial enterprise for capital accumulation; similar to the corporate behavior of intercollegiate athletics. The following are multiple streams of revenue that are being tapped by youth and interscholastic sports administrators: the selling of naming rights of gymnasiums and stadiums, acquiring sponsorship, and also in a few cases the selling of broadcasting rights.

Naming Rights, Stadium Construction, and Broadcasting Rights

In 2004, Brooklawn, New Jersey's Alice Costello Elementary School became the first school to sell naming rights to its gymnasium. ShopRite is a local supermarket that has agreed to pay $100,000 over the next 20 years for the rights to have the gymnasium named the *ShopRite of Brooklawn Center*.[6] The price list is seeking more buyers where for $5,000 a company/corporation or an individual could sponsor the jump circle at the center of the gym floor, for $2,500 a company/corporation or an individual could have an advertisement on the baseline of the gym floor, and finally for $500 a company/corporation or an individual could have a banner on the wall.[7]

In 2004, TITUS Sports Marketing of Dallas was able to acquire naming rights for an East Texas high school football stadium from a health care company that is worth $1.2 million over 12 years.[8] In Florida and Texas where high school football is tremendously popular and well supported, several high schools have sold the naming rights to their football stadiums to local businesses.

Along with the sale of naming rights, there has been enormous investment into the construction of football stadiums at the high school level.

Stadium constructions including track fields, AstroTurf fields, or natural grass have an average cost of $17–$22 million with seating capacities ranging from 5,000 to 15,000 people.[9]

Other examples to illustrate how interscholastic sports has shifted from character development to capital accumulation is in the sponsorship of football and basketball championship games and media rights for televising interscholastic sports. For example, Toyota donates $165,000 to sponsor a regional basketball tournament in southern California. Also in California, a high school football championship has been named the San Joaquin Section/Les Schwab Tires Division I Championship because Les Schwab Tire Company donated $183,000. Finally, James F. Byrnes High School in Duncan, South Carolina is known for its $320,000 JumboTron and its financial support from Nike, which equals about $20,000 annually. It is important to mention that the JumboTron cost was raised by the Rebels Touchdown Club.[10]

Furthermore, there has been an explosion of media coverage of interscholastic football in the past five years, which has generated revenue for high schools from the sell of media rights. Major networks like MTV (Music Television), ESPN, and Fox Sports Net are televising more interscholastic sports (especially football, basketball, and girl's softball), which generates revenue for these athletic programs. For example, for football coverage, each game televised equates to a payout ranging from $1,000 to $2000 for each team, plus travel expenses for the traveling team. ESPNU, ESPN, and ESPN2 *Old Spice High School Showcase* are televising 19 interscholastic football games during the 2008 season; up from 14 televised games in 2007, 13 in 2006, and only 4 in 2005.

Popularity and commercialization of interscholastic sports can also be seen in media coverage that includes dramatizations and reality show broadcasts of interscholastic sports. An example of this is with NBC converting the story of high school football in Texas, *Friday Night Lights*,[11] into a primetime show. Finally, a MTV's documentary, *Two-A-Days*, covers the season of high school football at Hoover High School in Hoover, Alabama. For the first season of coverage, Remote Productions paid Hoover High School $20,000 in media right fees, and a contract for a second season will garner Hoover High School a maximum of $21,000.

These are just a few examples to illustrate the direction and transition youth sports in the United States are making toward athletic capitalism. Despite the tremendous opportunity being afforded to millions of young athletes participating in interscholastic sports programs, this shift has bought both criticism and praise. Critics argue that this move toward athletic capitalism undermines the educational mission of the school system and efforts of developing character in other interscholastic sports programs, while the proponents of this shift to athletic capitalism argue that the revenue is needed because of the cuts in public education and government-supported community sports programs. They argue that the benefits of increased opportunity for youth to play in better facilities, with better equipment, and the opportunity of providing more sporting opportunities for youth is a good justification for the increased commercialization of interscholastic sports.

This wave of athletic capitalism is sweeping throughout small towns across the United States. One rural community where this is taking place is in Madison, Florida. This next section will examine how athletic capitalism is contributing to athletic demands that foster dreams deferred and delusions of grandeur.

Madison County High: A Case Study in Friday Night Lights

Nestled in the panhandle of Florida between Jacksonville and Tallahassee, Florida on Interstate 10 is the city of Madison, FL. Known as a quiet and peaceful community, Madison County was created in 1827 and named after the fourth U.S. president, James Madison. To further frame the location, Greenville, Florida, one of the towns within Madison County, is the birthplace of the legendary rhythm and blues giant Ray Charles. Growing up in this region of the Florida Panhandle between the ultraconservatives, Bible fundamentalist, and the "Juke-Joint" entrepreneurs undoubtedly provided Ray Charles with the experiences needed to sing the Blues.

With a population of 3,050, the town of Madison is located in Madison County, where the greater Madison County has a population of 18,957.[12] In 2007, the racial demographics for the city of Madison are as follows: Black (62.4 percent), White Non-Hispanic (34.4 percent), Hispanic (2.2 percent), two or more races (0.9 percent), and Native American (0.6 percent). For the Madison County, the racial demographics are: White Non-Hispanic (55.4 percent), Black (40.3 percent), Hispanic (3.2 percent), two or more races (1.0 percent), Native American (0.8 percent), and Others race (0.5 percent).[13] In 2007, the estimated median household income was $21,545 compared to $47,804 for the state of Florida.[14]

One can easily draw from this demographic data that Madison County is predominantly White, while the city of Madison is predominantly Black, a fairly poor small town, and probably not your next booming metropolis. Unfortunately, there are only two factories in the area (GoldKist Poultry Processing Plant and Deer Park Water Bottling Plant) and seasonal labor in farming or commuting to factories in neighboring counties provide most of the employment for Madison County residence. Madison County is a dry county so the only sources of entertainment are the parking lots at the local grocery store or strip mall, or a vacant building converted into a "nightclub." Even to attend a movie theater, one must travel about 30 miles to Valdosta, Georgia, or 55 miles to Tallahassee, Florida.

Madison County High School (MCHS) services the towns of Madison, Greenville, and Lee, Florida. MCHS is mounted on Boot Hill located on the outskirts of the city of Madison on Highway 90. Though the county is predominantly made of White Non-Hispanic residents, the public school paints a totally different picture. There are two private Christian schools that service Madison County, and 79 percent of the students who attend these institutions are White Non-Hispanic. Table 8.1 illustrates the racial demographics of the Madison County High School.[15] Table 8.1 also illustrates that Blacks make up the majority of the student body population at 53 percent. Again, although Whites represent the largest percentage of the Madison County population, they make up only 46 percent of the MCHS population; alternatives for the Whites include private schools or homeschooling. Regarding race and gender, Black males represent the largest percent of the student body population at 27 percent, Black females were 26 percent, White males were 24 percent, and White females were 22 percent.

Finally, table 8.2 illustrates the demographic breakdown of the number of students graduating from MCHS.[16] This data highlights the number of

Table 8.1   Racial demographics of Madison County High School, 2006–2007

	Males	*Females*	*Total*	*Percentages*
Black (Non-Hispanic)	230	222	452	53.2
White (Non-Hispanic)	200	191	391	46
Hispanic	3	3	6	0.7
Asian/Pacific Islander	0	1	1	0.1
Native American/Alaskan	0	0	0	0
Total	433	417	850	

Source: Racial demographic data was collected from the following Web site: *"Public School Report: Public School Information and Data,"* http://schools.publicschoolsreport.com/Florida/Madison/MadisonCountyHighSchool.html (accessed on September 26, 2008).

Table 8.2   Madison County High School Student completing high school, 2006–2007

		White, Non-Hispanic	*Black, Non-Hispanic*	*Hispanic*	*Multiracial*	*Total*
Standard	Female	45	25	3	1	74
Diplomas	Male	36	25	0	0	61
	Total	81	50	3	1	135
Special	Female	1	11	0	0	12
Diplomas	Male	2	12	0	0	14
	Total	3	23	0	0	26
Certificates of	Female	0	12	0	0	12
Completion	Male	0	11	0	0	11
	Total	0	23	0	0	23
Equivalency	Female	0	0	0	0	0
Diplomas	Male	20	8	0	0	28
	Total	20	8	0	0	28

Source: Graduation and Drop-out rate information was collected from the following website: Florida Department of Education, Education Information & Accountability Services—Madison County School District, http://www.fldoe.org/eias/flmove/madison.asp (accessed September 27, 2008).

students completing high school and the types of diplomas they received.[17] MCHS total graduation rates for 2006–2007 were 66.9 percent: Whites graduate at a rate of 74 percent and Blacks at 58.5 percent. MCHS graduation rates are similar to the state of Florida graduates rates, which are: 72.4 percent overall, 81 percent for Whites, and 58.7 percent for Blacks.[18] The national graduation rates were 78 percent for White students and 55 percent for Black students; therefore, MCHS graduation rates patterns were also similar to the average U.S. high school graduation rates.[19] The alarming data is reported regarding national graduate rates is found in the *Schott 50 State Report on Public Education and Black Males*, where 2005–2006 graduation rates averages for Black males was 47 percent whereas the averages for White males were 75 percent.[20]

Additional breakdown of the MCHS graduating data for Black males provides some relevant information for this chapter: they represent 48 percent of those receiving certificates of completion, 46 percent of those receiving special degrees, 29 percent of those receiving equivalency diplomas, and only 18 percent of those receiving standard diplomas (see table 8.2). This data is alarming because, although Black males are graduating in some form, only 18 percent of them receive standard diplomas. This data explicitly denotes how a significant population of Black males is being neglected and limited in career opportunities. It also speaks to a variety of conditions that plague rural communities: at the community level, there are issues concerning the socioeconomic status of families, family dynamics and their educational expectations, as well as school environment and curriculum; at the state level the issues include resource allocation and program development to meet the needs of a variety of school districts.

Madison County High School Cowboys

A great analogy when constructing an image for the MCHS Cowboys is the biblical story of David and Goliath. David was a small-town shepherd with unwavering faith and a warrior's spirit, while Goliath was an obstacle and arch enemy to the Israelites. The Cowboys, though small regarding geographic location and population size, have overcome these obstacles and gained national recognition and prominence by being ranked number 14 in the nation in 2008–2009 by *USA Today*'s High School Football Pre-Season Rankings: a David among Goliaths.

The Cowboys are one of 40 teams that compete in the Class 2A division, which is situated in District 2 of the Florida High School Athletic Association. The Florida High School Athletic Association has a total of eight classifications: Class 6A—schools with populations of 2,584 or more students; Class 5A—schools with populations of 2,055–2,583 students; Class 4A—schools with populations of 1,708–2,054 students; Class 3A—schools with populations of 1,067–1,707 students; Class 2A—schools with populations of 617–1,066 students; Class 2B—schools

with populations of 411–616 students; Class 1A—schools with populations of 233–410 students; and Class 1B—schools with populations of 232
or fewer students.[21]

The Cowboys have developed into a powerhouse football program.
The have won the District title 12 times straight and were state champions
twice; their last state champion victory was in 2007. They have several
players who have made it to the National Football League (NFL) from
these humble beginnings and two players are currently on NFL rosters:
Geno Hayes is the most recent Cowboy drafted in the 2008 NFL draft.
Furthermore, MCHS athletic department reports that 42 players have
gone on to college to compete at the intercollegiate level since 2002. This
is when Coach Frankie Carroll took over the football program. Therefore,
despite its size, the Madison County Cowboys is a feeder school for intercollegiate athletic programs.

Another example of the Cowboys growth into a 2A powerhouse can be
witnessed with game attendance and fan support. The Cowboys 5,000-
seat stadium has been known to pack over 15,000 fans in layers around
the field for premium games during the season. Similar to Odessa, Texas,
most business activity in the city of Madison stalls on Friday nights during football season. The focus of this town is directed toward the lights
sparkling on Boot Hill, where the Cowboys, like David, welcome the
opportunity to exhibit faith, determination, and the sheer opportunity to
display their athletic skills against their worthy opponents.

Of importance to this chapter are the racial demographics of the MCHS
Cowboys. Based on the overall racial demographics of the school population, one could conclude that the football team would reflect this makeup.
Of the 56 players listed on the 2008 varsity team rosters, Black males
make up 73 percent (41) of the team.

On the surface, it is hard to argue against the fact that football is providing opportunities for this group of Black males who may otherwise
have extremely limited opportunities given the economic conditions in
the city of Madison and Madison County, in general. Clearly, football has
been a ticket to a better life for a small percentage of Black males who have
made it to the intercollegiate level and especially those who have made
it to the professional level. Even the argument regarding the byproducts
(discipline, character development, work ethic, etc.) received from participating in interscholastic sports is hard to refute. Or, even the indirect
social mobility argument is hard to contest when these athletes will have
the opportunity to make contacts with alumni who could become potential employers once they graduate from high school. Finally, the exposure
and travel opportunities open up experiences for these athletes that other
students are not privileged to encounter. These are all benefits of interscholastic competition, which upon graduation can spark new interests
and desires to adventure beyond the confines of Madison County.

It is beneath the surface where the controversy exists; where the dream
deferred often turns into delusions of grandeur. In dialogue with teachers

and administration about Black males' academic and athletic pursuit, they ashamedly admit the horrors of how very few Black male athletes, specifically, have a balanced pursuit. In this community, athletic performance, aspiration, and dreams overshadow academics. Academics have been relegated to something to fall back on or a necessary venture to endure in order to pursue athletics.

Some teachers and parents have voiced their concerns to me regarding the overemphasis some of the Cowboys are putting on football, while showing meager interest and passion toward academics. This myopic view is creating foreseeable problems for the academic success of those athletes seeking to play college football. As a feeder system for college athletic programs, MCHS is reproducing the behavior of other interscholastic programs that have succumbed to the increased commercial demands.

Therefore, what is being perpetuated is a system that is thriving on the athletic prowess of Black males, yet it is neglecting to motivate and prepare them academically; again, similar to some intercollegiate programs. The horrors of communities like Madison, FL is that, if these Black males athletes do not graduate, their dreams deferred often become dreams unfulfilled. It is interesting to note that the architects of this system include all of the citizens, parents, and friends who assist in emphasizing and validating these Black males' athletic dreams, and who see athletics as the only way out for these young men. Whenever education is promoted as "something to fall back on," seeds of doubt are being planted that education is secondary and it is not a worthy pursuit in and of itself. Often these are the seeds that are being sowed in the lives of these young Black males, when they are constantly lauded for their athletic abilities.

It is in these communities where the arm of academic reform needs to extend. Cities like Madison function as feeder schools for intercollegiate athletic programs and will need reform in order to narrow the gap between athletic and academic performances; because they are not mutually exclusive.

Summary and Conclusion

Interscholastic sports has made a shift from its primary responsibilities of socializing youth to having a capitalist focus. Some critics see this as detrimental to the educational mission of the school, while proponents of this shift see it as part of the evolutionary process of interscholastic sports. The increased commercialization of interscholastic sports is also increasing the performance demands placed on the young athletes. Unfortunately, Black males are not performing as well academically in their attempts to use sports as a means of social mobility. Small town interscholastic programs like MCHS is only provide a glimpse into the feeder systems for intercollegiate athletic programs that are breeding an athletically trained labor pool that is academically unprepared.

To minimize the role and image as colonizers, universities that have a history of recruiting Black talent from communities like Madison County should invest in the academic infrastructures of these institutions to better equip the athletes they are recruiting, specifically, and the general student body population who have aspirations of attending one of the state higher educational institutions. The opposition for this practice would argue that there is no guarantee that there will be a return on the investment they make in the life of an athlete or student, or that there is no insurance that the athlete will attend the specific institution that is investing the most. These are legitimate concerns, yet a risk these institutions can afford to take, especially when the return on investment will increase the educational success for a student regardless if they compete athletically at the collegiate level, or if they compete at another institution. Investing in a life that ultimately has the potential to contribute positively to society, should be the ultimate focus, not whether this blue-chip athlete is going to stay eligible and help this institution make it to a BCS Bowl game or the NCAA Tournament.

The feeder systems of interscholastic athletics are replicating the behavior of intercollegiate athletics in regard to academic integrity and commercialization. In all honesty, I have mixed emotions about the practices of athletic programs in rural communities like Madison, FL. These programs, especially football, are permanent fixtures that add to the social landscapes of these depressed communities. They provide a sense of identity, community, meaning, and entertainment for thousands who cheer for their home teams.

For the Black athletes, who comprise a significant percentage of Madison County High Cowboys, football is a source of hope and dream for a grander life and an avenue to succeed socially. However, this dream is being deferred by too many and has become a delusion of grandeur.

CHAPTER NINE

Athletic Reform and Decolonization

The liquidation of colonization is nothing but a prelude to complete liberation, to self-recovery. In order to free himself from colonization, the colonized must start with his oppression, the deficiencies of his group. In order that his liberation may be complete, he must free himself from those inevitable conditions of his struggle.

—Albert Memmi, *The Colonizer and the Colonized*

What you do speaks so loudly that I cannot hear what you say.

—Ralph Waldo Emerson

The history of intercollegiate athletics and its relationship with the National Collegiate Athletic Association (NCAA) has been a history of reform. Plainly, reform in intercollegiate athletics, and more specifically football, was the major catalyst that sparked the development of the NCAA (originally named the Intercollegiate Athletic Association of the United States—IAAUS). In 1905, at the request of President Theodore Roosevelt, athletic leaders from 13 different colleges convened at the White House on two different occasions to address athletes' physical safety due to the numerous injuries and deaths occurring in football.[1]

In 1929, a report by the Carnegie Foundation for the Advancement of Teaching expressed the challenges in college athletics. This report highlighted how recruiting scandals had created a culture of professionalism and commercialism in college athletics, which further informed the need for reform.[2] Again, the history of college athletics has involved episodes of controversy and contradictions requiring a need for governance and oversight; consequently, requiring reform. Thus, reform has been an ongoing process instead of a one-shot vaccination that cures all the ills of college athletics. As the challenges that strain the relationship between education and athletics have evolved, it has demanded governance that is innovative and pliable in meeting these challenges.

Since its inception, the NCAA has evolved from an advisory group with the authority to create policies to govern intercollegiate athletics into a multibillion dollar corporate enterprise. Several scholars have written concerning intercollegiate athletic reform in various formats, and they have presented provocative recommendations to contribute to reform.[3] This chapter will examine the NCAA efforts to reform intercollegiate athletics, additional organizations that have emerged to address the need for athletic reform, and finally what does all this mean to Black athletes' intercollegiate sporting experiences. First, a brief overview of the NCAA and its effort to reform intercollegiate athletics will provide a backdrop for discussing reform and the decolonization of intercollegiate athletics.

The NCAA: Born to Reform

Intercollegiate athletics were birthed out of extracurricular activities that were student controlled, funded, and managed. According to Ronald Smith,

> Students were almost the sole force in developing athletics within the larger college extracurriculum, including the first five intercollegiate sports. Crew, baseball, cricket, football, and track and field were all contested intercollegiately by the early 1870s. Later in the nineteenth century other intercollegiate sports would be developed under student leadership. These included the first intercollegiate contests in rifle (1877), lacrosse (1877), bicycling (1880), tennis (1883), polo (1884), cross country (1890), fencing (1894), ice hockey (1895), basketball (1895), golf (1896), trap shooting (1898), water polo (1899), swimming (1899), and gymnastics (1899).[4]

As these activities grew in popularity, both negatively and positively, faculty began to take note and exhibit control in order to address the following issues: professionalism, academic integrity, recruiting and eligibility, and physical safety of students competing in football.

The brutal nature of intercollegiate football during the late 1800s and early 1900s contributed significantly to the need for greater institutional control and ultimately a governing body that could establish rules and policies that would insure the safety of student participants. With the negative publicity being broadcasted about the violence ensuing in intercollegiate athletics, it took the words, "Reform or Abolish" declared by President Theodore Roosevelt to birth the reform of intercollegiate football, specifically; thus the inception of the IAAUS in 1905, which was officially establish on March 31, 1906. In 1910, the IAAUS changed its name to the National Collegiate Athletic Association (NCAA). Forged under the pressure to reform intercollegiate football, the NCAA has expanded exponentially in governance and enforcement since its inception.

As intercollegiate athletics expanded in its variety of sport offerings and complexity, the NCAA also expanded to meet increasing legislative demands. Initially concerned with issues involving professionalism, academic integrity, recruiting and eligibility, and player safety, the NCAA has had to address issues revolving around some of the initial concerns of intercollegiate athletics and additional challenges involving commercialization, antitrust, anti-betting or sport wagering, and so on. Thus, the NCAA history of reform has been a history rich with opportunity and opposition.

Joseph N. Crowley highlights some of the legislation the NCAA has instituted to address some of the re-occurring issues of reform. The following list is a brief overview of key reform issues from 1909 to 2005:

- In 1909, the IAAUS instituted rules to reduce the violence and eliminate the deaths occurring in college football.
- In 1922, a ten-point code was adopted to address the following: conferences, amateurism, freshman rule, ban on playing pro football, three-year participation, no graduate students, faculty control, anti-betting, ban on playing for non-collegiate teams.
- In 1946, the Conference of Conferences was conducted in Chicago, resulting in "Principles for the Conduct of Intercollegiate Athletics" (five points of the principles —known as "Sanity Code"—formally adopted in 1948).
- In 1951, the Sanity Code was revised (financial aid and enforcement provisions).
- In 1952, a limited television plan was adopted.
- In 1965, a 1.600 rule for initial academic eligibility is adopted.
- In 1971, freshman eligibility in all championships except University Division basketball and postseason football was approved.
- In 1972, freshman eligibility in basketball and football was approved.
- In 1973, the 1.600 legislation was abolished.
- In 1973, membership votes in a Special Convention to reorganize into three divisions.
- In 1975, NCAA marketing program initiated through agreement with Descente Ltd. to use NCAA mark in marketing sportswear and accessories in Japan.
- In 1975, Second Special Convention addresses recruiting limitations, financial aid limits, and football and basketball staff and squad sizes.
- In 1976, 70th Convention and third Special Convention stages first roll-call vote in Convention history (need-based aid is rejected in the vote).
- In 1979, first two-year agreement with ESPN is signed to televise selected championships; programming begins September 7.
- In 1983, Division I approves Proposal No. 48, which requires prospective student-athletes to reach specified grade-point averages and standardized-test scores.

- In 1984, the creation of NCAA Presidents Commission was approved.
- In 1984, Supreme Court upholds ruling that NCAA Football Television Plan violates Sherman Antitrust Act.
- In 1987, Southern Methodist University football program suspended for one year in NCAA's first (and to date only) application of the "death penalty" for assorted and ongoing rules violations.
- In 1989, Proposal No. 42, withholding athletically related aid from partial academic qualifiers, is approved.
- In 1989, Knight Foundation Commission on Intercollegiate Athletics formed.
- In 1989, NCAA and CBS sign $1 billion television agreement for 1991 through 1997; Executive Director Richard Schultz moves to examine equitable distribution of revenue.
- In 1990, Proposal No. 42 rescinded; Convention also features lengthy debate over time demands on student-athletes.
- In 1991, the Knight Foundation Commission on Intercollegiate Athletics issues report concluding that chief executive officer control of intercollegiate athletics is essential.
- In 1991, NCAA Presidents Commission holds hearings directed at developing stronger academic standards.
- In 1992, Proposal No. 16, establishing an initial-eligibility index based on standardized-test scores and grade-point averages, is approved in Division I.
- In 1994, NCAA and CBS agree to $1.725 billion, eight-year television contract; ESPN agrees to expand coverage of the Division I Women's Basketball Championship.
- In 1997, membership restructuring is approved; new governance structure implemented in August. The new structure provides a more federated means of governance, along a greater leadership role for chief executive officers.
- In 1999, NCAA and CBS agree to $6 billion, 11-year contract for rights to Division I Men's Basketball Championship and other championships, including marketing opportunities.
- In February 2005, the Division I Board of Directors adopts an Academic Progress Rate (APR), subjecting teams that fail to meet established minimum scores to possible penalties ranging from loss of scholarships to postseason bans and membership restrictions.[5]

The above list of legislation and policy implementation informs us of how the NCAA has worked to reform and expand with the demands of intercollegiate athletics. The stress of adhering to the academic mission of institutions of higher education and grow commercially has often strained the relationship between athletic departments and the university; the athletic mission, at times, seemingly contradicts the academics mission of acquiring, advancing, and disseminating knowledge for social progress and improving social welfare.

Intercollegiate athletics (specifically NCAA Division I Institutions) has purely embraced commercialism and capitalist ideals, while the academic arm of the university has wavered between academic elitism and academic capitalism. There has been considerable resistance by members of the academy to the increased commercialization intercollegiate athletics has embraced. Whether it is because of the degree of media attention (positive or negative) athletics have acquired for the institution, the high salaries of athletic coaches and administrators, or the revenue generated and expenses occurred, there is significant cause that has produced an alarm and a call for greater reform. Although the NCAA and its member institutions are held responsible for the governance of intercollegiate athletics, however, there have emerged various commissions, groups, coalitions, and so on with vested interests in reforming intercollegiate athletics. These groups (some outside the institution, some operating within) have organized and armed themselves with proposals and specific recommendations for athletic reform. This section will address the mission and reform demands of some of these organizations, and hopefully capture how they envision intercollegiate athletics.

The Knight Commission on Intercollegiate Athletics

In 1989, the Knight Commission on Intercollegiate Athletics (KCIA) was formed by the John S. and James L. Knight Foundation as a result of college sport scandals that had achieved national attention and were threatening the integrity of higher education. The KCIA goal was to "recommend a reform agenda that emphasized academic values in an arena where commercialization of college sports often overshadowed the underlying goals of higher education."[6] In efforts to push reform and stay the tide of commercialism in college athletics, the KCIA convened in 1989 to examine the governance of intercollegiate athletics. At a cost of $3 million, it published three reports from 1991 to 1993 that outlined recommendations for reform: (1) *Keeping Faith with the Student-Athlete: A Model for Intercollegiate Athletics*; (2) *A Solid Start: A Report on Reform of Intercollegiate Athletics*; and (3) *A New Beginning for a New Century: Intercollegiate Athletics in the United States*; and ten years later, in 2001, it produced another report, *A Call to Action,* which identified the progress of the NCAA and it made further recommendations for reform.[7] It is important to add that the KCIA's focus on intercollegiate athletics was not because they loathed intercollegiate athletics, but as Chairman James Knight stated:

We have a lot of sports fans on our board, and we recognize that intercollegiate athletics have a legitimate and proper role to play in college and university life. Our interest is not to abolish that role but to preserve it by putting it back in perspective. We hope this Commission can strengthen the hands of those who want to curb the abuses, which are shaking public confidence in the integrity of not just big-time collegiate athletics but the whole institution of higher education.[8]

A re-occurring theme amid the KCIA's reports is the belief that college athletics is a vital part of the campus culture and college life, and it provides a service to millions. Therefore, the recommendations were a means to restore ethical standards, and "the public's 'deeply rooted faith in collegiate education'..., and the public's trust in the integrity of college sports."[9]

To summarize, the KCIA's 1991 report, *Keeping Faith with the Student-Athlete: A Model for Intercollegiate Athletics*, suggested that the major problem negatively impacting college athletics is increased commercialism. They suggested that it had been a culprit in creating unethical practices among coaches, specifically in the area of recruiting, who were trying to meet the increasing athletic demands of winning bowl games and championships. From the KCIA's analysis, recruiting has become the major source of NCAA violations, and it is the root of the problem where athletics is a higher priority than education. The KCIA asserts that "Increasingly, the team, the game, the season and 'the program'—all intended as expressions of the university's larger purposes—gain ascendancy over the ends that created and nurtured them."[10]

To address this problem, the KCIA admonishes the need for greater presidential control. It is their conclusion that several decades of "presidential neglect and institutional indifference" that has spiraled college athletics out of control.[11] In response, they proposed a "one-plus-three model" where "the one—presidential control" will be "directed toward the three—academic integrity, financial integrity, and accountability through certification."[12]

In order to implement greater presidential control, the KCIA determined the following requirements were needed:

1. Trustees should explicitly endorse and reaffirm presidential authority in all matters of athletics governance.
2. Presidents should act on their obligation to control conferences.
3. Presidents should control the NCAA.
4. Presidents should commit their institutions to equity in all aspects of intercollegiate athletics.
5. Presidents should control their institution's involvement with commercial television.[13]

Regarding the component "academic integrity" in the one-plus-three model, the KCIA suggested that "the fundamental premise must be that athletes are students as well," and therefore should be expected to have comparable experiences concerning admissions, academic progress, and graduation rates.[14] In addition, "No Pass, No Play," best captures their recommendations on academic integrity. Other recommendations to promote academic integrity are as follows:

1. The NCAA should strengthen initial eligibility requirements.
2. The letter of intent should serve the student as well as the athletic departments.
3. Athletic scholarships should be offered for a five-year period.
4. Athletics eligibility should depend on progress toward a degree.
5. Graduation rates of athletes should be a criterion for NCAA certification.[15]

The KCIA propose in the financial integrity component that institutions of higher education must be better stewards of the revenue they are allotted through "taxpayer's dollars, the hard-earned payments of student and their parents, the contributions of alumni, or the revenue streams generated by athletic programs."[16] Therefore, the KCIA make the following recommendation to advance financial integrity:

1. Athletics costs must be reduce.
2. Athletics grants-in-aid should cover the full cost of attendance for the very needy.
3. The independence of athletic foundations and booster clubs must be curbed.
4. The NCAA formula for sharing television revenue from the national basketball championship must be reviewed by university presidents.
5. All athletic-related coaches' income should be reviewed and approved by the university.
6. Coaches should be offered long-term contracts.
7. Institutional support should be available for intercollegiate athletics.

Finally, the last component in the one-plus-three model is certification. According to the KCIA:

Periodic independent assessments of a program can go a long way toward guaranteeing that the athletic culture on campus responds to academic direction, that expenditures are routinely reviewed, and that the president's authority is respected by the board of trustees, and that the trustees stand for academic values when push comes to shove in the athletics department.[17]

The KCIA makes the following recommendations to assist independent certification:

1. The NCAA should extend the certification process to all institutions granting athletic aid.

2. Universities should undertake comprehensive, annual policy audits of their athletic program.
3. The certification program should include the major themes put forth in this document.

The KCIA end this report by addressing the major actors involved in putting these principles into action, which include the following: college and university presidents, chairs and governing boards, faculty, athletic directors, coaches, alumni, student-athletes, secondary school officials, and the NCAA. They conclude by providing institutions that are committed to implementing the "one-plus-three" model with a statement of principles and several guiding principles to assist these institutions.[18]

In a follow-up to the first report, *Keeping Faith with the Student-Athlete . . .*, the KCIA's, *A Solid Start: A Report on Reform of Intercollegiate Athletics*, provided a report of the progress made toward reform. The following measures indicated that progress was being made: the Presidents Commission of the NCAA voted to raise academic standards enacting the "no pass, no play," a certification program was being tested by the NCAA, and that presidents were in charge of the reform process. For the KCIA, this was a "solid start" toward athletic reform.

In the KCIA's final report of the three part series, *A New Beginning for a New Century: Intercollegiate Athletics in the United States*, they expressed confidence that athletic reform was well under way. The "one-plus-three" model had been well received and enacted by the NCAA, presidents, and supporters of athletic reform. Regarding academic integrity, freshman entrance requirements had increased: in 1989 the requirements were for student-athletes to have a "C" average in 11 core academic subjects and a combined Scholastic Aptitude Test scores of 700; by 1995, freshman entry requirements were a 2.5 high school grade point average in 13 high school academic units where the 13 units were to include four years of English and one year of algebra and geometry.[19] Furthermore, regarding athletic finances, the KCIA reported that cost containment was being witnessed where the number of athletic scholarships for NCAA Division I and II men sports were reduced by 10 percent, coaching staffs had been reduced, and the certification process was reviewing athletic budgets. They concluded in this report that cost containment and gender equity will be the prevailing issues requiring future policy dialogue.[20]

Ten years after its initial report, in 2001 the KCIA produced, *A Call to Action: Reconnecting College Sports and Higher Education*. The tone of this report was mixed with discontent and optimism and wavered on a spectrum between hope and hopeless. It asserted that there had been some good intentions and positive efforts made toward reform; however, the report informs that "The good name of the nation's academic enterprise is even more threatened today than it was when the Knight Commission published its first report a decade ago."[21] According to the KCIA, low graduation rates in the sports of football and basketball, the escalating "arms race" of spending and building, and the increased commercialization of intercollegiate athletics were the reasons that threatened the good name of the nation's academic enterprise.

Yet, hope for reform and optimism was a re-occurring theme throughout this report. It was evident in their call for a grassroots effort "to restore the balance of athletics and academics on campus" from presidents and trustees, national higher education associations (e.g., American Council on Education and the Association of Governing Boards of Universities and Colleges), athletic conferences, faculty, athletic directors and coaches, and alumni.[22] It was evident in the reworking of the "one-plus-three" model with a new model that include "'one,' a Coalition of Presidents, directed toward an agenda of academic reform, de-escalation of the athletic arms race, and de-emphasis of the commercialization of intercollegiate athletics."[23]

For academic reform, they proposed that the Coalition of Presidents should concentrate on mainstreaming athletes, improving graduation rates, provide scholarships to athletes until they graduate, reduce the length of seasons and practice, and allow the National Basketball Association (NBA) and National Football League (NFL) to develop a minor league for students that lack interest in higher education.[24] The Coalition of Presidents should also focus on reducing expenditures, mainly in the sports of football and basketball, promote greater compliance to Title IX by supporting women sports, consider coaches compensation within the context of the academic institution, ensure that outside income of coaches should be negotiated with the institutions, revise revenue sharing to place values on improving academic performance, improving the experiences of athletes, and to achieve gender equity do not base the distribution of revenue on winning and losing.[25] Finally, in order to reduce commercialization, the Coalition of Presidents should focus on placing the control scheduling and the broadcasting of games in the hands of the institution, renegotiate all sport-related commercial contracts using traditional academic values as the context for evaluation, minimize commercial intrusions throughout sporting facilities, alleviate the exploitation of athletes as advertising vehicles, and seek federal legislation that bans gambling on college sports in the state of Nevada and illegal gambling on campuses.[26]

At the conclusion of this report, the KCIA gave a resounding message if reform is not accomplished;

> If it proves impossible to create a system of intercollegiate athletics that can live honorably within the American college and university, then responsible citizens must join with academic and public leaders to insist that the nation's colleges and universities get out of the business of big-time sports.[27]

This statement speaks volumes to the weightiness KCIA's has concerning athletic reform, and their belief in its need and urgency for the survival of intercollegiate athletics.

In summary, as an "outside" entity, the KCIA has given significant visibility to the issue of athletic reform. It has informed the public about athletic reform, and it has been a catalyst for generating reform policies for the NCAA. The KCIA has also illustrated how great the inertia and how strong the resistance are in creating athletic reform within the system of intercollegiate athletics. However, it has been one of the major privately funded organizations seeking to restore academic integrity and bring balance to the academic and athletic missions in institutions of higher education.

Coalition on Intercollegiate Athletics

Another organization created in 2002 to address athletic reform and to restore academic integrity is the Coalition on Intercollegiate Athletics (COIA). They are currently an alliance of 56 faculty senate members representing Division 1A universities, which provides a faculty voice in the national dialogue on academic reform. Their ultimate goal is to "preserve and enhance the positive contributions athletics can make to academic life by addressing longstanding problems in college sports that undermine those contributions."[28] It seeks to work with the following organizations in its efforts of achieving reform in intercollegiate athletics: the NCAA, the Association of Governing Boards (AGB), the American Association of University Professors (AAUP), the KCIA, the Division 1A Faculty Athletics Representatives (D1A-FARs), the Faculty Athletics Representatives Association (FARA), the National Association of Academic Advisors for Athletics (N4A), the Division 1A Athletics Directors Association, university presidents, and conference commissioners.[29] Similar to the KCIA, COIA has also compiled several position papers and reports in working toward a comprehensive plan to reform intercollegiate athletics.

In their initial charter adopted in March of 2003 and in their report, *A Framework for Comprehensive Athletics Reform*, developed in the fall of 2003, COIA outlined five areas that outlined their scope of reform:

1. Academics. This includes issues of initial and continuing eligibility, admissions, and student-athlete academic standards, etc.
2. Student Welfare. This includes issues of scholarship policies; academic advising, and other forms of student support; equity concerning matters such as gender and race; athletics scheduling; training expectations and time limits; athletes' engagement in campus life, etc.
3. Finances and Scale. This point toward issues related to the athletics "arms race," and includes the cost structure of athletics departments and revenue/non-revenue programs; financial planning, reporting, and monitoring; competitive equity within conferences and divisions; the relationship between winning programs and solvency; the constraints of anti-trust law, etc.

4. Commercialization. This concerns responses to financial impera-
tives that may lead to dependency on corporate and media funding,
requiring various forms of commercial behavior that may conflict
with academic missions or values, including corporate sponsorship contracts and branding control; media contracts and schedul-
ing/marketing control; high-stakes dependency on revenue streams
influenced by factors outside institutional control and not related to
institutional priorities, etc.

5. Governance. This includes the shared governance roles among faculty, presidents, athletics administrators and trustees on individual
campuses over such matters as academic standards and support for
student-athletes, athletics personnel decisions, supervision of financial planning and performance of athletics auxiliaries, programmatic
athletics department decisions, etc.[30]

In the spring of 2004, COIA adopted a statement that addresses governance
issues at NCAA Division IA Institutions: *Campus Athletics Governance,
the Faculty Role: Principles, Proposed Rules, and Guidelines.* This document
details how the Faculty Athletics Representative (FAR), the Campus
Athletics Board (CAB), and the Faculty Governance Body (FGB) are the
three major groups, along with the support and oversight of the president and in collaboration with athletic directors and coaches that provide
effective governance and management of college athletics.[31] According to
COIA, this document:

> articulates a set of principles, proposes a set of uniform rules, and
> discusses in detail guidelines that, when adapted and applied by indi-
> vidual campuses, can help ensure the proper function of the faculty
> role.[32]

In April of 2005, the COIA generated another policy paper, *Academic
Integrity in Intercollegiate Athletics: Principles, Rules, and Best Practices*, and in
December 2005 it provided a report to the NCAA Presidential Task Force
members simply entitled, *A Report to the NCAA Presidential Task Force.*
The *Academic Integrity in Intercollegiate Athletics: Principles, Rules, and Best
Practices* policy paper proposed recommendations or "best practice guidelines" in five areas applicable to NCAA Division I schools: admissions,
scholarships, curricular integrity, time commitment, missed class time,
and scheduling of competitions, and policies concerning the office of academic advising for athletes.[33] COIA specified that three specific areas
should result directly into NCAA bylaw or rule changes for all NCAA
Division I schools. The three specific areas and recommendations are as
follows:

2. Scholarships—2.1 Athletics scholarships shall be awarded on a
year-by-year basis with the presumption that they will be renewed

up to four times for a total award of five years, or until graduation, whichever comes first, for students who are in good academic standing, conform to campus codes for student behavior, conform to the athletics department's standards of conduct, and adhere to team rules. If a student graduates in fewer than five years an institution may renew the scholarship if the student has athletic eligibility remaining. Institutions shall establish criteria and a mechanism for revoking a scholarship. The final authority for revoking a scholarship shall rest with the chief academic officer. A student awarded an athletics scholarship who is no longer participating in athletics will be counted against the NCAA maximum number of awards for that sport, unless the scholarship is revoked or unless the student has exhausted athletic eligibility.

　　3. Curricular Integrity—3.1 Campuses shall collect data on athlete enrollments and grades by course section, including indication of course GPAs, and data on choice of majors, for each individual sport, and shall convey that information to the campus Faculty Governance Body, ensuring that the anonymity of individual students is protected to the degree provided by law. Where no campus Faculty Governance Body exists, the information shall be conveyed to the Campus Athletics Board.

　　4. Time Commitment, Missed Class Time, and Scheduling of Competitions—4.3.2 NCAA bylaws should be amended so that divided competition seasons are not permitted.[34]

Finally, COIA adopted another policy paper in June of 2007, *"Framing the Future: Reforming Intercollegiate Athletics."* It delineates 28 proposals in four major areas: academic integrity and quality, student-athlete welfare, campus governance of intercollegiate athletics, and fiscal responsibility.[35] This position paper is extensive in outlining specific proposals for reform, the specific levels of implementation for each suggested reform, and five key reforms that will require "changes in or enforcement of existing NCAA legislation."[36]

　　In summary, COIA, similar to the KCIA, has sought to provide guidance to the movement of reform in intercollegiate athletics. Unlike the KCIA, it functions as an alliance within institutions of higher education to seek to collaborate with various groups in its efforts to "ensure that college sports are fully integrated within the academic goals, values and missions of our universities and colleges."[37]

The Drake Group

The final organization I will discuss that has organized to address issues involving reform in intercollegiate athletics is The Drake Group (TDG). TDG was conceived by Drake University professor, Jon Ericson, in 1999 as the National Association for College Athletic Reform (NAFCAR). It later changed its name to TDG denoting its origins—Drake University. Its original mission focused on restoring academic integrity to college athletics. This organization mainly consists of current and former faculty members with a vision

> to create an atmosphere on college campuses that encourages personal and intellectual growth for all students, and demands excellence and professional integrity from faculty charged with teaching.[38]

Similar to the KCIA and COIA, TDG has created a proposal with recommendations that they believe, if implemented, will assist in narrowing the gap between athletics and academics and contribute to reforming intercollegiate athletics. TDG proposals are in three phases that address academic transparency, academic priority, and academic based participation. The following is a summary of the recommendations and rationale:

> Phase I: Academic Transparency—Ensure that universities provide accountability of trustees, administrators and faculty by public transparency of such things as a student's academic major, academic advisor, courses listed by academic major, general education requirements, electives, course grade point average (GPA) and instructor—without revealing the names of individual students. In addition, TDG requests that average SAT and ACT scores for revenue producing sports teams be reported along with those of athletes in non-revenue sports, and scholarship students in the symphony orchestra, band, and other extra-curricular activities. Similar comparisons should be made regarding independent studies taken, grade changes by professors, and classes missed because of extracurricular demands.
> *Rationale:* The goal of TDG with regard to academic transparency is to seek to ensure that all college athletes are afforded the full and equal opportunity to earn an education. The Drake Group simply wants to ensure that athletes are afforded the opportunity to earn a college education as promised to them when they accept an academic scholarship and/or agree to participate on a team. Academic transparency is the first step toward creating an atmosphere on college campuses that encourages personal and intellectual growth for all students, and demands excellence and professional integrity from all faculty charged with teaching.
> Phase II: Academic Priority—Require students to maintain a cumulative GPA of 2.0 each semester to continue participation in intercollegiate athletics.
> *Rationale:* Students whose cumulative grade point average falls below 2.0 in any given semester need to give immediate attention to academic performance.... Given the often low graduation rates

for athletes, most notably in the revenue-producing sports, and the acknowledged stressors on the lives of athletes, this measure would provide a safety net for those athletes who are most academically at risk.

Make the location and control of academic counseling and support services for athletes the same as for all students.

Rationale: The NCAA's stated basic purpose is to maintain intercollegiate athletics as an integral part of the educational program and the athlete as an integral part of the student body. This proposal further reinforces the notion that athletes are students and should be integrated into the general student body. Separate athletic counseling centers have been spawned by the separation and control of the athlete—a philosophy TDG rejects. Academic counseling should be rooted in a genuine concern for assisting athletes in the pursuit of their education, not a short-sighted goal of keeping them athletically eligible. This goal cannot be accomplished in a setting that is compromised by pressure to produce winning athletic teams. Faculty Senates can and should act to ensure equal access to education for all students.

Establish university policies that will ensure that athletic contests and practices do not conflict with scheduled classes.

Rationale: To protect the athletes' right to have equal access to educational opportunities, faculty need to enforce the policy that class attendance should take priority over athletic participation. Whenever there are scheduling conflicts between sports and course requirements, faculty members, and administrative staff members, have a professional responsibility to enforce attendance policies that support quality instruction.

Phase III: Academic-Based Participation—Replace one-year renewable scholarships with need-based financial aid (or) with multi-year athletic scholarships that extend to graduation (five year maximum).

Rationale: As long as coaches and athletics directors use factors related to athletics to determine whether financial aid will be renewed, athletes are under considerable pressure to make sports their main priority during enrollment. This highlights the inherent hypocrisy in the term "athletic scholarship," a term that should relate to educational opportunities. To ensure that education remains the priority, renewal of athletic scholarships should be unrelated to athletic performance or athletic scholarships themselves replaced with educational grants awarded on the basis of financial need. In either case, universities should be committed to athletes as students whose value to the university exceeds their role in athletics.

Require one year in residency before an athlete can participate in intercollegiate sport. This rule would apply to transfer students as well as to first year students.

Rationale: Keeping first year students and transfer students out of varsity competition until they have completed one year of residency would assist them in transitioning into to college life without added pressure and time commitment inherent in athletic participation. A one-year residency rule would also discourage coaches from recruiting high school and junior college players as a quick fix to turn around a losing program.[39]

In summary, similar to the KCIA and COIA, TDG has provided national visibility to the need for reform in intercollegiate athletics. It has worked with faculty who have been ostracized by universities and had their job security threatened because of their stance against academic abuse and athletic exploitation. Members of TDG have written extensively and published in scholarly journals and in the popular press to consistently bring to the public's attention many of the controversies and contradictions that exist with academics and intercollegiate athletics, as well as, providing constructive criticism to improve academic integrity in college sports.

NCAA and the Academic Progress Rate

It is important to note that the NCAA has been instrumental in instituting policy to promote athletic reform. Crowley highlights some of the NCAA legislation that has been implemented to improve academic integrity and narrow the gap between athletics and academics. One major reform measure instituted by the NCAA in 2005 that warrants attention in this chapter is the Academic Progress Rate (APR). According to the NCAA, "the APR is the fulcrum upon which the entire academic-reform structure rests."[40] Some have labeled it as a means to prevent the age old practice of "majoring in eligibility," where athletes took classes that were not coherent with a specific program of study.

With the APR, the NCAA has developed a rating system that awards a team two points each term for student-athletes who meet academic-eligibility standards and who remain with the institution. Basically,

> A team's APR is the total points earned by the team at a given time divided by the total points possible. [A score of 925] is the cut score the Division I Board of Directors approved for immediate (or contemporaneous) penalties. APR scores have already become meaningful numbers to the NCAA membership and general public. Based on current data, an APR score of 925 (out of 1,000) translates to an approximate 60 percent Graduation Success Rate [GSR].[41]

Regarding penalties for not meeting the minimum score of 925, the NCAA has different penalty levels to administer to teams: contemporaneous and historical penalties.

> Contemporaneous penalties...are the most immediate penalties and occur when a team with an APR score below 925 loses a

student-athlete who would not have been academically eligible had he or she returned.... An immediate penalty means that the team cannot re-award that grant-in-aid to another player. In effect, a team's financial aid limit is reduced by the amount of countable aid awarded to the student-athlete who did not earn eligibility and was not retained. This penalty is not automatically applied when teams fall below the APR cut point; it is applied only when teams below that line do not retain an academically ineligible player.[42]

A score of 900 converts into a 45 percent GRS and eventually necessitates historical penalties.

Historically based penalties carry more significant sanctions for teams that the APR identifies as chronic under-performers. The penalties will be incremental in nature, beginning with a warning once teams fall below a 900 APR cut score. Historical penalties progress to practice and financial aid restrictions, postseason bans and ultimately restricted membership in Division I. Teams scoring below 900 are subject to further examination to determine if historical penalties are warranted.[43]

In summary, the goal of the NCAA implementation of the APR is to improve athletes' academic success or degree completion and graduation rates. According to the NCAA,

The NCAA's Academic Performance Program (APP) is creating positive behavioral change among Division I institutions, according to new four-year data released May 6. The multi-year Academic Progress Rate (APR) data—with four years of data collection available for the first time—show upward trends in several categories, especially from 2005–06 to 2006–07.[44]

Therefore, progress appears on the reform horizons given measures the NCAA has implemented and the recommendation other organizations have proposed to improve academic integrity and reform intercollegiate athletics.

This brief overview of "reform" organizations and movements highlight some re-occurring themes that have existed since the inception of NCAA. There are other organizations, conferences, institutions, and so on that are staking a claim in addressing these persistent challenges to academic integrity and athletic reform. The work of the National College Players Association (NCPA) (mentioned earlier in chapter 7) is noteworthy because its mission and goals overlap with the mission and goals of the organizations previously noted in this chapter.

Another noteworthy effort in restoring academic integrity to higher education took place at Vanderbilt University in 2008. Despite this school's image of being academically rigorous, Gordon Gee, the president of Vanderbilt, noticed the gap expanding between athletics and academic life. President Gee's answer to this problem was in disbanding the Vanderbilt's athletic department and placing it under the division of student life. Disregarding heavy criticism from colleagues and public critics, Vanderbilt has forged ahead in making confrontational policy decisions that break from traditional paths as a means to restore academic integrity and reform intercollegiate athletics. Other institutions such as Rice and Arizona have implemented similar practices: at Rice, academic counseling for athletics and athletic compliance have been placed under the authority of the dean of undergraduates; while at Arizona, the athletic director has been given a vice presidential title to connect the position with the larger scope of the university.

The journey to athletic reform has been a long, uphill, and winding road. Intercollegiate athletics and higher education remains a controversial union. Raymond Kent's description made in 1930 still reigns true today:

> Athletics in the American colleges are paradoxical. They are the most severely criticized activity of college life and they are the most loved. They are the most rational channel into which to direct the energies of youth, and they are, when improperly administered, the most dangerous and diseased. They are the most vulnerable activity of American college life, and they are one of the most vital. . . . College professors steeped in habits of mind-training and hard work see them largely as misspent effort. Herein are the two extremes in overvaluation—youth in an overvaluation of athletics, and middle age in an overvaluation of academic training. These two extremes are still far apart. The problem of the modern administrator is to find a middle ground.[45]

Finding a middle ground between the academic mission of training the mind and the athletic mission of entertaining the masses reside at the core of making athletics and academics work efficiently in higher education.

Yet an enemy to finding this middle ground has been commercialization and the advancement of capitalist ideals in intercollegiate athletics.[46] History illustrates that academic integrity and commercialization have consistently been re-occurring challenges that face intercollegiate athletics. It is easy to draw the conclusion that as commercialization of intercollegiate athletics has increased it has simultaneously threatened the academic integrity at many NCAA Division I Institutions; especially those institutions that make up the Football Bowl Series Division and many of the institutions that compete to reach the coveted NCAA Men's Basketball Tournament. Therefore, if reducing commercialization will restore academic integrity the accompanying question is, can the public's demand for college athletics and the wave of ultra-commer-cialization[47] being experienced in intercollegiate athletics be restrained? Furthermore, since the increased commercialization has placed a demand on Black athleticism and talent, what would be the need for the Black athlete if there is no longer a demand for his talent and athletic abilities? In paraphrasing the words of Sidney Wilhelm, "Who then would need the Negro?"

★   ★   ★

Decolonization, Reform, and the Black Athlete

The KCIA, COIA, TDG, and so on have skirted around the race issue in their reform efforts. One can conclude from some of the reform demands and recommendations, especially as it relates to academic standards, that there is an attempt to ethnically cleanse and re-Whiten college athletics; especially football and basketball. There are some specific areas of reform that are necessary to address, which involve the plight of Black athletes and their status as internally colonized individuals. I couch these reform recommendations within the process of decolonization.

Decolonization in its purest sense, which has yet to be fully implemented, is the shifting of power from colonial powers into the hands of the indig-enous people in colonized territories; it consists of emancipatory strategies to equalize the imbalance in power. Generally, power shifts when there is a redistribution of resources. In countries that have experienced some form of colonization and decolonization (e.g., throughout South Asia, African, Caribbean, etc.), there was an attempt to shift economic and political power back into the hands of the indigenous inhabitants.[48] Even in the United States, emancipatory strategies resulted in failed attempts to redistribute economic power and resources in the hands of slaves dur-ing the era of reconstruction. For example, the short-lived "Forty Acres and a Mule" compensation package was a decolonization attempt or an emancipatory strategy implemented after the abolition of slavery. It ended abruptly with President Andrew Jackson restoring the land allotted to former slaves back to the White land "owners." Even the Lyndon B. Johnson's "Great Society" legislation can be considered another lofty but failed attempt of redistributed power to combat the social ills of poverty and racial injustices.

To expound further on decolonization, it is not merely an appeal to a moral adjustment but a fundamental change in structural arrangements and the distribution of resources, and an access to services previously denied. Claud Anderson paints a clear picture of the tragedy of appealing to the moral character in the process of decolonization. He states:

> The flaw in the abolitionists' strategy was that they did not recog-nize or treat slavery as the economic issue that it was. They made

the abolishment of slavery a moral issue, which it was not. As a moral issue, the abolitionists appealed to the conscience of slaveholders' concerning right and wrong. These appeals did not damage the slaveholders' profits from slavery.[49]

Beyond the moral appeal, decolonization creates emancipatory strategies (political, economic, and social) that promote empowerment and liberation among the colonized territories and the previously colonized. It also represents ideological changes, where attitudes and behaviors of both the colonizer and the colonized are radically altered requiring the acceptance of an interdependence and an understanding that they share a common fate. There are some emancipatory strategies and changes in ideologies that are requirements in the decolonization process, which can assist in athletic reform.

But first, it is important to reiterate, although it is rather apparent, that at the current rate of commercialization in intercollegiate athletics, PWIs have created a long-term demand for Black athletic labor. Black male athletes have clearly elevated the intercollegiate sports of football and basketball and created a perpetual demand for their athletic labor. And, needless to say that in order to maintain this high level of performance, entertainment, and commercial appeal, these institutions will need Black male athletes. Conversely, Black male basketball players, specifically, may have a diminishing dependency on these institutions as paths to professional sporting careers in other countries emerge and compete with intercollegiate athletics. Especially, if the Black athletes are willing to make the cultural adjustments, endure the language barriers, and have the fortitude to be away from their family and friends.

Black athletes should never see themselves at the mercy of these institutions and victims to its hegemony, but rather co-creators in this is commercial entity and creators of their academic and athletic futures. The decolonization process should not only include efforts to restore academic integrity, but also the self-empowerment of Black athletes.

It should be evident that the need to restore academic integrity and reform intercollegiate athletics were problems long before Black athletes were recruited and allowed to attend PWIs. Again, the very inception of the NCAA in 1905 was due to the need to reform intercollegiate athletics. Many of the re-occurring challenges were evident long before Black athletes were allowed to grace these campuses. Therefore, this is not necessarily a "Black athlete problem"; however, Black athletes are severely and disproportionately affected by it. Unfortunately, current reform efforts are in a strange quagmire with Black male athletes. This section will highlight how some of the recommendations put forth earlier may be irrelevant to producing reform (e.g., limiting practice times and adjusting competition schedules) and how some of the recommendations may have adverse impact that will directly affect Black male athletes (e.g., initial eligibility, admission recommendations, APR standards, etc.).

First, it is important to mention that many of the individuals working on behalf of reform are well-intentioned individuals, competent leaders, and credentialed scholars. I have had the privilege of serving with many of them on national committees and boards, debating issues regarding athletic reform with them, and collaborating with them on common issues about reform.

Unfortunately, the issue of reforming intercollegiate athletics is a bit misguided because as it relates to initial eligibility, academic standards, progression, and achievement, because, as major pieces of the reform movement, these issues target the wrong stage in the process. By the time an athlete arrives at the university with low academic credentials or through special admits, s/he is behind and will remain behind during his/her tenure at that institution. The ability to "catch-up" academically is only possible with the right infrastructure and a sufficient amount of time; however, the athletic time demands make it impossible for athletes to make meaningful strives in keeping up with their cohort of students and excelling academically. Even adhering to the 20 hours a week is unrealistic and loosely enforceable.

One of the reasons is because you can limit the practice times, alter weight-lifting schedules, and time analyzing film, but the hours mentally absorbed by ones respective sport is hard to regulate. For example, I competed at a small private school that on a good week, when we were on a winning streak, our game was broadcast on the radio (yes, I said the radio, and this was in the late eighties, early nineties—big-time, right). In classes on a game day, I was only there in physical form; my mind was absorbed with strategies to employ given a variety of situations and preoccupied with anxiety and fears. I can only imagine what these athletes are thinking in class during the weeks their games are nationally televised. I have personally witnessed that hazed look from athletes in my classes the week of the big game, or in some cases the first part of the week after a big game; their bodies were occupying a seat in my class, but their minds were executing plays and their bodies were battling anxieties. When you combine these factors together, the end result is unfavorable and has been for athletes in revenue generating sports, in general, and many Black male athletes, specifically.

Even the efforts of the propositions (Prop. 48 or 16[50]) that have been instituted to send a message to high school administrators, coaches, and parents of potential college athletes about academic preparation have not fully achieved desired outcomes. Therefore, reform must start within the communities these athletes migrate from, and with the school system, these institutions have a pipeline to for athletic recruitment. Not merely in sending messages by raising academic standards to promote academic achievement. The reform must run deeper. If athletes with phenomenal athletic talent are being targeted by an athletic department during the seventh or eighth grade, along with inviting them to camps that provide them with the necessary training to develop their athlete talents, these athletes should receive the necessary academic training to develop their intellectual abilities to prepare them for admission into college. Adding an academic component that seeks to enhance specific academic skills (SAT preparation, study skills, time management, etc.) to athletic camps is an emancipatory strategy that could be implemented as a reform measure. Furthermore, the same athletic infrastructures that are created in the communities where universities recruit require these institution's investments in creating academic infrastructures that produce academically prepared as well as athletically talented students. This will obviously alter the recruiting philosophy and process, because current recruiting limits will have to be expanded in order to ensure the academic preparation of potential recruits.

There are programs that are trying to meet this need. For example, in 1998, the National Football Foundation (NFF) created *Play It Smart*. *Play It Smart* is "an educational program targeted at high school football players from economically disadvantaged environments where family and community support are often lacking."[51] It has six measures of success:

> 1) Improve Grade Point Average; 2) Increase Number of Students Taking the SAT/ACT & Improved Scores on Tests; 3) Increase Graduation Rate & Opportunities for Higher Education; 4) Enhance Life Skills Development; 5) Increase Opportunities for Community Service; and 6) Increase Parental & Family Involvement.[52]

Its limitations are that they only target high school football players, funding, and the limited amount of communities they serve. I have spoken with students who have worked with this program and they have expressed their frustration because of the lack of structure, support from high school officials, and overall funding. Clearly, the NCAA and its member institutions have an opportunity here to invest in the precollegiate experiences of athletes by expanding on the NFF's concept and underwrite the funding needed to provide this service to include high school basketball players. It can only enhance their image and improve the academic success of athletes migrating to these institutions.

The proposed recommendations and those that are instituted regarding initial eligibility, admission, academic standards, APR, etc., within the current context and given the academic preparation of many athletes, have done more in penalizing the victims, rather than motivating them to excel academically. The object of decolonization in intercollegiate athletics is to empower, where every academic resource necessary is available for athletes recruited into the athletic labor pools; especially when the rate of "special" admits (sometime referred to as presidential admits or faculty sponsorships) are increasing and are becoming indispensable on many of the top football programs in the nation. For example, Mark Alesia reported the following regarding "special admits":

> Many of the nation's largest universities rely on special admits—students admitted under exceptions to normal admission standards for reasons including "special talent"—to stock their football teams.... At these schools, the percentage of special admits among students overall is extremely small. The disparity can be stark: The University of California in 2004 reported that 95 percent of its freshman football players on scholarship were special admits, compared with 2 percent of the student body; Texas A&M in 2004, 94 percent to 8 percent; and Oklahoma in 2002, 81 percent to 2 percent.[53]

Clearly, these athletes are at a disadvantage from their first day and in legitimately meeting the progression requirements instituted by the NCAA.

Significantly altering institutional arrangements are necessary, if the NCAA and its member institutions are truly concerned with adhering to its shared belief in and commitment to its core purpose:

> to govern competition in a fair, safe, equitable, and sportsmanlike manner, and to integrate athletics into higher education so that the educational experience of the student-athlete is paramount.[54]

Meaningful alterations are necessary if they are truly willing to practice the idea that:

> The overwhelming majority of student-athletes will never earn a dime as a professional athlete. That's why the terms "student" and "athlete" are synonymous within the NCAA: When the athlete can no longer play, the student can still succeed.[55]

Therefore, it seems illogical to bring athletes to academic institutions that are academically unprepared, place enormous athletic time demands on them, and expect them to compete with the regular student body. This is clearly a disaster waiting to happen and violations waiting to occur. Too often I have had to encourage athletes who enter my class that I know just left some early morning training or practice to make sure they keep their fellow team member awake in class. The quality of their educational experiences diminishes when they are academically unprepared, pushed to their limits athletically, and tired. So when they are "in season" (if there is such a time where they are out of season), the window of opportunity to achieve a quality educational experience is challenged by athletic time demands.

Having the option to reduce their course load from 12 hours to 6–9 hours to increase their chances of learning and performing well academically is another emancipatory strategy that should be available to athletes who are obviously unprepared and are challenged with time demands.

This will definitely extend the time the athlete is at a university, but the average student takes 5–6 years to graduate, or longer depending on their work demands.

This could also remedy the complaint athletes are voicing regarding majoring in programs where they have no interest, but were convenient in enabling them to maintain eligibility; or what is better known as "majoring in eligibility," where athletes take the "paths of least resistance."[56] This practice places unwarranted pressure on academic advisors to meet academic demands instituted by the NCAA, work within the time constraints of athletic demands (which is a full-time occupation with over-time), as well as, be compassionate to the fact that many of the athletes they are working with are academically unprepared. David Radpith, former compliance director and liaison to academic services for athletes at Marshall University's athletics department and current university professor at Ohio University, informs of the pressures academic advisors incur when trying to manage academic and athletic demands.[57] Also, Donna Lopiano, former Texas' director of women's athletics from 1975 to 1992 and currently the president of Sports Management Resources, "thinks the imperative of staying eligible sometimes trumps the best interests of athletes who get nudged into majors they might not otherwise choose."[58] Therefore, the controversies and contradictions prevail for academic advisors to keep athletes eligible and progressing toward viable major increases as commercialism in athletics increases.

Many of the reform efforts by the organization and groups listed above avoid or do not feel that athletes in revenue generating sport should be paid beyond their yearly athletic scholarships. Generally, the ones who are making this claim do not have contact with the athletes who require having their "full" athletic scholarships supplemented with income from their parent(s), grandparent(s), girlfriend, and so on. The illusions that all football and basketball players ride around in SUVs and live luxuriously in off-campus condominiums are definitely not the norm and certainly escape the experiences of many Black athletes I have known; the testimonies of those living at or below the poverty line are frequent and disheartening, especially when they have to delay their gratification while everyone, except them, are benefiting off of their abilities. Therefore, to increase their athletic scholarships or provide a monthly stipend to offset basic living expenses is another emancipatory strategy and minimally empowers athletes. For example, increasing the athletic scholarship by $500 a month for 85 football players and 13 basketball players would cost an athletic department roughly $582,000 extra each year; and just more than $1 million if it increased to $1,000 per month.

To fund this venture should be considered when negotiating multimillion dollar coaches' salary packages, including bonuses and buyout clauses. Therefore, funding for this expenditure could be in redirecting some of the bonuses that line coaches' coffers and putting it into the pockets of needy athletes. I am well aware that job security for coaches is dismal in this "you must-win big" era of intercollegiate sport, and I sympathize with many coaches who are threatened, harassed, and fired because they did not win the "right" games. However, the job security of athletes competing is also dismal. Career ending injuries are a constant threat to their health and well-being, not to mention the future livelihood of these athletes. I am amazed each semester at the young 19–20-year-old athletes, especially football players and more specifically linesmen, who have to take the elevator because they cannot walk a flight of steps (this was often advised by athletic training staff). I remember, on my way to class, I would frequently share an elevator with one football lineman—he would get off on the second floor and I would head to the third floor. Regarding his use of the elevator, he informed me of his future health outlook. He mentioned that his doctor's prognosis was that at the current rate of competing and the pounding his body was taking he would have to have both hips replaced by the time he was 30. The list is extensive of athletes I have known who have had one of the following injuries: too many concussions, back or neck injuries, or those who must submit to living with pins and rods in their bodies due to athletic injuries. Athletes' security must also be considered in the equation in regards to compensation, which again is an emancipatory strategy.

The major ideological change regards PWIs acknowledging and accepting Black athletes as partners in this intercollegiate athletic enterprise. This would be a quantum leap in their belief system because it has been a difficult process for many Whites to relate to Blacks as equals or partners in any endeavor given the history of race relations in this country. However, current sociopolitical, sociocultural, and socioeconomic situations demand their evolution from archaic racial ideologies. The current economic configuration of intercollegiate athletics is such a situation. Accepting Black athletes as partners is an emancipatory strategy that can potentially enhance loyalty to universities' brand, as well as, improve brand identity, especially in Black communities.

To materialize this shift in ideology, this partnership should materialize in some type of contractual agreement between the two parties, which outline the specific and desired outcomes of both parties. With a contractual agreement, why not create incentives for elite athletes to consider staying in college instead of the "one and done" approach we see occurring in college basketball, or where underclassmen or declaring themselves eligible for the NFL/NBA draft? Why not ensure athletes, who have participated in revenue generating sports and do not make it to the professional level, with financial support for graduate school, medical benefits for life if they incur a life-altering injury, or career counseling support[59] after they have graduated? Furthermore, as lettermen and athletic laborers they should be vested to have emeritus status at their respective institutions; especially if the institution is a public institution, which is supposedly owned by the citizens of that respective state. Emeritus status should go beyond having access to tickets or sideline appearances, but it should more substantial services for the services they have rendered. For example, emeritus status could provide them with student privileges and access to community events, the library, career counseling services, and so on.

Future research should examine how this partnership approach impacts brand identity and loyalty among members throughout Black communities, and how contractual agreements can be motivating factors for academic eligibility and excellence. Future research should also consider additional emancipatory strategies and ideological changes to decolonized intercollegiate athletics. In addition, future research should engage how developing emancipatory strategies to ensure that the educational experiences of athletes is paramount impact NCAA legislation.. The few suggestions put forth in this chapter would require greater flexibility in NCAA policies and institutional governance.

★   ★   ★

In summary, Table 9.1 highlights some additional recommendations for decolonization that focuses on structural changes, and includes the internal colonial components that relate to the particular recommendations. Unlike previous efforts of reform, these structural changes do not penalize the victim. It requires PWIs to assimilate to the changing racial, sociocultural, and political structures of the larger U.S. society they operate in, and it requires them to be proactive in educating individuals to function within this multiracial and multicultural society.

To conclude, this chapter has provided an overview of the history of intercollegiate athletic reform. It has highlighted several organizations that are contributing recommendations to fuel the reform movement. These organizations' major concern centers on restoring academic integrity to institutions of higher learning. Unfortunately, many of their recommendations have a tendency to penalize the victim, especially the majority of the recommendations that have been instituted. Thus, in the words of Ralph Waldo Emerson, what they (NCAA/PWIs) are doing speaks so loudly that what they are saying cannot be heard. In other words, it is a bit hypocritical to say that the educational experiences of student athletes are paramount, yet athletic demands shape their lives and significantly impact these experiences.

The process of decolonization seeks to provide emancipatory strategies to empower athletes and provide them with the resources needed to be competitive academically and athletically. This process begins years before the athlete steps onto the campus, more so during the time athletic departments start showing interests in the physical abilities and talents of an athlete; seventh and eight grades. Once they are on campus, there must be greater concessions made to balance the academic and athletic demands, especially in cases where athletes have limited academic preparation.

Finally, self-empowerment is the most vital empowerment for athletes and more specifically Black male athletes. It begins with PWIs and Black athletes understanding that they are partners in this commercial enterprise. This empowerment for Black athletes should manifest during the recruiting process where letter of intents become more of contractual agreements with specific demands that detail specific expectations of this business arrangement. If these demands are not met, they should have "free agency" rights to seek opportunities at another institution that is capable of meeting these demands.

Self-empowerment for Black athletes can also be achieved through uniting and developing grassroots organizations among themselves or by uniting with organizations like NCPA. This organization was founded by Ramogi Huma, former UCLA linebacker, as an advocacy group for college athletes.[60] Athletes in revenue generating sports, in general, and Black athletes, specifically, must understand the amount of power they possess with their athletic labor. The practices that prevail in keeping athletes unaware, fragmented, and tolerant of their conditions cannot be taken lightly in their quest for self-empowerment. However, history documents that momentum and justice is on the side of those who unite with a common cause and have faith to persist in the face of adversity will eventually altered oppressive institutional arrangements.

Table 9.1 Components of the internal colonial model & decolonization

Components	Dynamics/Functions	Reform/Decolonization
Colonizer and the Colonized Relationship	The colonizer's privileges are directly and illegitimately based on the exploitation and pauperization of the colonized.	Black athlete self empowerment & understand and negotiate rights as a student & athlete; parents function as agents during the recruitment process; establish contractual partner agreements
Economics	The main purpose for internal colonialism; to enrich the lives of the colonizer.	Decrease commercialization and exploitation or increased scholarship funding to meet expenses; cost of living increases; post-graduate financial support.
Politics	Political decisions for the colonized are made by the colonizer.	Diversify leadership structure; democratic process. Incorporate voice of the Black athlete in the political/governing process.
Racism (Individual and Institutional)	Racial (biological) characteristics (skin color, specifically) have been ways that the colonizer identifies, controls, and exploits the colonized.	Increase racial diversity throughout university structure: administrative, faculty, and student body; seek to reflect global community.
Social	Colonized are not a permanent resident, therefore they do not identify with the colonizer's social setting.	Increase racial diversity throughout university structure: administrative, faculty, and student body to minimize the drastic difference in migration points; seek to reflect global community.
Cultural	The colonized are removed from their cultural context. It is suppressed or exterminated by the colonizer in the internal colonial situation.	Increase cultural diversity throughout university structure: administrative, faculty, and student body to minimize the drastic difference in migration points; seek to reflect global community.

CHAPTER TEN

Conclusion

> Come, then, comrades; it would be as well to decide at once to change our ways. We must shake off the heavy darkness in which we were plunged, and leave it behind. The new day which is already at hand must find us firm, prudent, and resolute.
>
> —Frantz Fanon, *The Wretched of the Earth*

The use of the internal colonial or plantation model places the experiences of Black athletes at predominantly White National Collegiate Athletic Association (NCAA) Division I institutions (PWIs) into a broader social context. It outlined the structural challenges that are present at these institutions, and how the institutional settings contribute to the experiences of Black athletes. The use of an internal colonial analysis helps draw upon the similarities that exist between the experiences of Black athletes and internally colonized people. This also suggests that the structures in which they exist also have some similarities. In other words, the economic, political, social, and cultural patterns of each share marked resemblances.

To reiterate, colonial situations exist to enrich the lives of the colonizer.[1] The main interests of the NCAA and its member institutions with respect to revenue generating sports of football and basketball are power and money. The monopolistic or cartel-like behavior of the NCAA ensures that it exercise a certain degree of power and control over intercollegiate athletics, including the image and commodity produced by men and women who participate in revenue generating sports.

It has been shown that Black athletes are a large percentage of the athletic labor class (specifically in the sports of football and basketball), and this labor class generates the revenue for PWIs. This pattern is repeated throughout history, where a disproportionate percentage of Blacks in the United States have served as physical laborers advancing the motives of White capitalists. Blacks, in the context of intercollegiate athletics, continue to be exploited for their physicality. The presence of Black athletes at PWIs sustains ideals of scientific racism and reproduces the notion of the physically superior Black body similar to how it was represented in the internal colonial system of slavery in North America and other internal colonial situations throughout the world.

The economic and political systems and the social and cultural settings at these institutions function in a manner that hinders the merging of Black athletes' two identities. The ability to enjoy these institutions as students and athletes, despite their contributions to them through athletic participation, has been a "dream deferred" that has cost many Black athletes their chances of getting an education, obtaining a college degree, and increasing their chances of social mobility.

The oscillating migrant laborers expectations to help their families and villages are purely motivated by the need for financial subsistence, thus they migrate to distant areas to labor sites. Similarly, the hopes of many Black athletes resemble the hopes of these oscillating migrant laborers. Unfortunately, the rate of Black athletes graduating from these institutions has been low, and their chances of making it to the level of professional sports has been very slim. Therefore, instead of being in a position to help their families, an unfortunate number have become a burden to their families and communities. This is discouraging because the families and communities that bore the burden of developing this athletic skill benefit the least.

The internal colonial nature of these institutions contributes to their experiences and lack of success at PWIs as well as impacts their abilities in navigating these contested terrains. The fact that too many Black athletes enter these institutions academically unprepared and are required to maintain a rigorous athletic schedule impacts their chances of graduating. This challenge increases drastically when these students must deal with different sociocultural settings, endure the racism, and the political and economic exploitation at these institutions.

Restructuring and diversifying PWI's athletic departments are suggestions and an effort that is put forth by the current NCAA administration. Although the NCAA is committed on paper to diversifying athletic administration departments at these institutions, the efforts have yet been token concessions because there has been no significant or enduring changes in Blacks being hired in administrative positions: athletic directors, associate athletic directors, administrative assistants, head coaches, assistant coaches, academic advisors, compliance officers, business managers, auxiliary services, equipment managers, faculty athletics representatives, graduate assistants, promotion and marketing directors, strength coaches, sports information directors, ticket managers, and trainers.[2] Instead of a significant increase in these positions, there has been considerable recycling of Black coaches and administrators who have already been in the system. According to the Institute for Diversity and Ethics in Sport, at Football Bowl Subdivision (FBS) institutions:

> 92.5 percent of the presidents, 86.7 percent of the athletics directors, 92.6 percent of the faculty athletics reps, 83.3 percent of the faculty

and 100 percent of the conference commissioners... whites hold 328 (90.6 percent) of the 362 campus leadership positions.[3]

Individuals in these are potential role models who could inspire Black athletes to excel academically, or motivate them "to pursue a career in athletic administration where they would have some input into the future of student athletes."[4]

Decolonization basically suggests that there is a transfer of power (resources) from the colonizer's hands *back* to the colonized's. The history of colonialism in Africa and internal colonialism in the United States illustrates that in many cases this shift of power has been superficial and without the needed substance to qualify the colonized as completely liberated and independent. The use of indirect rule has been and still is an effective means that gives an illusion that power has changed hands; when in fact there have mainly been cosmetic changes.

Besides the emancipatory strategies outlined earlier, the ability of Black athletes to recognize and understand their common goals, potential destinies, and collective efforts, and then organize to form a united voice is a key emancipatory strategy. While the efforts of NCAA officials seek to diversify its leadership, an important need of Black athletes for self-empowerment and collective self-actualization is to organize to insure that the efforts by the NCAA go beyond the current superficial cosmetic changes. The organization of Black athletes in a democratic manner and use of a democratic approach is a prerequisite to fully realizing the transfer of power and necessary resources into their hands or accessible to them as a collective body.

I emphasize this strategy because the athletic culture presents a severe process of domestication, which breeds conservatism and political inactivity. When I competed in sports, from Little League Baseball to college sports, it was under a type of dictatorship. We were being trained to take orders and follow through on those orders regardless of our physical limitations. There was no democratic process in deciding whether we wanted to run in 100 degree weather, or to negotiate the practice schedule if our sleep patterns requested a siesta. No, coach said, "Run!" We said, "How far and how fast coach?" If the coach said, "Jump!" We said, "How high and how long?" For us, during the era of capital punishment in the home and school, confronting coach or the system was like talking back to your parents—you might as well pack your bags. Therefore, because of the nature of the athletic culture, motivating athletes to organize around weightier matters could present a challenge.

However, organizing for political input, that is, the ability to make valid input and vote on the policy decisions that govern their lives and the resources they produce, is imperative for Black athletes. Kwame Nkrumah suggests that a people without political independence cannot exist freely or be respected.[5] Economic exploitation and political, racial, social, and cultural oppression will not be minimized for Black athletes at these institutions without obtaining political independence. According to Nkrumah:

> No people without a government [political independence] of its own can expect to be treated on the same level as peoples of independent sovereign States. It is far better to be free to govern, or misgovern, yourself than to be governed by anyone else.[6]

Nkrumah's statement expresses the necessity for Black athletes to organize. The alternative is to be continually disrespected, that is, economically exploited, politically, racially, socially, and culturally oppressed.

Organizing can be problematic because all Black athletes may not have the same goals of graduating and becoming better educated. Some may be looking for a way into the professional ranks, and unfortunately, they must endure one or two years in a college or university environment; in my experience, fortunately, this group has been the minority. However, with the increased opportunities in professional sport (e.g., Arena Football, expanding franchise teams in the NBA, professional basketball leagues in other countries, etc.) and the increased number of athletes opting to leave prior to finishing their eligibility, could pose a problem to uniting. Fortunately, the majority of Black athletes who I have come in contact with have generally shared the goals of graduating and becoming better educated at these institutions, thus, they could benefit from the emancipatory strategies of uniting.

For Black athletes, two of their strongest allies in uniting and organizing are the National College Players Association and the existing Black student organizations. Together Black students and Black athletes should seek to use their collective power to better their living and educational conditions on these campuses. No longer can Black athletes be discouraged by athletic department staff members from joining and supporting Black organizations. Even though the schedules of Black athletes are restrictive and may cause conflict in them participating in some of the meetings of these organizations, sacrifices must be made by both groups to unite and do strategic planning that will produce agendas and tactics to aid in changing these unaccepting environments.

If staff members in the athletic department (coaches, counselors, athletic directors, and other administrators) are concerned about the well-being and academic success of Black athletes, they should understand and accept Black athletes organizing with Black students. They must become less demanding of Black athletes' time and adhere to NCAA ruling that limits the athletic participation of all student athletes to 20 hours a week during the season of competition and 8 hours a week during the off-season. Basically, they must be willing to relinquish some of the power and control they have over the lives of Black athletes. Although a lot about life can be learned through the collegiate athletic experience, they still need more freedom to enjoy collegiate life beyond the playing fields and arenas.

White athletes can also be allies when it comes to the shift of economic and political power from the hands of NCAA and institutional officials. Both groups are definitely exploited economically and can benefit in uniting to overthrow economic exploitation. Despite the different structural positions Black athletes and White student athletes hold as laborers, they can both benefit from united efforts aimed at having a voice into the expenditure of the revenues they generate and in creating ways they may be compensated beyond the yearly grant-in-aid (athletic scholarship). The option of compensating student athletes beyond athletic scholarships is an emancipatory strategy that is a viable option in the process of decolonization and can take the form of increasing scholarship amounts to meet the cost of living expenses and travel. As the commercialization of collegiate sport increases, compensating athletes will become a logical alternative to receive a desired outcome and to minimize illegal activity.

Additional concerns of decolonization is the need to reduce the social, racial, cultural, and other deficiencies at these institutions and change these unaccepting environments into environments that produce higher graduation rates and decrease the negative experiences of Black athletes and Black students in general. Diversifying the student body, administration, and so on must move beyond theory and become praxis.

There are areas that many PWIs are deficient in and it is mainly out of ethnocentric arrogance and neglect. I see an assumption being made on the part of these institutions that suggests that all cultures, races, and ethnic groups outside of the Euro-American race are supposed to assimilate or else it minimizes the chances of success. Because of this assumption, cultural diversity and multiculturalism have lagged in being fully accepted and implemented at many of the institutions, which do not see a problem in receiving national exposure and generating revenue off of the athletic labor of Black male athletes. Some of these deficiencies can be minimized once these campuses become more culturally diverse, especially among these institutions' powerbrokers (faculty and administrators).

Having multicultural curriculums and cultural diversity among faculty and staff members is part of the decolonization process that will assist in decentering these monolithic Euro-American centered environments. The ultimate goal of decolonization must be in creating environments where all students can learn, live, and be creative, and become productive with some level of comfort having multiple roles and identities without the fear of being stigmatized, minimized, and often ostracized. The true tests of being an institution of higher learning will be whether are not these institutions seek to become less monolithic in behavior instead of in just rhetoric, and whether or not they seek to reduce, rather than contribute to or neglect, the problems of diversity (race, culture, religion, etc.) we face in this country.

Direction for Future Research

Examining the structural and ideological issues that continue to impact the experiences of Black athletes at PWIs is a necessary direction for future analysis. Furthermore, developing ways to de-emphasize the intellectual inferiority of Black athletes and emphasize the social, cultural, political, racial, and economic conditions these students are challenged with at predominantly White institutions should be a continual line of inquiry for future research. This does not mean that we should neglect the fact that some Black athletes have academic concerns upon entering these institutions, but attention needs to be given to the problems these institutions have in assisting these students in graduating and becoming better educated.

This study intended to focus more on the systems Black athletes were entering rather than on their academic unpreparedness. Future research on the experiences of Black athletes or their graduation rates needs to focus on the structure these students are entering as well as the high school structures they are leaving. One inquiry along this line of thinking can be if and how historically Black colleges and universities (HBCUs) may be a better fit to meet the needs of Black athletes who are academically unprepared. It is only my speculation but the philosophy and the social and cultural settings of HBCUs may be more conducive in equipping Black male athletes for academic and career success. This speculation is based on anecdotal data and personal interactions with Black male athletes that have graduated from HBCUs and have voiced having more of a quality "well-rounded" educational experience.

One of the discouragements for Black athletes *remigrating* back to HBCUs is that many HBCUs lack the athletic financial infrastructure in comparison to many PWIs that are capitalizing off of Black athletic labor. However, as HBCUs develop comparable athletic infrastructures, this remigration can prove beneficial for Black athletes requiring an environment that can nurture them academically and athletically. This is possible as long as the increased commercialization does not cause HBCUs to forsake their philosophy of taking students where they are academically and assisting them to where they need to be—better educated.

Another direction for future research is whether modifying the internal colonial model can be used to examine the experiences of all athletes at PWIs. Besides the racial and cultural aspects of the Black athletes' experiences, White student athletes in revenue generating sports face some of the same challenges regarding the political, economic, and social structures of these institutions.

This study lends support to the need for these institutions to make efforts toward reforming: encouraging athletes to excel more as students than as athletes. It is a challenge that must begin at the youth sports and interscholastic levels so that athletes are motivated in taking full advantage of educational opportunities that are available to them and not just focus on athletics. Black athletes, specifically, must be encouraged from an early age to see athletics not as an end in and of itself but more as a means to an end and the end being becoming better educated and productive citizens.

In our homes, we must require that our young athletes spend two hours of academic related activities (reading, writing, etc.) to every one hour they spend at the gym or on the playground. It is important to reward them more for their academic achievements than we do for their athletic accomplishments. History teaches us the consequences of placing too much emphasis on athletics than on developing the mind. It is paramount to emphasize and stress to young Black male athletes, especially, that they can be "book smart" and still be masculine and Black—Black scholar-ballers are a part of collective experiences and historical make-up. This ideology among many of our young Black male athletes who equates intelligence with femininity and Whiteness must be repudiated.

Youth programs and junior high and high school programs must emphasize the need for athletes to put in just as much time in academics as they do with athletics. The scholar athlete must be the image we epitomize in all our athletic programs for our young people. These programs must not settle for anything less than this or else we will continue to lose lives who are chasing an elusive dream and young minds who are set at an early age on becoming a professional athlete and only a professional athlete. Our goal with future research is not to discourage athletic participation, that is, stop the dreamer from dreaming, but to encourage academic excellence as part of fulfilling their dreams.

★ ★ ★

Despite the election of the first Black male president of the United States, there are yet structural arrangements that must be made and ideologies that require altering among institutions in this country to fully accommodate the humanitarian vision and proclamation that:

> We hold these truths to be self-evident, that all men [and women] are created equal, that they are endowed by their Creator with certain unalienable Rights, which among these are Life, Liberty, and the Pursuit of Happiness.[7]

Although this statement may not have been conceived with Blacks being considered as "men or women," it is applicable to the potential lying dormant for many in this country who have been perplexed, persecuted, and abused because of their race or ethnicity. Until the actualization of this truth, Black athletes must navigate the current institutional arrangements at PWIs. Though we should not be content with the current arrangements, academic success is achievable in spite of these arrangements.

I have asserted that the experiences of Black athletes at PWIs are a part of the broader struggle for racial justice against glaring racial inequalities; similar to colonized people who endured economic exploitation, political oppression, and sociocultural marginalization. I have sought to provide an alternative perspective regarding the experiences of Black athletes at PWIs. Athletic and academic excellence is the standard that many Black athletes have achieved because of and in spite of the statistical odds consistently professed against them. You are competing against historical forces and making history, and I share in your tragedy and triumphs and in your defeats and victories.

EPILOGUE

We are hard pressed on every side, but not crushed; perplexed, but not in despair; persecuted, but not abandoned; struck down, but not destroyed.

—Apostle Paul's Letter to the Church at Corinth,
II Corinthians 4:8–9.

History presents the fact that structures are unstable and institutional arrangements are erratic. With this said, there is hope for Black athletes' acceptance into the full educational intercollegiate experience. They can relinquish the title of being *modern day gladiators*, as coined by Dr. Harry Edwards, who are specifically used to entertain the White masses and accumulate capital for predominantly White institutions (collegiate and corporate). In this current paradigm, their athletic brawn has been their means; their ticket to educational opportunities or fortune and fame through professional athletic careers. A paradigm shift is required to bring about a greater balance between athletic services rendered and educational services received, as well as, academic achievement and athletic aspiration.

For my colleagues who are in the athletic and academic trenches hard pressed and seeking to reach one to teach one, our work of educating, researching, and liberating must continue, regardless of how insurmountable the odds may seem. Many of you can identify with being "hard pressed on every side, but not crushed; perplexed, but not in despair; persecuted, but not abandoned; [and] struck down, but not destroyed." Our work is connected to a greater cause and grounded in the historical fight against oppression and injustices everywhere. I believe reform is inevitable because the divine nature of the human condition will prevail against all inhumanity and evolve to embrace all humanity.

I believe we are capable of creating a collegiate athletic model that is conducive to both educating our youth and providing them with the skills they need to live productive lives, and one that is athletically competitive and entertaining. I believe it is possible to have our actions congruent with what we say, so that what we do bears witness with what we are saying. The progress we have made thus far, including putting a Black face in a high place, speaks loudly and precisely to our ability to not only make progress in everything, but to also created visible and permanent change. In the spirit of the recent election and inauguration, I leave you with these three words of hope: Yes, We Can!

NOTES

Preface

1. Derrick Bell, *And We Are Not Save: The Elusive Quest for Racial Justice* (New York, NY: Basic Books, 1989), p. 10.
2. Dr. Martin L. King, Letter from Birmingham Jail, April 16, 1963.

Introduction

1. H. G. Bissinger, *Friday Night Lights: A Town, a Team, and a Dream* (Cambridge, MA: Da Capo Press, 1990). This ethnographical account of the Permian Panthers of Odessa, Texas, captures the power of high school football captivating the lives of many individuals across racial, ethnic, economic, etc., lines in this small community.
2. There were degrees of academic success where for certain subjects such as physical education, vocational technical classes, math, etc., we were expected to excel in whereas for other subjects such as home economics, art, and other "non-masculine" classes we were expected to perform poorly.
3. Black athlete will be used instead of Black student athletes because the reason Black students with athletic abilities are on at these institutions are primarily because of their athletic abilities. This is not to say that they are not intellectually capable of performing well academically, but to say that the dominant role they perform, especially in revenue generating sports, are as athletes; being a student is a byproduct of their experience at predominantly White NCAA Division I institutions.
4. I will use fictitious names or first names in some cases to protect the privacy of those individuals.
5. When speaking of intercollegiate athletics or NCAA Division I institutions, I will be mainly focusing on those institutions that are from the "equity leagues" or are a part of the Bowl Championship Series (BCS), which include the following conferences: the Atlantic Coast Conference (ACC), Big East, Big 10, Big 12, Pacific-10, and the Southeastern Conference (SEC). These institutions have the largest operating budgets, the largest expenses, and generate the most revenue among the NCAA Division IA second-tier institutions and the Division IAA and IAAA programs. There are actually 12 conferences that makeup the BCS. The other six include Conference USA, Mid-American Conference, Mountain West Conference, Sun Belt Conference, Western Athletic Conference, and NCAA Division Independent schools.
6. Some of the structural inequalities that impact the decisions and options for young Black males include some challenges mentioned previously—also educational achievement levels and unemployment rates.
7. The ideology of Black physical/athletic superiority is a belief system that has it origins in racist propaganda, which was used to justify slavery in the United States, has also been co-opted into the ethos of many Blacks. It is not uncommon to hear Blacks, especially young Black males,

express pride in their athletic prowess and speak of their ability to dominate other racial groups in certain sports. The adoption of this belief is a means of racial uplift gone bad.

8. Dr. Harry Edwards has elaborated on the process of funneling Black youth into the avenue of athletics at the expense of other academic and occupational pursuits. William Rhoden describes this process as a conveyer belt system that young Black males are put on early in life and for some continue on throughout their college athletic careers.

9. Oliver Cromwell Cox, *Race: A Study in Social Dynamics* (New York: Monthly Review Press, 2000), 43.

10. See the following reference for more information concerning personal troubles and public issues: C. Wright Mills, *Sociological Imagination* (New York: Oxford Press, 1959). Although the original intent of the application of these concepts was to be applied to larger sociostructural issues, such as unemployment, divorce rates, etc., applying these concepts to examine structural deficiencies within social institutions can be instructive.

11. Adam Himmelsbach, "First Impressions Can Create Unrealistic Expectations Basketball Recruits," http://www.nytimes.com/2009/03/10/sports/10recruiting.html (accessed March 10, 2009).

12. Graduation Rate Rata, http://web1.ncaa.org//app_data/instAggr2008/1_0.pdf (accessed March 10, 2009).

13. 2008–2009 NCAA Division I Manual, http://www.ncaapublications.com/Uploads/PDF/Division_1_Manual_2008-09e9e568a1-c269-4423-9ca5-16d6827c16bc.pdf (accessed July 27, 2008). For a more in-depth analysis of amateurism and collegiate sports, see Allen L. Sack and Ellen J. Staurowsky, *College Athletes for Hire: The Evolution and Legacy of the NCAA's Amateur Myth* (Westport, CT: Praeger, 1998).

14. Eugene Genovese, *Roll, Jordan, Roll: The World the Slaves Made* (New York: Random House, 1974). Genovese further expounds on paternalism and its operation within the system of slavery.

15. Random House, *The Random House College Dictionary (Revised Edition)* (New York: Random House, 1980).

16. Mary R. Jackman, *The Velvet Glove: Paternalism and Conflict in Gender, Class, and Race Relations* (Berkeley: University of California Press, 1994), 10.

17. Brent Kallestad, "NCAA gives Florida State 4 years' Probation," http://rivals.yahoo.com/ncaa/football/news?slug=ap-floridast-cheating&prov=ap&ty (accessed March 10, 2009).

18. This analogy is borrowed from the following source: Jackman, *The Velvet Glove.*

19. *Athletic industrial complex* is a term used by scholars and sport writers that examines the institution of intercollegiate athletics. See e.g., Earl Smith, *Race, Sport and the American Dream* (Durham, NC: Carolina Academic Press, 2007); William C. Rhoden, *Forty Million Dollar Slaves: The Rise, Fall, and Redemption of the Black Athlete* (New York: Crown Publishers, 2006).

20. I intend to use the terms, *internal colonialism* and *plantation system*, interchangeably.

21. Robert Staples, "Race and Colonialism: The Domestic Case in Theory and Practice" *The Black Scholar* 7, no. 9 (1976): 39.

22. Ibid., 44.

23. Several researchers have examined the issue of White privilege. Peggy McIntosh has labeled it as an invisible knapsack of unearned assets that Whites can cash in on daily. For example, Whites can go shopping and be assured that they will not be harassed or followed, or they will never be asked to speak for all the people of their racial group. For more see Peggy McIntosh, "White Privilege: Unpacking the Invisible Knapsack," *Independent School* 49, no. 2 (Winter 1990): 5, 31.

24. Robert M. Sellers, "Black Student-Athletes: Reaping the Benefits or Recovering from the Exploitation," in D. Brooks and R. Althouse (eds.), *Racism in College Athletics: The African-American Athlete's Experience* (Morgantown, WV: Fitness Information Technology 1993), 149.

25. The following references provide insight into the concept of a class fraction: Annie Phizacklea and Robert Miles, *Labour and Racism* (Boston: Routledge & Kegan Paul, 1980); Robert Miles, *Racism and Migrant Labour* (Boston: Routledge & Kegan Paul, 1992); and Nicos Ar Poulantzas, *Political Power and Social Classes* (London: New Left Books, 1973).

26. Phizacklea and Miles, *Labour and Racism*, 6.

27. Ibid.

28. Gary Sailes, "An Investigation of Campus Stereotypes: The Myth of Black Athletic Superiority and the Dumb Jock Stereotype," *Sociology of Sport Journal* 10, no. 1 (1993): 88–97; Robert M.

Sellers, Gabriel P. Kuperminc, and Andrea S. Waddell, "Life Experiences of Black Student-Athletes in Revenue Producing Sports: A Descriptive Empirical Analysis," *Academic Athletic Journal* (1991): 21–38.

29. Dean Purdy, D. Stanley Eitzen, and Rick Hufnagel, "Are Athletes also Students? The Educational Attainment of College Athletes," *Social Problems* 29, no. 4 (1982): 439–448; Beth J. Shapiro, "Intercollegiate Athletic Participation and Academic Achievement: A Case Study of Michigan State University Student Athletes, 1950–1980." *Sociology of Sport Journal* 1, no. 1 (1984): 46–51; Leroy Ervin, Sue A. Saunders, H. Lee Gillis, and Mark C. Hogrebe, "Academic Performance of Student Athletes in Revenue-Producing Sports," *Journal of College Student Personnel* 26, no. 2 (1985): 119–124; Robert M. Sellers, "Racial Differences in the Predictors of Academic Achievement of Division I Student Athletes," *Sociology of Sport Journal* 9 (1992): 48–59.

30. Excerpts from the West India Emancipation Speech delivered by Frederick Douglass at Canandaigua, New York, August 4, 1857. Also included in the following source: Philip S. Foner (ed.), "West India Emancipation Speech," *The Life and Writings of Frederick Douglass, Vol. 2* (New York: International Publishers, 1950), 437.

One   Brief Historical Overview and the Experience of Black Athletes and Students at Predominantly White Institutions: A Mind Is a Terrible Thing to Waste

1. Cheikh Anta Diop, *Pre-colonial Black Africa: A Comparative Study of the Political and Social Systems of Europe and Back Africa from Antiquity to the Formation of Modern States That Demonstrates the Black Contribution to the Development of Western Civilization* (Europe: Lawrence Hill Books, 1987); Cheikh Anta Diop, *The African Origin of Civilization: Myth or Reality* (Europe: Lawrence Hill Books, 1989); Ivan Van Sertima, *They Came before Columbus: The African Presence in Ancient America* (New York: Random House, 1976); Chancellor Williams, *The Rebirth of African Civilization* (Chicago, IL: Third World Press, 1993); Chancellor Williams, *The Destruction of Black Civilization: Great Issues of a Race from 4500 B.C. to 2000 A. D.* (Chicago, IL: Third World Press, 1987).

2. The debate between E. Franklin Frazier and Melville Herskovits denotes notions of African retention. In other words, did Africans completely lose their cultural identities (assimilate into the dominant America Culture) or were their remnants of African cultures maintained through-out the plantation life. Frazier suggests that there was no retention, while Herskovits argues that there are some remnants of Africanism preserved in African American cultural expressions in the United States (e.g., in worship, cuisine, music). Scholars from various disciplines began to provide credence to Herskovits argument in their works on African American culture. For additional readings regarding this debate, see the following: E. Franklin Frazier, *The Negro Family in the United States* (Chicago: University of Chicago Press, 1939); Melville Herskovits, "What Has Africa Given America?" *New Republic, 84* (1935): 92–94; Melville Herskovits, *The Myth of the Negro Past* (Boston: Harper and Brothers, 1941).

3. See Frederick Douglass, *Life and Times of Frederick Douglass* (New York: Collier Books, 1892), 79. In this quote, Douglass is recalling a conversation Master Hugh is having with his wife explaining the necessity in not teaching Douglass, specifically, and slaves in general to read.

4. Faustine C. Jones-Wilson provides a brief overview in the preface of the *Encyclopedia of African-American Education* detailing the law and policies that were barriers to Blacks' opportunity to partake in the educational system in the United States (see p. vii). This encyclopedia is a great source for information examining education and the Black experience; see, e.g., Faustine C. Jones-Wilson, Charles A. Asbury, Margo Okazawa-Rey, D. Kamili Anderson, Sylvia M. Jacobs, and Michael Fultz (eds.), *Encyclopedia of African-American Education* (Westport, CT: Greenwood, 1996).

5. I will use both Black student and Black athlete at times. There are times when I will make a distinction and use only Black athlete. When speaking in general about their experiences, I will use the term *Black students*.

6. For additional reading on Historically Black Colleges and Universities (HBCUs) also called Traditionally Black Institutions (TBIs), see the following: Susan T. Hill and National

Center for Education Statistics, *The Traditional Black Institutions of Higher Education, 1860 to 1982* (Washington, DC: U.S. Department of Education, Office of Educational Research and Improvement, National Center for Educational Statistics, 1985). Also, for bibliography on HBCUs see Fredrick Chambers, *Black Higher Education in the United States: A Selected Bibliography on Negro Higher Education and Historically Black Colleges and Universities* (Westport, CT: Greenwood, 1978).

7. Ibid.

8. The Morrill Act of 1890; it is the second Morrill Act. The Morrill Land Grant Act of 1862 was the initial act that provided states with land or proceeds from the sale of the land to be used in developing educational institutions with an emphasis on agriculture and the mechanic arts. For the Second Morrill Act see, *Morrill Land Grant Act of 1890 The Second Morrill Act.* Act of August 30, 1890, ch.841, 26 Stat.417, 7 U.S.C. 322 et seq.

9. Several Black athletes competed at predominantly White northern colleges and universities during the late 1800s. For example, Moses Fleetwood Walker played baseball at Oberlin College in 1878 and his brother enrolled and competed in 1881, William Henry Lewis and William Tecumseh played and excelled at Amherst in 1889; Lewis enrolled in Harvard Law School, and he also played on its football team. George Jewett was the starting fullback at the University of Michigan in 1890, William Arthur Johnson competed at MIT (Massachusetts Institute of Technology) in 1890, and in 1892, George A. Flippin played halfback for Nebraska. Other Black players starred at predominantly White northern colleges and universities and received All-American honors as well as excelled academically: see, e.g., Arthur R. Ashe, Jr., *A Hard Road to Glory: A History of the African-American Athlete 1619–1918,* Volumes 1 (New York: Amistad Press, 1993).

10. Dr. David Livingstone was known for his philanthropic efforts and for his expedition throughout the continent of Africa as an explorer and missionary.

11. Other intercollegiate athletic associations that governed HBCUs included the following: Southern Intercollegiate Athletic Conference (SIAC, 1912), Southwestern Athletic Conference (SWAC, 1920), Midwestern Athletic Association (MWAA, 1932), South Central Athletic Conference (SCAC, 1930), Eastern Intercollegiate Athletic Conference (EIAC, 1940), and the Mid-eastern Athletic Conference (MEAC, 1970). The four major HBCUs that remain to date are CIAA, SIAC, SWAC, and the MEAC. The SWAC and MEAC members are classified as NCAA Division I-AA schools and the SIAC and CIAA members are classified as NCAA Division II schools.

12. For additional information on HBCUs conference champions see the following: Ashe, *A Hard Road to Glory.*

13. The Victorian ideology and masculine hegemony during this era placed restrictions on female athletic participation. It typecast womanhood as docile, physically weaker, and delicate. See, e.g., the following: M. Ann Hall, *Feminism and Sporting Bodies: Essays on Theory and Practice* (Champaign, IL: Human Kinetics, 1996); Paula J. Giddings, *When and Where I Enter: The Impact of Black Women on Race and Sex in America* (New York: William Morrow, 1984); Cindy Himes, *The Female Athlete in American Society: 1860–1940* (unpublished Ph.D. dissertation, University of Pennsylvania, 1986); Akilah R. Carter, *Negotiating Identities: Examining African American Female Collegiate Athlete Experiences in Predominantly White Institutions* (unpublished Ph.D. dissertation, University of Georgia, 2008).

14. See, e.g., Carter, *Negotiating Identities.*

15. For additional information on college athletic departments revenue and expenses, see Office of Postsecondary Education, *"The Equity in Athletics Data Analysis Cutting Tool,"* Office of Postsecondary Education, http://www.ope.ed.gov/athletics/GetOneInstitutionData.aspx (accessed March 30, 2008).

16. James R. Mingle, "The Opening of White Colleges and Universities to Black Students," in *Black Student in Higher Education: Condition and Experiences in the 1970s,* ed. G. E. Thomas, 18–29 (Westport, CT: Greenwood, 1981).

17. Gaynelle Evans, "Black Students Who Attend White Colleges Face Contradictions in Their Campus Life," *Chronicle of Higher Education* (1986, April 30): 29–30.

18. Barry Beckham, "Strangers in a Strange Land: The Experience of Blacks on White Campuses" *Educational Record* 68, no. 4 (1988): 74–78.

19. Jacqueline Fleming, *Blacks in College: A Comparative Study of Students' Success in Black and in White Institutions* (San Francisco, CA: Jossey-Bass, 1985).

20. Audwin Anderson and Donald South, "Racial Differences in Collegiate Recruiting, Retention, and Graduation Rates" in *Racism in College Athletics: The African-American Experience 2nd Ed*, ed. D. Brooks and R. Althouse, 155–172 (Morgantown, WV: Fitness Information Technology, 1999); Douglas Lederman, "Black Athletes Who Entered Colleges in Mid-80's Had Much Weaker Records than Whites, Study Finds," *Chronicle of Higher Education* (1991, July 10): A31; Robert M. Sellers, Gabriel P. Kuperminc, and Andrea S. Waddell, "Life Experiences of Black Student-Athletes in Revenue Producing Sports: A Descriptive Empirical Analysis," *Academic Athletic Journal* (1991): 21–38; Donald Spivey and Thomas A. Jones, "Intercollegiate Athletic Servitude: A Case Study of the Black Illini Student-Athletes, 1931–1967," *Social Science Quarterly* 55, no. 4 (1975): 939–947. One description that dates back to the early 1920s examines this topic of Blacks at PWIs.

21. Research examining position segregation and race is abundant. Some of the studies listed provide examples of the research in this area: Laura R. Davis, "The Articulation of Difference: White Preoccupation with the Question of Racially Linked Genetic Differences among Athletes," *Sociology of Sport Journal* 7, no. 2 (1990): 179–187; Forrest J. Berghorn, Norman R. Yetman, and William E. Hanna, "Racial Participation and Integration in Men's and Women's Intercollegiate Basketball: Continuity and Change, 1959–1985," *Sociology of Sport Journal* 5, no. 2 (1988): 87–106; James V. Koch, and C Warren Vander Hill, "Is This Discrimination in the Black Man's Game?" *Social Science Quarterly* 69, no. 1 (1988): 83–94; Wilbert M. Leonard, "Stacking in College Basketball: A Neglected Analysis," *Sociology of Sport Journal* 4, no. 4 (1987): 403–409; Barry D. McPherson, "Minority Group Involvement in Sport: The Black Athlete" in *Sport Sociology* ed. A. Yiannakis, T. D. McIntyre, M. J. Melnick, and D. P. Hart, 153–166 (Dubuque, IA: Kendall/Hunt, 1976); Norris R. Johnson and David P. Marple, "Racial Discrimination in Professional Basketball," *Sociological Focus* 6 (1973): 6–18; John W. Loy and Joseph F. McElvogue, "Racial Segregation in American Sport," *International Review of Sport Sociology* 5 (1970): 5–23; Rufus Clement, "Racial Integration in the Field of Sports," *Journal of Negro Education* 23 (1954): 222–230.

22. This account on collegiate athletics provides insight into the role conflict experienced by athletes that compete in major college sports. It expresses how the athletic demands often overshadow the athlete's academic responsibilities, thus, relegating academics to a lower priority. Patricia A. Adler and Peter Adler, *Backboards and Blackboards: College Athletics and Role Engulfment* (New York: Columbia University Press, 1991).

23. Forms of racism include covert and overt practices and institutionalize acts of racism, such as, admission policies, hiring of faculty of color, etc. Racism will be defined more in-depth later in this chapter.

24. Some of the studies and commentary that examines Black students experiences on PWIs include the following: Walter R. Allen, "Black Student, White Campus: Structural Interpersonal and Psychological Correlates of Success," *Journal of Negro Education* 54 (1985): 134–147; David P. Claerbant, *Black Student Alienation: A Study*. San Francisco, CA: R&E Research Associates, 1978); Evans, "Black Students Who Attend White Colleges, 29–30; Fleming, *Blacks in College*; Hoi K. Suen, "Alienation and Attrition of Black College Students on a Predominantly White Campus" *Journal of College Student Personnel* 24 (1983): 117–121; Joe R..Feagin, Heman Vera, and Nikitah Imani, *The Agony of Education: Black Students at White Colleges and Universities* (New York: Routledge, 1996); Joe Feagin, "The Continuing Significance of Racism: Discrimination against Black Students in White College," *Journal of Black Studies* 22, no. 4 (1992): 546–578; Walter R. Allen, Edgar G. Epps, and Nesha Z. Haniff (eds). *College in Black and White: African American Students in Predominantly White and in Historically Black Public Universities* (Albany: State University of New York Press, 1991); Sylvia Hurtado, "The Campus Racial Climate: Contexts of Conflict," *Journal of Higher Education* 63, no. 5 (1992): 539–569.

25. Fleming, *Blacks in College*.

26. An in-depth discussion on race and racial categories is beyond the scope of this book; therefore, for additional information of race and racial classifications, see the following examples: Margaret Mead, Theodosius Dobzhansky, Ethel Tobach, and Robert E. Light (eds.), *Science and the Concept of Race* (New York: Columbia University Press, 1968); Claude Lévi-Strauss, *Race and History* (Paris: Unesco, 1952).

27. Laws against miscegenation or race mixing did not start in the United States; however, these laws were enforced during the seventeenth century during slavery and throughout the Jim Crow era. Works that have examined the concept of race mixings and efforts to maintain

racial purity: see, e.g., F. James Davis, *Who Is Black? One Nation's Definition* (University Park: Pennsylvania State University Press, 1991); Elise Lemire, *"Miscegenation": Making Race in America* (Philadelphia: University of Pennsylvania Press, 2002); George Yancey, "Experiencing Racism: Differences in the Experiences of Whites Married to Blacks and Non-Black Racial Minorities," *Journal of Comparative Family Studies* 38, no. 2 (2007, March 22): 197–213; George Fredrickson, "Mulattoes and Métis. Attitudes toward Miscegenation in the United States and France since the Seventeenth Century," *International Social Science Journal* 57 (2005, March): 103–112.

28. Several scholars have examined the practice of White supremacy and its impact throughout the world, especially as it relates to people of color: Francis C Welsing, *The Isis Papers: The Keys to the Colors* (Chicago, IL: Third World Press, 1991); Bobby E. Wright, *The Psychopathic Racial Personality and Other Essays* (Chicago, IL: Third World Press, 1984); Neely Fuller, Jr. *The United-Independent Compensatory Code/System/Concept: A Textbook/Workbook for Thought, Speech, and/or Action, for Victims of Racism (White Supremacy)* (Washington, DC: Library of Congress, 1969).

29. William Julius Wilson asserts that economic class position trumps race. He states on page one that "Race relations in America have undergone fundamental changes in recent years, so much so that now the life chances of individual blacks have more to do with their economic class position than with their day-to-day encounters with whites." See, e.g., William J. Wilson, *The Declining Significance of Race: Blacks and Changing American Institutions* (Chicago: University of Chicago Press, 1978).

30. Feagin, "Continuing Significance of Racism," 546–578.

31. Stokely Carmichael and Charles V. Hamilton, *Black Power: The Politics of Liberation in America* (New York: Random House, 1967).

32. Louis Knowles and Kenneth Prewitt provide a broader sociological description and examination of institutional racism in America. Louis Knowles and Kenneth Prewitt, *Institutional Racism in America* (Englewood Cliffs, NJ: Prentice-Hall, 1969).

33. The debate over whether the standardized tests (ACT and SAT) are racially biased and poor predictors of academic success in college dates back to the late sixties and early seventies. See for example reference # 29. For a summary of the origin, uses, and shortcomings of SAT see James Crouse and Dale Trusheim, *A Case against the SAT* (Chicago: University of Chicago Press, 1988). Another example of scholars engaging this topic and the gap in standardized tests in general can be found in the following: Christopher Jencks and Meredith Phillips (eds.), *The Black-White Test Score Gap* (Washington, DC: Brookings Institution, 1998). This work looks at factors that contribute to the gap in test scores between Blacks and Whites, as well as, provides suggestions for reducing this disparity.

34. James M. Jones, "The Concept of Race in Social Psychology: From Color to Culture" in *Black Psychology* ed. R. L. Jones (3rd ed.), 441–467 (Berkeley, CA: Cobb & Henry, 1991).

35. The following are some of the leading scholars who have been proponents of multiculturalism in education: James A. Banks, "Approaches to Multicultural Curriculum," *Multicultural Leader* 1, no. 2 (1988): 1–3; James A. Banks, *Cultural Diversity and Education* (4th ed.). (Boston: Allyn & Bacon, 2000); James A. Banks and Cherry A. McGhee Banks (eds.), *Multicultural Education: Issues and Perspectives* (4th ed.) (New York: John Wiley & Sons, 2002); Geneva Gay, *Culturally Responsive Teaching: Theory, Research, and Practice* (New York: Teachers College Press, 2000); Carl A. Grant and Christine E. Sleeter, *Making Choices for Multicultural Education; Five Approaches to Race, Class, and Gender* (Columbus, OH: Merrill, 1988); Arlene Lenaghan, "Reflections of Multicultural Curriculum," *Multicultural Education* 7, no. 3 (2000): 33–36.

36. Bhikhu Parekh, *The Concept of Multicultural Education: The Interminable Debate* (London: Falmer Press, 1986).

37. Renee D. Turner, "The Resurgence of Racism on White Campuses," *The Black Collegian* 16, no. 1 (1985): 18–24.

38. Because of the significance of this topic and the fact that it contributes to a major distortion about Black athletes, it will be examined in more detail in a later chapter.

39. The University of Michigan at Ann Arbor came under media scrutiny and public criticism for their general studies major, which inexplicably caters to athletes, and the fact that a disproportionate amount of athletes were taking independent study hours with a psychology professor. Starting on March 16, 2008, the *Ann Arbor News* did a four-day series entitled *Academics and Athletics*. For more information on this four-part series, see the following: "Academics

and Athletics," *Ann Arbor News*, http://www.mlive.com/wolverines/academics/stories/index. ssf/2008/03/athletes_steered_to_prof.html (accessed June 24, 2008).

40. Having a Black experience is the reverse of White privilege. It is a "knapsack" of racialized experiences Blacks typically encounter routinely, for example, it can range from being called a nigger, to being denied a taxi or housing in a certain community, to being racially profiled in department stores or while driving.

41. Athletic identity is an area of inquiry that has received considerable attention in the sports research literature. Adler and Adler, *Backboards and Blackboards* at 20, examined this topic within the context of athletic role engulfment. Britton W. Brewer and Allen E. Cornelius developed the Athletic Identity Measurement Scale (AIMS), which examines the dichotomous relationship between student and athlete. See, e.g., Britton W. Brewer and Allen E. Cornelius, "Norms and Factorial Invariance of the Athletic Identity Measurement Scale," *Academic Athletic Journal* 15 (2001): 103–113.

42. Sylvester Monroe, "Guest in a Strange House: A Black at Harvard," *Saturday Review of Education*, 14 (1973, February): 45–48.

43. Ralph Ellison, *Invisible Man* (New York: Random House, 1947), 7–8.

44. W. E. B. Du Bois, *The Soul of Black Folks* (New York: Fawcett, 1961), 16.

45. George H. Sage, "Introduction," in *Racism in College Athletics: The African-American Athlete's Experience*, ed. D. Brooks and R. Althouse, 9 (Morgantown, WV: Fitness Information Technology, 1993).

46. Within the discipline of sociology and in the framework of critical social theory, *alienation* is defined as an individual's separation from the immediate community and others in general. *Racial isolation* refers to isolation based on race and social isolation pertains more to Black athletes social status as athletes on campus. For the sake of this paper, racial and social isolation will be referred to as isolation.

47. Chalsa M. Loo and Garry Rolison, "Alienation of Ethnic Minority Students at a Predominantly White University," *Journal of Higher Education* 57 (1986): 76–77.

48. Suen, "Alienation and Attrition of Black College Students," 117–121.

49. Several studies have examined or addressed the topics of alienation and isolation as it relates to the plight of Black students at PWIs, e.g., Alberto F. Cabrera and Amaury Nora, "College Students' Perceptions of Prejudice and Discrimination and Their Feelings of Alienation: A Construct Validation Approach," *Review of Education/Pedagogy/Cultural Studies* 16, no. 3–4 (1994): 387–409; Anthony D'Augelli and Scott Hershberger, "African American Undergraduates on a Predominantly White Campus: Academic Factors, Social Networks, and Campus Climate," *Journal of Negro Education* 62, no. 1 (1993): 67–81; Robbie J. Steward, "Alienation and Interactional Styles in a Predominantly White Environment: A Study of Successful Black Students," *Journal of College Student Development* 31, no. 6 (1990): 509–515; Walter Allen, "The Education of Black Students on White College Campuses: What Quality the Experience," In *Toward Black Undergraduate Student Equality in Higher Education*, ed. M. Nettles (Albany: State University of New York Press, 1988), 57–86; Walter R. Allen, "Correlates of Black Student Adjustment, Achievement, and Aspirations at a Predominantly White Southern University," in *Black Students in Higher Education: Conditions and Experiences in the 1970s*, ed. G. Thomas (Westport, CT: Greenwood, 1981), 126–141; Allen, "Black Student, White Campus," 134–147; Adler and Adler, *Backboards & Blackboards*; Claerbant, *Black Student Alienation*; Fleming, *Blacks in College*; Michael T. Nettles, *Toward Black Undergraduate Student Equality in American Higher Education* (New York: Greenwood, 1988).

50. Monroe, "Guest in a Strange House," 45–48.

51. Junius A. Davis and Anne Borders-Patterson, "Black Students in Predominantly White North Carolina Colleges and Universities, 1986: A Replication of a 1970 Study," *College Board Report No. 86-7* (New York: College Board Publications, 1986).

52. Douglas Lederman, "Blacks Make up Large Proportion of Scholarship Athletes, yet Their Overall Enrollment Lags at Division I Colleges," *Chronicle of Higher Education* (1992, June 17): 30–34.

53. William C. Rhoden, "Athletes on Campus: A New Reality," *New York Times* (1990, January 8): A1.

54. Ibid.

55. These dorms were abolished in the sense of allowing regular students of the student body to be housed in these dorms. Therefore, athletes make up a certain percentage and a certain percentage is students that are not athletes.

56. Jack Olsen, "Pride and Prejudice," *Sports Illustrated* 29, no. 2 (1968, July): 18–31.
57. This unequal exchange has been a consistent practice between White people and people of color throughout the world. In regards to Black people, European's extraction of human capital and natural resources from Africa demonstrated an unequal exchange. The concept of unequal exchange is associated with the works Marxism are ecological economics where an analysis is provided for forms of exploitation regarding profit and wages, owners and laborers, or what Immanuel Wallerstein refer to in his World Systems Theory, exploitative relations between core and periphery nations. Thomas Sowell is a Black economist who has elaborated on the concept of unequal exchange regarding European nations transferring wealth and resources from Africa. Finally, the following source also outlines this concept of unequal exchange and how it underdeveloped Africa: Claud Anderson, *Black Labor, White Wealth: The Search for Power and Economic Justice* (Edgewood, MD: Duncan & Duncan, 1994), 112–113.

Two   The New Plantation Model: A Conceptual Framework for Diagnosing the Experiences of Black Athletes at Predominantly White NCAA Division I Institutions

1. Recreational basketball provides an interesting example of racially segregated experiences at my university. Courts are segregated racially among Asian, Mid-eastern, White, and Black participants. There is some interracial competition among Whites and Blacks but very limited. Some of this may be due to perceived performance levels or stereotypical assumptions about Black athletic superiority.
2. Albert Memmi, *The Colonizer and the Colonized* (Boston: Beacon Press, 1965), xii. Memmi initially set forth to comprehend his own self-identity and his status as a Tunisian in the larger society of others, and in doing so he provides a conceptual framework that described the conditions of oppressed people in general; especially as it relates to Blacks that have come into contact with various European nations.
3. Robert Blauner, "Internal Colonialism and Ghetto Revolt," *Social Problems* 16, no. 4 (1969): 395.
4. Lerone Bennett, *The Shaping of Black America: The Struggles and Triumphs of African-Americans, 1619–1990s* (Chicago: Johnson Publishing, 1975), 209.
5. Frantz Fanon, *The Wretched of the Earth* (New York: Grove Press, 1963), 250.
6. Bennett, *Shaping of Black America*, 209.
7. The following works are examples of analyzing the living conditions of Black Americans using a type of internal colonial conceptual framework: Robert L. Allen, *Black Awakening in Capitalist America: An Analytic History* (New York: Doubleday, 1970); Blauner, "Internal Colonialism and Ghetto Revolt"; Stokely Carmichael and Charles V. Hamilton, *Black Power: The Politics of Liberation in America* (New York: Random House, 1967); Harold Cruse, *The Crisis of the Negro Intellectual* (New York: William Morrow, 1967).
8. Bennett, *Shaping of Black America*, 209.
9. Blauner, "Internal Colonialism and Ghetto Revolt," 395.
10. Ibid.
11. Ibid., 396.
12. Bennett, *Shaping of Black America*, 209.
13. Ibid., 211. Bennett speaks of the colonizer's ability to employ judges who legislate laws, where they have sheriffs to enforce these laws and jails to condemn those who refuse to submit to the colonial situation.
14. Memmi, *Colonizer and the Colonized*, 8.
15. For additional information on the colonial situation and alienation, see for e.g., Renate Zahar, *Frantz Fanon: Colonialism and Alienation* (New York: Monthly Review Press, 1974).
16. Ibid. and Memmi, *Colonizer and the Colonized* both provide insight into the creation of the colonial situation.
17. Memmi, *Colonizer and the Colonized*, 8.
18. Ibid., 82–83.

19. Ibid., 89.
20. The recruiting process has evolved into a very elaborate and complex system. Bruce Feldman's *Meat Market: Inside the Smash-Mouth World of College Football Recruiting* (New York: ESPN Books, 2007) provides an interesting perspective on the world of football recruiting. He outlines the four stages in which the NCAA regulates the recruiting process: The Quiet Period, The Dead Period, The Contact Period, and the Evaluation Period, and asserts how these confusing and sometimes confounding rules create a system that operates on its own independent calendar.
21. Adam Himmelsbach, "First Impressions Can Create Unrealistic Expectations Basketball Recruits," http://www.nytimes.com/2009/03/10/sports/10recruiting.html (accessed March 10, 2009).
22. Kwame Nkrumah, *Ghana: The Autobiography of Kwame Nkrumah* (New York: International Publishers, 1957), vii.
23. Carmichael and Hamilton, *Black Power*, 17. It is a good resource for information that examines the economic motives of the internal colonial situation.
24. Bennett, *Shaping of Black America*, 211.
25. Carmichael and Hamilton, *Black Power*, 17.
26. Kenneth B. Clark, *Dark Ghetto* (New York: Harper and Row, 1965), 27–28.
27. Carmichael and Hamilton, *Black Power*, 13.
28. Martin L. Kilson, *Political Change in a West African State: A Study of the Modernization Process in Sierra Leone* (Cambridge, MA: Harvard University Press, 1966), 24.
29. Carmichael and Hamilton, *Black Power*, 10.
30. Ibid., 11.
31. Ibid., 12.
32. Nkrumah *Ghana: The Autobiography of Kwame Nkrumah*, 18.
33. Bennett, *Shaping of Black America*, 212.
34. Blauner, "Internal Colonialism and Ghetto Revolt," 397.
35. Frantz Fanon, *Black Skin, White Masks* (New York: Grove Weidenfeld, 1967). In Fanon's psycho-analysis of Black identity and psyche under colonial rule, he excavates the idea that the Black body is an identifying source of meaning that also enslaves the colonized; especially chapter four, entitled, "The So-Called Dependency Complex of Colonized People."
36. Carmichael and Hamilton, *Black Power*, 22–23.
37. Both of the following references give insight into institutional racism and its affect within the internal colonial situation: Carmichael and Hamilton, *Black Power*; Bennett, *Shaping of Black America*, 212.
38. Carmichael and Hamilton, *Black Power*, 5.
39. For an example of research examining the stereotypical belief regarding their intellectual inferiority and athletic superiority, the differences in their demographic and academic background, overall college life experiences, mental health issues, and social support, see, e.g., Gary A. Sailes, "The African American Athletes: Social Myths and Stereotypes," in *African Americans in Sport: Contemporary Themes,* ed. G. A. Sailes, 183 (New Brunswick, NJ: Transaction, 1998); Dean Purdy, D. Stanley Eitzen, and Rick Hufnagel, "Are Athletes also Students? The Educational Attainment of College Athletes" *Social Problems* 29, no. 4 (1982): 439–448; Beth J. Shapiro, "Intercollegiate Athletic Participation and Academic Achievement: A Case Study of Michigan State University Student Athletes, 1950–1980" *Sociology of Sport Journal* 1, no. 1 (1984): 46–51; Gary Kiger and Deana Lorentzen, "The Relative Effect of Gender, Race, and Sport on University Academic Performance" *Sociology of Sport Journal* 3, no.2 (1986): 48–59; Robert M. Sellers, Gabriel P. Kuperminc, and Andrea S. Waddell, "Life Experiences of Black Student-Athletes in Revenue Producing Sports: A Descriptive Empirical Analysis" *Academic Athletic Journal* (1991, Fall): 21–38.
40. The following works provide an understanding of migrant labor patterns: Sharon Stichter, *Migrant Labour in Kenya: Capitalism and African response 1895–1975* (Great Britain: Longman Group, 1982); Sharon Stichter, *Migrant Laborers* (Cambridge: Cambridge University Press, 1985); Francis Wilson, *Migrant Labour in South Africa* (Johannesburg: The South African Council of Churches, 1972).
41. Wilson, *Migrant Labour in South Africa*, v.
42. Ibid., 2.
43. Ibid.

44. Stichter, *Migrant Laborers*, 29.

45. Isaac Schapera, *Migrant Labour and Tribal Life: A Study of Conditions in the Bechuanaland Protectorate* (London: Oxford University Press, 1947).

46. Stuart B. Philpott, *West Indian Migration: The Montserrat Case* (London: Athlone Press, 1973), 188.

47. Aaron Victor Cicourel, "Living in Two Cultures: The Everyday World of Migrant Workers," in *Living in Two Cultures: The Socio-Cultural Situation of Migrant Workers and Their Families* (Paris: Unesco, 1982), 17–66.

48. Patricia A. Adler and Peter Adler, *Backboards & Blackboards: College Athletics and Role Engulfment* (New York: Columbia University Press, 1991), 107.

48. W. E. B. Du Bois, *The Soul of Black Folks* (New York: Fawcett, 1961), 16.

49. Ibid., 39.

50. This diagram was constructed using the following sources: Memmi, *Colonizer and the Colonized*; Fanon, *The Wretched of the Earth*; Fanon, *Black Skin, White Masks*; Carmichael and Hamilton, *Black Power*; Blauner, "Internal Colonialism and Ghetto Revolt."

Three   Intellectually Inferior and Physically Superior: Racist Ideologies and the Black Athlete

1. Anton L. Allahar, "When Black First Became Worth Less" *International Journal of Comparative Sociology* 34, no. 1–2 (1993): 39–55.

2. Ideology has remained an elusive term to define. John Storey summarizes the works of Graeme Turner, James Carey, Stuart Hall, Louis Althusser, and Roland Barthes to illustrate various meaning of the concept ideology: see John Storey, *Cultural Theory and Popular Culture: An Introduction*, 3rd ed. (Harlow, England: Pearson/Prentice Hall, 2001), 2–5. He suggests that ideology can be considered in the following ways: (1)"a systematic body of ideas articulated by a particular group of people"; (2) A process of "masking, distortion, [and] concealment" used in the "interests of the powerful against the interests of the powerless"; (3) A use of "ideological forms" or "texts (television fiction, pop songs, novels, feature films, etc.), which work to convey meaning and persuade collective consciousness"; (4) A "material practice" where "certain rituals and customs have the effect on binding us to the social order"; (5) "a terrain [level of connotations] on which takes place a hegemonic struggle to restrict connotations, to fix particular connotations, [and] to produce new connotations." Finally, it is important to note that ideology is not necessarily a negative concept. There are dominant ideas, material practices, etc., that can be considered neutral or nonthreatening, simply of means of distinction (religious doctrinal beliefs held by a group of people); however, as it relates to power relations and hegemony, ideology takes on a different form and denotes different uses.

3. For information on White privilege and possessive investment in Whiteness, see the following sources: for white privilege see, e.g., Peggy McIntosh, "White Privilege and Male Privilege: A Personal Account of Coming to See Correspondences through Work in Women's Studies," (Center for Research on Women, Wellesley College, Wellesley, MA, 1988). For possessive investment in Whiteness see, e.g., George Lipsitz, "The Possessive Investment in Whiteness: Racialized Social Democracy and the 'White' Problem in American Studies," *American Quarterly* 47, no. 3 (1995): 369–387; George Lipsitz, *The Possessive Investment in Whiteness: How White People Profit from Identity Politics* (Philadelphia, PA: Temple University Press, 2006).

4. PWI will be used when speaking collectively of the NCAA and its predominantly White member institutions.

5. Richard J. Herrnstein and Charles Murray, *The Bell Curve: Intelligence and Class Structure in American Life* (New York: Free Press, 1994).

6. Ibid., 551–552.

7. Several scholars have examined the portrayal of Blacks in the mass media: see, e.g., Donald Bogle, *Toms, Coons, Mulattoes, Mammies, and Bucks: An Interpretive History of Blacks in American Films* (New York: Continuum, 1989); Joseph Boskin, "Sambo and Other Male Images in Popular Culture" in *Images of Blacks in American Culture: A Reference Guide to Information Sources*, ed. J. C. Smith, 257–272 (New York: Greenwood, 1988); Winthrop D. Jordan, *White over*

Black: American Attitudes toward the Negro, 1550–1812 (New York: W. W. Norton, 1968); Daniel J. Leab, *From Sambo to Superspade: The Black Experience in Motion Pictures* (Boston: Houghton Mifflin, 1975); Jan Nederveen Pieterse, *White on Black: Images of Africa and Blacks in Western Popular Culture* (New Haven, CT: Yale University Press, 1992); Karen Ross, *Black and White Media: Black Images in Popular Film and Television* (Cambridge, MA: Polity Press, 1996).

8. Also known as the "separate but equal" doctrine, *The Homer Plessy v. The State of Louisiana* case also *Plessy v. Ferguson* was a U.S. Supreme Court decision made on May 18, 1896 supporting racial segregation in public accommodations.

9. "Separate but equal" remained standard doctrine in U.S. law until *Brown v. Board of Education of Topeka, Kansas* in 1954. In this case, the U.S. Supreme Court ruled against this doctrine of separate but equal by pronouncing in their decision that separate was not equal as it relates to public school education between Black and White children.

10. Jonathan Kozol, *Savage Inequalities: Children in America's Schools* (New York: Crown Publishers, 1991). Kozol case studies and statistical data provides detailed information on the inequalities in the distribution of resources between schools that are predominantly Black or Latino (usually urban) and schools that are predominantly White (usually suburban).

11. For an excellent resource that examines scientific racism and Black athletic achievement from a historical perspective see the following: Patrick Miller, "The Anatomy of Scientific Racism: Racialist Responses to Black Athletic Achievement" in *Sport and the Color Line: Black Athletes and Race Relations in Twentieth-Century America*, ed. P. B. Miller and David K. Wiggins, 327–344 (New York: Routledge, 2004).

12. Some of the works that document the tragedies of racist ideologies about Blacks' intellectual inferiority include the following: Rayford W. Logan, *The Betrayal of the Negro from Rutherford B. Hayes to Woodrow Wilson* (New York: Collier Books, 1965); August Meier and Elliott M. Rudwick, *From Plantation to Ghetto* (New York: Hill and Wang, 1963).

13. These percentages will be discussed in a later chapter.

14. W. E. B. Du Bois, *The Soul of Black Folks* (New York: Fawcett, 1961), 16–17.

15. Jordan, *White over Black*, 217.

16. Although the history of the Chain of Being can be traced back to the works of Plato's *Idea of the Good* and Aristotle's *Ladder of Nature*, it played a major role in seventeenth- and eighteenth-century thought. The following works detail the history, theory, and utility of the Chain of Being: Arthur O. Lovejoy, *The Great Chain of Being: The Study of the History of an Idea* (Cambridge, MA: Harvard University Press, 1936); William F. Bynum, "The Great Chain of Being after Forty Years: An Appraisal," *History of Science* 13 (1975): 1–28.

17. Winthrop D. Jordan, *The White Man's Burden: Historical Origins of Racism in the United States* (New York: Oxford University Press, 1974), 100.

18. Ibid., 9, 105.

19. Jose Parry and Noel Parry, "Sport and the Black Experience" in *Sport, Racism and Ethnicity*, ed. G. Jarvie, 155 (New York: Falmer Press, 1991).

20. Jay J. Coakley, *Sport in Society* (St. Louis: C. V. Mosley, 1978), 304.

21. *The Chicago Tribune*, "Bannister Speculates on Sprinters," sec. 4, p. 7 (August 14, 1995).

22. William Shockley, "The Apple-of-God's-Eye Obsession," *The Humanist* 32 (1972): 16–17; Thomas Gladwin and Ahmad Saidin, *Slaves of the White Myth: The Psychology of Neocolonialism* (Atlantic Highlands, NJ: Humanities Press, 1980).

23. Harry Edwards, "The Black 'Dumb Jock': An American Sports Tragedy," *The College Board Review*, no. 131 (1984): 8.

24. Some of the works that have documented the PWI discrepancies in valuing athletic ability over intellectual include the following: Gary D. Funk, *Major Violation: The Unbalanced Priorities in Athletics and Academics* (Champaign, IL: Leisure Press, 1991); Richard Lapchick, *Five Minutes to Midnight: Race and Sport in the 1990s* (Lanham, MD: Madison Books, 1991); John Valenti and Ron Naclerio, *Swee' Pea and Other Playground Legends: Tales of Drug, Violence, and Basketball* (New York: Michael Kesend, 1990).

25. For additional information on Black athletes who competed at PWI in the late 1800s and early 1900s see the following: Arthur R. Ashe, Jr., *A Hard Road to Glory: A History of the African-American Athlete*. Volumes 1 and 2 (New York: Amistad Press, 1993).

26. Tom Friend, "Pro Football; for Manley, Life without Football Is Impossible to Tackle," *New York Times*, February 26, 1995, http://query.nytimes.com/gst/fullpage.html?res=990CE5DC103DF935A15751C0A963958260&sec=&spon=&pagewanted=1.

27. Nathan Aaseng, *The Locker Room Mirror: How Sport Reflects Society* (New York: Walker, 1993). For information about the lawsuit see: *Ross v. Creighton University*, 957 F.2d 410 (7th Cir. 1992); also available at http://www.altlaw.org/v1/cases/490747.

28. For an autobiographical account of Lloyd Daniels sporting experiences see the following: Valenti and Naclerio, *Swee' Pea and Other Playground Legends.*

29. For works on the notion of "acting White," see the following: Signithia Fordham and John U. Ogbu, "Black Students' School Success: Coping with the 'Burden of 'Acting White,'" *The Urban Review* 18, no. 3 (1986): 176–206; Signithia Fordham, *Blacked Out: Dilemmas of Race, Identity, and Success at Capital High* (Chicago: University of Chicago Press, 1996); John U. Ogbu, *Black American Students in an Affluent Suburb: A Study of Academic Disengagement* (Mahwah, NJ: Lawrence Erlbaum, 2003). There have been several critiques regarding this notion of "acting White." It has been misinterpreted to mean that Black would rather earn poor grades than to earn good grades and be perceived as acting White, thus, an explanation for other social problems endemic in Black communities. Other misinterpretations have labeled this phenomenon within the framework of cultural deprivation, see, e.g., John W. McWhorter, *Losing the Race: Self Sabotage in Black America* (New York: Free Press, 2000). Yet others studies have found contradicting evidence to this notion of "acting White," see, e.g., Philip J. Cook and Jens Ludwig, "The Burden of 'Acting White': Do Black Adolescents Disparage Academic Achievement" in *The Black-White Test Score Gap*, ed, C. Jencks and M. Phillips, 375–400 (Washington, DC: Brookings Institution, 1998); James W. Ainsworth-Darnell and Douglas B. Downey, "Assessing the Oppositional Cultural Explanation for Racial/Ethnic Differences in School Performance," *American Sociological Review* 63, no. 4 (1998): 536–553.

30. Cool Pose incorporates distinctive behavioral expressions (demeanor, patterns of speech, walk, etc.) to maintain some level of equilibrium in a society that has administered inequity in distributing favor and opportunities. See, e.g., Richard Majors and Janet M. Billson, *Cool Pose: The Dilemmas of Black Manhood in America* (New York: Lexington Books, 1992).

31. See the following source for additional information: American Institute for Research, "Report #2: Methodology of the 1987–88 National Study of Intercollegiate Athletes," *Studies of Intercollegiate Athletics* (Palo Alto, CA: Center for the Study of Athletics, 1988).

32. Austin Murphy, "Goodbye, Columbus (Ohio State tailback R. Smith quits)," *Sports Illustrated* 75 (September 9, 1991): 46–49.

33. John A. Cooper and Elwood C. Davis, "Athletic Ability and Scholarship: A Resume of Studies Comparing Scholarship Abilities of Athletes and Non-athletes," *Research Quarterly* 5, no. 4 (1934): 68–79.

34. Bob Case, H. Scott Greer, and James Brown, "Academic Clustering in Athletics: Myth or reality?" *Arena Review* 11, no. 2 (1987): 48.

35. Jay J. Coakley, *Sport and Society: Issues & Controversies* (New York: McGraw-Hill, 2004).

36. Kevin M. Teno, "Cluster Grouping Elementary Gifted Students in the Regular Classroom: A Teacher's Perspective," *Gifted Child Today Magazine* 23, no. 1 (2000): 44–53; Susan Winebrenner and Barbara Devlin, "Cluster Grouping of Gifted Students: How to Provide Full-time Services on a Part-time Budget," *Teaching Exceptional Children* 30 (Jan/Feb 1998): 62–66; Stephen M. Hoover, Michael Sayler, and John F. Feldhusen, "Cluster Grouping of Gifted Students at the Elementary Level," *Roeper Review* 16, no. 1 (1993): 13–15; Jennifer L. Crissman, "The Impact of Clustering First Year Seminars with English Composition Courses on New Students' Retention Rates," *Journal of College Student Retention* 3, no. 2 (2002): 137–152; Carl J. Huberty, Christine DiStefano, and Randy W. Kamphaus, "Behavioral Clustering among School Children," *Multivariate Behavioral Research* 32 (1997): 105–134; Leslie Rescorla, "Cluster Analytic Identification of Autistic Preschoolers," *Journal of Autism and Developmental Disorders* 18, no. 4 (1988): 475–492.

37. John Heuser, Dave Gershman, and Jim Carty, "University of Michigan Athletes' 'Safe Harbor' Is General Studies," *Ann Arbor News* (March 18, 2008). http://www.mlive.com/wolverines/academics/stories/index.ssf/2008/03/athletes_safe_harbor_is_genera.html.

38. Ibid., 24

39. Jill Lieber Ste8om/sports/college/2008-11-18-majors-cover_N.htm?POE=click-refer (accessed November 19, 2008).

40. Ibid.

41. Ibid.

42. Ibid.

43. Charles S. Farrell and Peter Monagham, "University of Maryland Athletic Director Quits: Task Force Faults Sports Departments for Players' Ills," *Chronicle of Higher Education* (October 15, 1986): 45, 48.

45. Welch Suggs, "Jock Majors: Many Colleges Allow Football Players to Take the Easy Way Out." *Chronicle of Higher Education* 49 (2003): A33–A34.

45. Data on universities' athletic revenue and expenses is a result of the Equity in Athletics Disclosure Act, which requires co-educational institutions of postsecondary education that participate in a Title IV, federal student financial assistance program, and have an intercollegiate athletic program, to provide the Department of Education with an annual report on athletic participation, staffing, and revenues and expenses, for men's and women's teams. For athletic revenue and expenses information, see the following Web site: http://ope.ed.gov/athletics/main.asp.

46. It is important to note that Arts and Sciences consist of 4 divisions and 30 programs. Therefore, within the college of Art and Sciences, student athletes' majors could range from Art to Theater and Film to Genetics or Statistics. This college appears to be used as a holding pattern for athletes, until decisions are made about their specific majors.

Four   Operating in the "Black" Financially: On the Back of the Black Athletic Body

1. Lerone Bennett, *The Shaping of Black America: The Struggles and Triumphs of African-Americans, 1619–1990s* (Chicago: Johnson Publishing, 1975).

2. David Eltis, "A Brief Overview of the Trans-Atlantic Slave Trade," Voyages: The Transatlantic Slave Trade Database, http://www.slavevoyages.org/tast/database/index.faces (accessed February 21, 2009).

3. Eric Williams, *Capitalism and Slavery* (Chapel Hill: University of North Carolina Press, 1994). Williams concludes that the Atlantic slave trade contributed to the European Merchant capitalism, which ultimately funded the lucrative New World plantation system. He also suggests that it was the slave trade that contributed significantly in financing the English Industrial Revolution.

4. Marcus Rediker, *The Slave Ship: A Human History* (New York: Viking, 2007), 43.

5. David Brion Davis, *Inhuman Bondage: The Rise and Fall of Slavery in the New World* (New York: Oxford University Press, 2006), 298.

6. Sidney M. Willhelm, *Who Needs the Negro?* (Garden City, NY: Doubleday, 1971), 223.

7. Ibid., 233.

8. Michael Brush, "3 Prison Stocks Poised to Break Out," *MSN Money*, http://moneycentral.msn.com/content/P105034.asp (accessed May 15, 2008). This article illustrates incentives for investing in the private prison industry.

9. David M. Oshinsky, *Worse than Slavery: Parchman Farm and the Ordeal of Jim Crow Justice* (New York: Free Press, 1996).

10. Ibid., 137.

11. Ibid., 139.

12. Cited in Oshinsky, *Worse than Slavery*.

13. Ibid., 252.

14. Ibid.

15. Douglas A. Blackmon, *Slavery by another Name: The Re-Enslavement of Black People in America from the Civil War to World War II* (New York: Doubleday Books, 2008).

16. For additional information of the Sentencing Project and its research on the racial demographics of the U.S. prison system and the sentencing of Black males see http://www.sentencingproject.org/Default.aspx.

17. National Association of State Budget Officers, *2007 State Expenditure Report*, http://www.nasbo.org/publications.php (accessed March 5, 2009). An additional source that illustrates the growing cost of the prison system is Pew Centers of the States, *One in 31: The Long Reach of American Corrections*, http://www.pewcenteronthestates.org/uploadedFiles/PSPP_1in31_report_FINAL_WEB_2-27-09.pdf (accessed March 5, 2009).

18. Several scholars have concluded that the institution of slavery was not profitable economically. For example, Ulrich B. Phillips, *American Negro Slavery: A Survey of the Supply, Employment and Control of Negro Labor as Determined by the Plantation Regime* (New York: D. Appleton, 1918); and Charles S. Sydnor, *Slavery in Mississippi* (New York: D. Appleton, 1933) both speak of the system of slavery as economically unprofitable. Furthermore, Robert W. Fogel and Stanley L. Engerman, *Time on the Cross: The Economics of American Negro Slavery* (Boston: Little Brown, 1974) informs of how the cliometric methodology has exposed the shortcomings of the traditional interpretation of slavery as a decrepit economic institution.

19. Eugene D. Genovese, *The Political Economy of Slavery: Studies in the Economy and Society of the slave South* (New York: Random House, 1965), 158.

20. The following works provide validity to the economic feasibility of slave labor: Robert W. Fogel, *The Slavery Debates, 1952–1990: A Memoir* (Baton Rouge: Louisiana State University Press, 2003); Fogel and Engerman, *Time on the Cross.*

21. Roger L. Ransom and Richard Sutch, *One Kind of Freedom: The Economic Consequences of Emancipation* (New York: Cambridge University Press, 2001), 2.

22. Alfred H. Conrad and John R. Meyer, "The Economics of Slavery in the Ante Bellum South," *Journal of Political Economy,* 66 (1958): 95–130.

23. Ransom and Sutch, *One Kind of Freedom* and Fogel and Engerman, *Time on the Cross* both provide information regarding the significance of sugar to the Atlantic slave trade and the sugar production wrought by slave labor; especially on the sugar cane plantations in the Caribbean, Mexico, and Brazil. In the United States, sugar was second to cotton in output and third to cotton and corn in price and value of crop output.

24. Lawrence Goldstone, *Dark Bargain: Slavery, Profits, and the Struggle for the Constitution* (New York: Walker), 69.

25. Ibid., 70. Rawlins Lowndes was South Carolina's second president.

26. Rediker, *The Slave Ship,* 347–348.

27. Ibid., 348.

28. Robin Blackburn, *The Making of New World Slavery: From the Baroque to the Modern, 1492–1800* (London: Verso, 1997), 581.

29. Rediker, *The Slave Ship,* 348.

30. E. N. Elliott, *Cotton Is King and Pro-Slavery Arguments* 3rd ed (Augusta, GA: Pritchard, Abbott, and Loomis, 1860), vii.

31. Examples of the NCAA institutions control and profit off of the images and the "rights to the athlete labor" are with the sale of uniforms and the recent NCAA ruling that prohibits athletes from profiting off of the use of their names and statistics by CBS Sports College Fantasy Football. Although the NCAA protested that CBS Sports violates their bylaws that prohibit companies from profiting or trading on the likeness or image of specific athletes, a Federal Court of Appeals opened the door for CBS Sports to use the college players names and statistics in the ruling that statistics and names that are in the public domain are not the property of the entity in the *Major League Baseball Advanced Media v. CDM Fantasy Sports Corp* case.

32. Michael Smith and John Ourand, "ESPN Pays $2.25B for SEC Rights," *SportsBusiness Journal,* http://www.sportsbusinessjournal.com/article/59824 (accessed October 25, 2008).

33. Ibid.

34. "Million-dollar Coaches Move into Mainstream," *USA Today,* http://www.usatoday.com/sports/college/football/2006-11-16-cover-coaches-media_x.htm (accessed October 25, 2008).

35. National Collegiate Athletic Association, *1999–00—2005–06 NCAA Student-Athlete Race and Ethnicity Report,* http://www.ncaapublications.com/Uploads/PDF/2005-06_race_ethnicity_reportf05055c6-deb3-45de-ab1c-cbeeb4c19584.pdf (accessed September 13, 2006); National Consortium for Academics and Sport, *Racial and Gender Report Cards,* http://www.ncasports.org/press_releases.htm (accessed September 13, 2006).

36. Mark Alesia, "Tourney Money Fuels Pay-to-Play Debate: Fewer Than 1% of Athletes Help Make More Than 90% of the NCAA's Money," *Indy Star,* April 1, 2006, www.indystar.com/apps/pbcs.dll/article?AID=/20060401/SPORTS/604010509 (accessed April 6, 2006).

37. Andrew Zimbalist, "March Madness It Is, Economically," *Wall Street Journal,* http://online.wsj.com/article/SB123664681664078731.html (accessed April 3, 2009).

38. *The Oakland bracket* consisted of the following schools: Memphis, Oral Roberts, Arkansas, Bucknell, Pittsburgh, Kent, Kansas, Bradley, Indiana, SDSU, Gonzaga, Xavier, Marquette,

Alabama, UCLA, and Belmont. *The Atlanta bracket* consisted of the following schools: Duke, Southern, GW, UNC-Wilmington, Syracuse, Texas A&M, LSU, Iona, West Virginia, S. Illinois, Iowa, Northwestern, California, NC State, Texas, and Penn State. *The Minneapolis bracket* consisted of the following schools: Villanova, Monmouth, Arizona, Wisconsin, Nevada, Montana, Boston College, Pacific, Oklahoma, UW-Milwaukee, Florida, S. Alabama, Georgetown, N. Iowa, Ohio State, and Davidson. *The Washington DC bracket* consisted of the following schools: U. Conn., Albany, Kentucky, University of Alabama-Birmingham, Washington, Utah State, Illinois, Air Force, Michigan State, George Mason, University North Carolina, Murray State, Wichita, Steton Hall, Tennessee, and Winthrop.

39. National Collegiate Athletic Association, "NCAA Approves 31 Bowls for '06," http://www.ncaafootball.com/index.php?s=&url_channel_id=32&url_subchannel_id=&url_article_id=6676&change_well_id=2 (accessed February 21, 2007).

40. According to the Title IX of the Educational Amendments of 1972 to the 1964 Civil Rights Act states that "No person in the United States shall, on the basis of sex, be excluded from participation in, be denied the benefits of, or be subject to discrimination under any educational program or activity receiving federal financial assistance." According to the NCAA Gender Equity Task Force, "An athletics program can be considered gender equitable when the participants in both the men's and women's sports programs would accept as fair and equitable the overall program of the other gender. No individual should be discriminated against on the basis of gender, institutionally or nationally, in intercollegiate athletics." National Collegiate Athletic Association, *NCAA Gender Equity*, http://www.ncaa.org/wps/ncaa?ContentID=286 (accessed April 3, 2009).

41. Welch Suggs, *A Place on the Team: The Triumph and Tragedy of Title IX* (Princeton, NJ: Princeton University Press, 2005), 180.

42. Myles Brand, "The Principles of Intercollegiate Athletics," *2006 NCAA State of the Association Address*, http://www.ncaa.org (accessed January 30, 2006): 2.

43. Ibid., 6.

44. Ibid., 8.

45. Ibid., 7.

46. Ibid.

47. Ibid., 8.

48. Ibid., 7.

Five   The Black Athlete's Racialized Experiences and the Predominantly White Intercollegiate Institution

1. William J. Wilson, *The Declining Significance of Race: Blacks and Changing American Institutions*, 2nd ed. (Chicago: University of Chicago Press, 1980), 1. Wilson argues that race is declining in significance as a determinant of economic achievement and success.

2. W. E. B. Du Bois, *The Soul of Black Folks* (New York: Fawcett, 1961), 19.

3. "Poll Shows Gap between Blacks and Whites over Racial Discrimination," http://news.yahoo.com/page/election-2008-political-pulse-race-in-america;_ylt=Asi3cIqr1O5eLvV_F8zHqll2KY54 (accessed September 24, 2008).

4. Academic clustering is an institutional racist practice that assumes the intellectual inferiority of athletes in general and Black athletes specifically. See chapter 3 for more information regarding academic clustering.

5. Manning Marable, "The Rhetoric of Racial Harmony: Finding Substance in Culture and Ethnicity" *Sojourners* 19, no. 7 (1990): 14–18.

6. For information on the social dynamics of racial inequality and the process of reinforcing and reproducing the ideology of White supremacy see George H. Sage, *Power and Ideology in American Sport: A Critical Perspective,* 2nd ed. (Champaign, IL: Human Kinetics, 1998).

7. Stokely Carmichael and Charles V. Hamilton, *Black Power: The Politics of Liberation in America* (New York: Random House, 1967), 4.

8. Ibid.

9. For data regarding 2008 College-Bound Seniors see *CollegeBoard: 2008 College-Bound Seniors: Total Group Profile Report*, http://professionals.collegeboard.com/profdownload/Total_Group_Report.pdf (accessed March 15, 2009).

10. For additional information of median earnings by racial groups and educational attainment see Income, Earnings, and Poverty Data from the 2007 American Community Survey, http://www.census.gov/prod/2008pubs/acs-09.pdf (accessed February 23, 2008).

11. Ibid. and for information regarding grade point averages, family income, and parental educational attainment see *CollegeBoard: College-Bound Seniors 2008*, http://professionals.collegeboard.com/data-reports-research/sat/cb-seniors-2008 (accessed March 15, 2009).

12. Carl C. Brigham, *A Study of American Intelligence* (Princeton, NJ: Princeton University Press, 1923), xxi.

13. Carmichael and Hamilton, *Black Power*, 4.

14. For additional information of prison statistics see U.S. Department of Justice: Office of Justice Programs, Bureau of Justice Statistics, http://www.ojp.usdoj.gov/bjs/ (accessed April 23, 2008), or The Sentencing Project, http://www.sentencingproject.org/ (accessed September 8, 2008).

15. Jawanza Kunjufu, *Countering the Conspiracy to Destroy Black Boys Vol. I* (Chicago, IL: African American Images, 1982), 7.

16. Shelby Steele, *The Content of Our Character: A New Vision of Race in America* (New York: HarperCollins, 1991), 41.

17. William B. Harvey, "The Data Speak: No Rest for the Weary," in *Making It on Broken Promises: Leading African American Male Scholars Confront the Culture of Higher Education*, ed. L Jones (Sterling, VA: Stylus Publishing, 2002), 16.

18. Six Black males (four juniors and two seniors) volunteered to meet and discuss issues involving race, sport, and their college experiences. Prior to the formation of this group, several of these Black males often engaged me in after-class discussions. I eventually asked if they would be interested in being a part of a focus group. I solicited other participants from on-campus interaction.

19. Nelson George, *Elevating the Game: Black Men and Basketball* (Lincoln: University of Nebraska Press, 1999).

20. Robert Miles, *Racism* (London: Routledge, 1989).

21. According to the NBA age limit rule, "Beginning in 2006, the age limit for entering the Draft will increase from 18 to 19 years of age. U.S. players must be at least one year removed from high school and 19 years of age (by the end of that calendar year) before entering the draft. An international player must turn 19 during the calendar year of the draft." Another stipulation includes the following: "Teams are allowed to assign players with less than 2 years experience to the NBA Development League. Players sent to the NBA Development League will continue to count on a team's inactive list"; "Every NBA team has a player development director who focuses on the individual needs of each player, particularly the younger players, providing essential support for their career and education opportunities"; and finally, "The NBA also has a '20 and under' program that provides additional support services for all players under the age of 20 as well as programs that are geared specifically toward international players helping them with their transition into the NBA." See, e.g., "NBA age limit," http://hoopedia.nba.com/index.php/NBA_Age_Limit (accessed September 22, 2008).

22. Several college basketball coaches from nationally ranked schools voiced their disagreement with young athletes opting to forego college and play in Europe. Pete Thamel, "Top Recruit Weighs the Benefits of a Trip of Europe," http://www.nytimes.com/2008/07/08/sports/basketball/08hoops.html?ex=1373256000&en=abf7837f87e8ec38&ei=5124&partner=permalink&exprod=permalink (accessed September 22, 2008).

23. Athletic identity is a body of research that speaks to how an individual identifies with being an athlete. I use it here as a cultural prescription, where whether one identifies with being an athlete or not he or she is assigned that role in a given context.

24. For additional information on the Scholar-Baller concept and movement, see Scholar-Baller: Bringing Education to Sport and Entertainment, http://www.scholarballer.org/index.htm (accessed September 22, 2008).

25. Stuart Hall, *Race: The Floating Signifier* (Media Education Foundation, 1997).

26. For national graduation averages for Black males at NCAA member institutions see 2007 NCAA Division I Federal Graduation Rate Data, http://www2.ncaa.org/portal/academics_and_athletes/education_and_research/academic_reform/grad_rate/2007/d1_school_grad_rate_data.html (accessed September 30, 2008).

Six The Sociocultural Environment of Predominantly White NCAA Institutions: The Black Athlete as Oscillating Migrant Laborers

1. Everett V. Stonequist, *The Marginal Man: A Study in Personality and Culture Conflict* (New York: Charles Scribner's Sons, 1937).

2. Robert E. Parks, "Human Migration and the Marginal Man," *American Journal of Sociology* 33, no. 6 (1928): 881.

3. Viktor E. Frankl, *Man's Search for Meaning: An Introduction to Logotherapy*, 3rd ed. (New York: Simon & Schuster, 1984), 45.

4. The concept of marginality has been addressed and expanded upon by a variety of scholars including the works of Robert E. Parks and Everett V. Stonequist. For example see, David Riesman, "Some Observations Concerning Marginality," *Phylon* 12, no. 2 (1951), 113–127; Peter A. Johnson, "The Marginal Man Revisited," *Pacific Sociological Review* 3, no. 2 (1960): 71–74; Dorothy Nelkin, "A Response to Marginality: The Case of Migrant Farm Workers" *British Journal of Sociology* 20, no. 4 (1969): 375–389; Jung Y. Lee, *Marginality: The Key to Multicultural Theology* (Minneapolis, MN: Fortress Press, 1995); Billie Davis, "Marginality in a Pluralistic Society" http://www.psichi.org/pubs/articles/article_145.asp (accessed October 8, 2008); Ghana S. Gurung and Michael Kollmair, "Marginality: Concepts and Their Limitations," http://www.nccr-pakistan.org/publications_pdf/General/Marginality.pdf (accessed October 7, 2008).

5. Aaron V. Cicourel, "In Living in Two Cultures," *United Nations Educational, Scientific and Cultural Organization (UNESCO)* (Great Britain: Unesco, 1982), 17–66.

6. See the following references for additional information on oscillating migrant laborers: Sharon Stichter, *Migrant Laborers* (Cambridge: Cambridge University Press, 1985); Sharon Stichter, *Migrant Labour in Kenya: Capitalism and African Response 1895–1975* (Great Britain: Longman Group, 1982); Francis Wilson, *Migration Labour in South Africa* (Johannesburg: The South African Council of Churches, 1972).

7. For a review of literature that examines the psychological impact of biculturalism, see Teresa LaFromboise, Hardin L. K. Coleman, and Jennifer Gerton, "Psychological Impact of Biculturalism: Evidence and Theory," *Psychological Bulletin* 114, no. 3 (1993): 395–412.

8. For additional information on types of capital see Pierre Bourdieu, "The Forms of Capital" in *Handbook for Theory and Research for the Sociology of Education,* ed. J. G. Richardson, 241–258 (Westport, CT: Greenwood, 1986).

9. Ibid., 242.

10. Ibid., 258. Bourdieu also expands on symbolic capital in: Pierre Bourdieu, *Distinction: A Social Critique of the Judgement of Taste* (London: Routledge, 1984).

11. Kimberly Torres, "'Culture Shock': Black Students Account for Their Distinctiveness at an Elite College," *Ethnic and Racial Studies* 31, no. 1 (2008): 1–23.

12. Some additional scholars not mentioned in chapter 2 include the following: Mark A. Chesler, Amanda E. Lewis, and James E. Crowfoot, *Challenging Racism in Higher Education: Promoting Justice* (Lanham, MD: Rowman & Littlefield, 2005); William E. Sedlacek, "Black Students on White Campuses: Twenty Years of Research," *Journal of College Student Development* 40, no. 5 (1999): 538–550; Michael J. Cuyjet, "African American Men on College Campuses: Their Needs and Their Perceptions," *New Directions for Student Services* 80 (1997): 5–16; Anthony R. D'Augelli and Scott L. Hershberger, "African American Undergraduates on a Predominantly White Campus: Academic Factors, Social Networks, and Campus Climate," *Journal of Negro Education,* 62, no. 1 (1993): 67–81; Walter R. Allen, Edgar G. Epps, and Nesha Z. Haniff (eds.), *College in Black and White: African American Students in Predominantly White and in Historically Black Public Universities* (Albany: State University of New York Press, 1991). For research that provides insight into areas ranging from achievement prediction, degree attainment, academic performance, and social support networks for Black students, see the following: Chalmer E. Thompson and Bruce R. Fretz, "Predicting the Adjustment of Black Students at Predominantly White Institutions," *Journal of Higher Education* 62, no.4 (1991): 437–450; Walter R. Allen, "The Education of Black Students on White College Campuses: What Quality Are the Experiences?" in M. Nettles (ed.), *Towards Black Undergraduate Student Equality in American Higher Education,* 57–86 (Albany: State University of New York Press, 1988).

13. Aaron V. Cicourel, "In Living in Two Cultures," *United Nations Educational, Scientific and Cultural Organization (UNESCO)* (Great Britain: Unesco, 1982), 17–66; Robert Miles, *Racism and Migrant Labour* (Boston: Routledge & Kegan Paul, 1992); Mamphela Ramphele, *A Bed Called Home: Life in the Migrant Labour Hostels of Cape Town* (Athens: Ohio University Press, 1993); Patrick Harries, *Work, Culture, and Identity: Migrant laborers in Mozambique and South Africa, c. 1860–1910* (Portsmouth, NH: Heinemann, 1994).

14. One of the most comprehensive studies funded by the NCAA provided insightful data regarding the experiences of Black athletes at PWIs. See the following resource: American Institute for Research, "Report #3: The Experiences of Black Intercollegiate Athletes at NCAA Division I Institutions," *Studies of Intercollegiate Athletics* (Palo Alto, CA: Center for the Study of Athletics, 1989).

15. Ralph Ellison, *Invisible Man* (New York: Random House, 1947), 7.

16. I define *acculturation* as adapting to a new cultural setting but maintaining your original cultural traditions, etc.—becoming bicultural; while assimilation is adopting a new culture and losing your previous cultural identity.

17. Harry Edwards, *Sociology of Sport* (Homewood, IL: Dorsey Press, 1973).

18. Mike Fish, "Where is the Justice?" *The Atlanta Journal-Constisution* (1997, March 2): E8–E9.

19. Allen Sack, *Sport Sociology: Contemporary Themes* (Dubuque, IA: Kendall-Hunt, 1979); James Michener, *Sports in America* (New York: Random House, 1976).

20. D. Stanley Eitzen and George H. Sage, *Sociology of North American Sport*, 3rd edition (Dubuque, IA: William C. Brown, 1986), 122.

21. Wilbert M. Leonard, "The Sport Experience of the Black College Athlete: Exploitation in the Academy," *International Review for the Sociology of Sport*, 21 no. 1 (1986): 44.

22. Sack, *Sport Sociology*; Michener, *Sports in America.*

23. Robert M. Sellers, Gabriel P. Kuperminc, and Andrea S. Waddell, "Life Experiences of Black Student-Athletes in Revenue Producing Sports: A Descriptive Empirical Analysis," *Academic Athletic Journal* (1991): 21–38; Ralph Wiley, "A Daunting Proposition," *Sports Illustrated* (1991, August 12): 27–25; Richard Lapchick, *Five Minutes to Midnight: Race and Sport in the 1990s* (Lanham, MD: Madison Books, 1991); Othello Harris, "African-American Predominance in Collegiate Sport," in *Racism in Collegiate Athletics*, ed. R. C. Althouse and D. D. Brooks, 51–74 (Morgantown, WV: Fitness Information Technology, 1993).

24. Harries, *Work, Culture, and Identity.*

25. Harry Edwards, "A Dual Challenge for College Sports: Demographic and Cultural Pluralism Must be Concurrent," *NCAA News* (1993, March 10): 4.

26. R. A. Schermerhorn, "Power as a Primary Concept in the Study of Minorities," *Social Forces* 35 (1956): 53–56.

Seven   Politics and the Black Athletic Experience

1. National Collegiate Athletic Association, "Legislation and Governance Overview," http://www.ncaa.org/wps/ncaa?ContentID=18 (accessed November 18, 2008).

2. I will use the term Predominantly White Institutions (PWIs) when referring to the NCAA and its member institutions because these are the institutions under observation regarding Black athletes experiences. I will use NCAA when I am referring only to the governing body.

3. Manning Marable, *Speaking Truth to Power: Essays on Race, Resistance, and Radicalism* (Boulder, CO: Westview Press, 1998), 76.

4. Ibid., 76–77.

5. Manning Marable, *Beyond Black and White: Transforming African American Politics* (Brooklyn, NY: Verso, 1995), xii.

6. 2008–2009 NCAA Division I Manual http://www.ncaapublications.com/Uploads/PDF/Division_1_Manual_2008-09e9e568a1-c269-4423-9ca5-16d6827c16bc.pdf (accessed July 27, 2008).

7. For a more in-depth analysis of amateurism and collegiate sports see Allen L. Sack and Ellen J. Staurowsky, *College Athletes for Hire: The Evolution and Legacy of the NCAA's Amateur Myth* (Westport, CT: Praeger, 1998).

8. Mary R. Jackman, *The Velvet Glove: Paternalism and Conflict in Gender, Class, and Race Relations* (Berkeley: University of California Press, 1994), 10.

9. Ibid.

10. United States Court of Appeals for the Eighth Circuit, *"C.B.C. Distribution and Marketing, Inc. vs. Major League Baseball Advanced Media, L.P. et. al.,"* http://www.ca8.uscourts.gov/opndir/07/10/063357P.pdf (accessed November 12, 2008). Specific court decision regarding this case is as follows: "The district court granted summary judgment to CBC. It held that CBC was not infringing any state-law rights of publicity that belonged to major league baseball players." *C.B.C.*, 443 F. Supp.2d at 1106-07. The court reasoned that CBC's fantasy baseball products did not use the names of major league baseball players as symbols of their identities and with an intent to obtain a commercial advantage, as required to establish an infringement of a publicity right under Missouri law (which all parties concede applies here). *Id.* at 1085-89. The district court further held that even if CBC were infringing the players' rights of publicity, the first amendment preempted those rights. *Id.* at 1091–1100. The court rejected, however, CBC's argument that federal copyright law preempted the rights of publicity claim. *Id.* at 1100-03. Finally, the district court held that CBC was not in violation of the no-use and no-contest provisions of its 2002 agreement with the Players Association because "the strong federal policy favoring the full and free use of ideas in the public domain as manifested in the laws of intellectual property prevails over [those] contractual provisions" (internal quotations omitted). *Id.* at 1106-07.

11. National Collegiate Athletic Association, "Bylaw 10.3 and Related Cases," http://www1.ncaa.org/membership/enforcement/gambling/toolkit/chapter_4?ObjectID=42728&ViewMode=0&PreviewState=0 (accessed November 11, 2008).

12. NCAA Student-Athlete Advisory Committees, "What Is a Student-Athlete Advisory Committee? (SAAC)," http://www1.ncaa.org/membership/membership_svcs/saac/index.html (accessed November 12, 2008).

13. Ibid.

14. Ibid.

15. NCAA Student-Athlete Advisory Committees, "Campus, Conference and Division SAACs," http://www1.ncaa.org/membership/membership_svcs/saac/campus-conf-div.html#campus (accessed November 12, 2008).

16. Ibid.

17. Participation—1981–82—2006–07 NCAA Sports Sponsorship and Participation Rates Report Executive Summary, "Executive Summary," http://www.ncaapublications.com/Uploads/PDF/PariticipationRates20084232c5b7-6441-412c-80f1-7d85f3536a51.pdf (accessed November 12, 2008).

18. NCAA Student-Athlete Advisory Committees, "Campus, Conference and Division SAACs."

19. Mike Freeman, "Pro Football: Notebook; Upshaw Deplores the Plight of Black Assistants," *New York Times* http://query.nytimes.com/gst/fullpage.html?res=9506EEDB163CF930A35751C1A9669C8B63 (accessed November 3, 2008).

20. Ibid.

21. Terry Bowden, "Uneven Playing Field," *Yahoo! Sports*, http://rivals.yahoo.com/ncaa/football/news?slug=tb-minoritycoaches062905&prov=yhoo&type=lgns (accessed November 11, 2008).

22. The tables were constructed using data from the following source that was collected from 283 NCAA Division I Institutions (HBCUs excluded): The NCAA Minority Opportunities and Interests Committee's Biennial Study, "2005–06 Ethnicity and Gender Demographics of NCAA Member Institutions' Athletics Personnel," http://www.ncaa.org/wps/ncaa?ContentID=354 (accessed November 13, 2008).

23. Black Coaches and Administrators, "The Number of Black Head Football Coaches in FBS Has Gone in the Erroneous Direction," http://bcasports.cstv.com/genrel/111208aaa.html (accessed November 17, 2008).

24. Ibid.

25. Richard E. Lapchick, "Think beyond the Competition: 2006–07 Racial and Gender Report Card," http://www.tidesport.org/RGRC/2007/2006-07_RGRC.pdf (accessed October 15, 2007).

26. Ibid.

27. Ibid.
28. National College Players Association (NCPA), "Mission and Goals," http://www.cacnow. org/our_mission.asp (accessed November 17, 2008). The goals of the NCPA are as follows: (1) Raise the scholarship amount: The NCAA admits that a "full scholarship" does not cover the basic necessities for a college athlete, but it refuses to change its rules to allow schools to provide more scholarship money. The NCPA's plan is to use a relatively small percentage of post–season revenues to assist universities in providing scholarships that cover costs; (2) Secure health coverage for all sports-related workouts: The NCAA does not require schools to cover sports-related injuries—it is optional. College athletes injured during sports-related workouts should not have to pay for medical expenses out of their own pockets. Universities should be mandated to ensure that their college athletes receive adequate medical care for all sports related workouts; (3) Increase graduation rates: The ultimate goal for a college athlete is not a scholarship, it's a degree. The graduation rate for Division I football players hovers around 50 percent while men's basketball players graduate at a rate of about 40 percent. The NCAA can help improve these rates by awarding a significant portion of the NCAA basketball tournament revenues to schools with the best graduation rates. In addition, the NCAA should work to reduce games that take place during the week. Although weekday games are in the interest of the TV networks, they hurt college athletes academically; (4) Allow universities to grant multiple year scholarships (up to five years) instead of one-year revocable scholarships: University recruiters mislead high school recruits by offering them "4 or 5 year scholarships" even though the NCAA does not allow multiple year scholarships. The NCAA only allows one-year scholarships that a university can refuse to renew for any reason (including injuries or personality conflicts). A university should be able to give multiple year scholarships and guarantee it in writing if it so chooses. This would help further protect college athletes and end deceptive recruiting practices; (5) Prohibit universities from using a permanent injury suffered during athletics as a reason to reduce/eliminate a scholarship: Such actions reduce the chance for such college athletes to graduate. College athletes put their bodies and lives on the line in their pursuit of higher education and the success of their university's athletic program. It is immoral to allow a university to reduce or refuse to renew a college athlete's scholarship after sustaining an injury while playing for the university; (6) Establish and enforce uniform safety guidelines in all sports to help prevent avoidable deaths: Several deaths in the college football off-season have highlighted the need for year round safety requirements that provide an adequate level of protections for college athletes from all sports. College athletes and athletic staff should be given the means to anonymously report breaches in such requirements; (7) Eliminate restrictions on legitimate employment: College athletes should have the same rights to secure employment as other students and U.S. citizens. Such a measure could be designed to increase graduation rates and allow universities to retain the most talented athletes for the duration of their eligibility; (8) Prohibit the punishment of college athletes who have not committed a violation: It is an injustice to punish college athletes for actions that they did not commit, that is, suspending a team's post–season eligibility for the inappropriate actions of boosters. Such punishments have significant negative impacts on the short college experience of many college athletes. Alternative forms of punishment are available and should be utilized to allow an adequate policing of the rules; (9) Guarantee that college athletes are granted an athletic release from their university if they wish to transfer schools: Schools should not have the power to refuse to release college athletes who choose to transfer. The NCAA currently gives universities the power to determine whether or not to allow college athletes to retain athletic eligibility after transferring. This contradicts the principle of sportsmanship that the NCAA is supposed to uphold; (10) Allow college athletes of all sports the ability to transfer schools one time without punishment; College athletes that participate in football, basketball, and hockey should not be denied the one-time no-penalty transfer option that is afforded to college athletes of other sports. Such a policy is coercive and discriminatory. All college athletes should have this freedom to ensure that they realize their academic, social, and athletic pursuits.
29. National College Players Association (NCPA), "NCPA-Backed Lawsuit Makes Over $445 Million Available to Athletes," http://www.ncpanow.org/news_detail.asp?ArticleID=38 (accessed November 17, 2008).
30. For more information on the BCA Hiring Report Card and the latest report, see the following source: Black Coaches Association, "Who You Know & Who Knows You: The Hiring Process

& Practice of NCAA FBS & FBC Head Coaching Positions," http://bcasports.cstv.com/auto_pdf/p_hotos/s_chools/bca/genrel/auto_pdf/08-hiring-report-card (accessed November 18, 2008).

31. For the latest hiring report card regarding head coaches in NCAA Division I Women's Basketball, see Black Coaches Association, "Scoring the Hire: A Hiring Report Card for NCAA Division I Women's Basketball Head Coaching Positions," http://bcasports.cstv.com/auto_pdf/p_hotos/s_chools/bca/genrel/auto_pdf/08-wbb-report-card (accessed November 18, 2008).

32. Excerpts from the West India Emancipation Speech delivered by Frederick Douglass at Canandaigua, New York, August 4, 1857. Also included in the following source: Philip S. Foner, "West India Emancipation Speech," *The Life and Writings of Frederick Douglass,* vol. 2 (New York: International Publishers, 1950), 437.

Eight   Friday Night Lights: A Dream Deferred or Delusions of Grandeur

1. Gerald Eskenazi, "Arena of Big-Time Athletics Is Showcasing a Younger Act," *New York Times,* http://query.nytimes.com/gst/fullpage.html?res=950DE4D8103AF936A35750C0A96F948260&n=Top/Reference/Times%20Topics/Subjects/C/College%20Athletics (accessed November 23, 2008). This article was part of a five-part series on the commercialization of high school athletics published in 1989.

2. H. G. Bissinger, *Friday Night Lights: A Town, a Team, and a Dream* (Cambridge, MA: Da Capo Press, 1990).

3. Elliott J. Gorn and Warren J. Goldstein, *A Brief History of American Sports* (Champaign, IL: University of Illinois Press, 2004), 162–163.

4. The Alfred University's national study on hazing in high school informs of the prevalence of hazing practices among high school students: "Initiation Rites in American High Schools: A National Survey," *Alfred University,* http://www.alfred.edu/hs_hazing/ (accessed February 20, 2009). For an additional source, the following article highlights the practices of hazing in high school sports: Tom Weir, "Hazing issue's lasting impact rears ugly head across USA," *USA Today,* http://www.usatoday.com/sports/preps/2003-12-09-hazing_x.htm (accessed February 20, 2009).

5. Harry Edwards exposed a belief system called the Dominant American Sport Creed, which consisted of ideals and beliefs achieved through sport participation that closely resembled the American Dream ideology. The American Dream ideology was a system of ideas centered on the belief that if individuals worked hard they would achieve a certain level of economic success (i.e., material possessions generally defined in terms of a two-car garage, house in suburban America, etc.). Therefore, sports promotes physical and mental fitness, builds character, teaches discipline, enhances competitiveness, prepares individual for a competitive market economy, and contributes to Judeo-Christian and patriotic belief systems. These ideals became applicable and common beliefs among advocates for interscholastic sports and youth sports programs in the United States, in general. Thus, interscholastic sports were seen as a practical vehicle to promote patriotism and to disseminate cultural values and socialize youth into having desirable cultural traits, while preparing them mentally and physically to be competitive and productive in a market economy. See Harry Edwards, *Sociology of Sport* (Homewood, IL: Dorsey Press, 1973).

6. Bill Pennington, "Reading, Writing and Corporate Sponsorships," *New York Times* http://www.nytimes.com/2004/10/18/sports/othersports/18sponsor.html (accessed October 11, 2006).

7. Ibid.

8. In September 11, 2007, the Dallas Associated Press reported the naming rights deal between East Texas high school football stadium and a health care company, see, "Texas High School Football Becoming Big Business," http://cbs11tv.com/business/texas.high.school.2.506554.html (accessed February 2009).

9. Gordon Dillow, "Bright Lights, Big Money," *Register,* http://www.ocregister.com/ocregister/news/columns/article_1338204.php (accessed November 12, 2006); Pennington, "Reading, Writing and Corporate Sponsorships."

10. Pennington, "Reading, Writing and Corporate Sponsorships"; "High School Football—A Growing Big Business," *Sport Business News,* http://sportsbiznews.blogspot.com/2006/09/high-school-football-growing-big.html (accessed October 11, 2006).

11. *Friday Night Lights* originally was a novel by H. G. Bissinger in 1990 that documents the coach and players of a high school football team and the small, economically depressed Texas town of Odessa that supports and is obsessed with them. This novel was converted into a movie in 2004, and finally into a primetime show that is into its third season airing on DIRECTV and NBC. For additional information regarding the novel, see, Bissinger, *Friday Night Lights.*

12. Data for the 2007 city and county census information for Madison, Florida, was retrieved from the following Web site: City-data—Madison, County Florida, http://www.city-data.com/city/Madison-Florida.html (accessed September 26, 2008).

13. Ibid.

14. Ibid.

15. Racial demographic data was collected from the following Web site: *"Public School Report: Public School Information and Data,"* http://schools.publicschoolsreport.com/Florida/Madison/MadisonCountyHighSchool.html (accessed September 26, 2008).

16. Graduation and Dropout rate information was collected from the following Web site: Florida Department of Education, Education Information & Accountability Services—Madison County School District, http://www.fldoe.org/eias/flmove/madison.asp (accessed September 27, 2008).

17. According to the Florida Department of Education, the following are the different description for diplomas: Standard Diploma are awarded to students who have accomplished one of the following: (1) passed both sections of the Graduation Test, successfully completed the minimum number of academic credits as identified in Section 1003.43, F.S., and successfully completed any other requirements prescribed by the state or the local school board; (2) received a Florida Comprehensive Assessment Test (FCAT) waiver, successfully completed the minimum number of academic credits as identified in Section 1003.43, F.S. and successfully completed any other requirements prescribed by the state or the local school board; (3) met all of the requirements to graduate base on the 18-credit college preparatory graduation option. Special Diploma are awarded to students who have been properly identified as educable mentally handicapped, trainable mentally handicapped, hearing impaired, specific learning disabled, emotionally handicapped, physically impaired, or language impaired. Certificates of completion are awarded to students who complete the required courses, but students who fail to meet the other diploma requirements may receive a certificate of completion. A certificate of completion is not a diploma. It certifies that the student attended high school. Students who receive a certificate of completion may enter the workforce, attend adult basic education classes, or possibly be enrolled in a community college or technical center. Students may be required to take the college placement test or a test of basic skills and complete remedial coursework. Finally, students who receive equivalency diplomas or General Equivalency Diplomas (GED) have successfully passed the General Education Development Test. For additional information regarding the state of Florida high school diploma requirements, see: Florida Department of Education, http://www.fldoe.org/default.asp (accessed September 27, 2008).

18. Florida Department of Education, Education Information and Accountability Services http://www.fldoe.org/eias/eiaspubs/default.asp (accessed October 2, 2008).

19. These rates are for the 2004–2005 school year. See the following Web site for additional information: U.S. Department of Education, Institute of Education Sciences—National Center for Educational Statistics, http://nces.ed.gov/programs/coe/2008/section3/table.asp?tableID=896 (accessed October 2, 2008).

20. "Given Half a Chance: The Schott 50 State Report on Public Education and Black Males," http://www.blackboysreport.org/ (accessed February 2009).

21. 20082009 FHSAA Football Manual, http://www.fhsaa.org/fb/manual/0809_fb_manual.pdf (accessed October 5, 2008).

Nine   Athletic Reform and Decolonization

1. See John N. Crowley, *The NCAA's First Century in the Arena* (Indianapolis, IN: National Collegiate Athletic Association, 2005), 7; National Collegiate Athletic Association, "History," http://www.ncaa.org/wps/ncaa?ContentID=1354 (accessed November 20, 2008), 18–19.

2. Howard J. Savage, *American College Athletics,* Bulletin no. 23 (New York: Carnegie Foundation for the Advancement of Teaching, 1929).

3. Some of the scholars who have written about intercollegiate reform include the following: Robert D. Benford, "The College Sports Reform Movement: Reframing the 'Edutainment' Industry," *Sociological Quarterly* 48 (2007):1–28; Murray Sperber, *Beer and Circus: How Big-time College Sports Is Crippling Undergraduate Education* (New York: Henry Holt, 2000), 262–275; James J. Duderstadt, *Intercollegiate Athletics and the American University: A University President's Perspective* (Ann Arbor: University of Michigan Press), see chapters 12–14, pages 263–318; James L. Schulman and William G. Bowen, *The Game of Life: College Sports and Educational Values* (Princeton, NJ: Princeton University Press, 2001) see Chapter 14, pages 289–309; Andrew Zimbalist, *"Unpaid Professionals - Commercialism and Conflict in Big-Time College Sports: Commercialism and Conflict in Big-Time College Sports"* (Princeton, NJ: Princeton University Press, 1999), see chapter 9, pages 188–205.

4. Ronald A. Smith, *Sports and Freedom: The Rise of Big-Time College Athletics* (New York: Oxford University Press, 1988), 119.

5. Crowley, *NCAA's First Century in the Arena,* 7; National Collegiate Athletic Association, "History," 230–251.

6. The Knight Commission on Intercollegiate Athletics, http://www.knightcommission.org/about/ (accessed November 23, 2008).

7. Ibid.

8. The Knight Commission on Intercollegiate Athletics, "The Foundation's Interest," http://www.knightcommission.org/images/uploads/1991-93_KCIA_report.pdf (accessed November 23, 2008), 3.

9. Ibid., 8.

10. Ibid., 22.

11. Ibid., 6.

12. Ibid., 25.

13. Ibid., 26–28.

14. Ibid., 28.

15. Ibid., 29–30.

16. Ibid., 31.

17. Ibid., 33.

18. On pages 40–41 of the report, *Keeping Faith with the Student-Athlete: A Model for Intercollegiate Athletics,* the KCIA outline "Principles for Action" in which they include a statement of principles complete with a preamble.

19. The Knight Commission, 62.

20. Ibid., 64.

21. The Knight Commission on Intercollegiate Athletics, *"A Call to Action: Reconnecting College Sports and Higher Education"* http://www.knightcommission.org/images/uploads/KCfinal-06-2001.pdf (accessed November 26, 2008), 12.

22. Ibid., 24.

23. Ibid., 26–29.

24. Ibid., 26.

25. Ibid., 27–28.

26. Ibid., 28–29.

27. Ibid., 31.

28. Coalition on Intercollegiate Athletics, "About COIA," http://www.neuro.uoregon.edu/~tublitz/COIA/aboutcoia.htm (accessed December 2, 2008).

29. Coalition on Intercollegiate Athletics, http://www.neuro.uoregon.edu/~tublitz/COIA/index.html (accessed December 2, 2008).

30. Coalition on Intercollegiate Athletics, "Charter of the Coalition on Intercollegiate Athletics," http://www.neuro.uoregon.edu/~tublitz/COIA/Charter.html (accessed December 2, 2008).

31. Coalition on Intercollegiate Athletics, "Campus Athletics Governance, the Faculty Role: Principles, Proposed Rules, and Guidelines," http://www.neuro.uoregon.edu/~tublitz/COIA/policypapers.htm (accessed December 2, 2008).

32. Ibid.

33. Coalition on Intercollegiate Athletics, "Academic Integrity in Intercollegiate Athletics: Principles, Rules, and Best Practices," http://www.neuro.uoregon.edu/~tublitz/COIA/AF.html (accessed December 2, 2008).

34. Ibid.
35. Coalition on Intercollegiate Athletics, "Framing the Future: Reforming Intercollegiate Athletics," http://www.neuro.uoregon.edu/~tublitz/COIA/FTF/FTFtext&appendix.htm (accessed December 2, 2008).
36. Ibid.
37. Ibid.
38. The Drake Group, http://www.thedrakegroup.org/index.html (accessed December 2, 2008).
39. The Drake Group, "The Drake Group Proposals," http://www.thedrakegroup.org/proposals. html (accessed December 2, 2008).
40. National Collegiate Athletic Association, "Defining Academic Reform" http://www.ncaa. org/wps/ncaa?ContentID=341 (accessed December 2, 2008).
41. Ibid.
42. Ibid.
43. Ibid.
44. Michelle B. Hosick, "Reform's Inroads Evident with APR Release" *NCAA News* (2008 May 06) http://www.ncaa.org/wps/ncaa?ContentID=331 accessed December 2, 2008).
45. Raymond A. Kent (ed.), *Higher Education in America* (New York: Ginn & Company, 1930), 587.
46. Allen Sack provides an informative analysis of college athletics and capitalist ideals in: Allen L. Sack, "Counterfeit Amateurs: An Athlete's Journey through the Sixties to the Age of Academic Capitalism" (University Park: Pennsylvania State University Press, 2008). His chapter addressing "College Sport in the Age of Academic Capitalism" illustrates how the capitalist model has impacted both the academic and athletic departments in higher education.
47. Since commercialization involves the process of promoting and marketing a (mainly new) product, for me, ultra commercialization is the process of developing multiple streams of revenue from that product, extending the brand identity vertically and horizontally, etc.
48. Works that have addressed the process of decolonization throughout the world, see e.g., Muriel Evelyn Chamberlain, *Decolonization: The Fall of the European Empires* (Malden, MA: Blackwell, 1999); Albert Memmi and Robert Bononno, *Decolonization and the Decolonized* (Minneapolis: University of Minnesota Press, 2006); Raymond F. Betts, *Decolonization: Making of the Contemporary World* (New York: Routledge, 2004).
49. Claud Anderson, *Black Labor, White Wealth: The Search for Power and Economic Justice* (Edgewood, MD: Duncan & Duncan, 1994), 19.
50. Proposition 48 legislation was passed in 1983. It required athletes to have a minimum SAT score of 700, or an ACT score of 17, and a minimum GPA of 2.0 in at least 11 courses in core classes. Proposition 16 had more rigorous requirements. It required athletes to have a 2.0 grade point average (GPA) in 13 approved academic "core" courses and an SAT of 1010 or a combined ACT of 86. If they scored lower on the SAT or ACT, they would need higher core course GPAs. Both have been shown to adversely impact Black athletes. For example, in 1994, the McIntosh Commission for Fair Play in Student-Athlete Admissions concluded that African American student-athletes who entered college the two years before the rule was instituted would have been declared ineligible at a rate six times as high as the rate for White student-athletes. More specifically, the McIntosh Commission concluded that Prop. 48 discriminate against Blacks, females, and lower-income athletes.
51. Play It Smart: A Program of the National Football Foundation & College Hall of Fame, "About Play It Smart," http://www.playitsmart.org/Play_about.php (accessed December 3, 2008).
52. Ibid.
53. Mark Alesia, "'Special' Treatment for Athletes," IndyStar.Com http://www.indystar.com/ apps/pbcs.dll/article?AID=/20080907/SPORTS/809070375/1069/SPORTS0601 (accessed December 5, 2008).
54. National Collegiate Athletic Association, "Our Mission," http://www.ncaa.org/wps/ ncaa?ContentID=1352 (accessed December 6, 2008).
55. National Collegiate Athletic Association, "Academics and Athletes," http://www.ncaa.org/ wps/ncaa?ContentID=8 (accessed December 6, 2008).
56. Jill L. Steeg, Jodi Upton, Patrick Bohn, and Steve Berkowitz, "College Athletes Academics Guided toward 'Major in Eligibility,'" http://www.usatoday.com/sports/college/2008-11-18-majors-cover_N.htm?POE=click-refer (accessed November 19, 2008).

57. Erik Brady, "Athletes' Academic Choices Put Advisers in Tough Balancing Act," *USA Today*, http://www.usatoday.com/sports/college/2008-11-20-athletes-advisers-cover_N.htm (accessed December 6, 2008).

58. Ibid.

59. Some athletic departments are beginning to provide this service for current and former athletes. However, it should be part of a contractual agreement and available as long as the services are needed by the athletes.

60. National College Players Association (NCPA), "Mission and Goals," http://www.cacnow.org/our_mission.asp (accessed December 7, 2008).

Ten   Conclusion

1. Stokely Carmichael and Charles V. Hamilton, *Black Power: The Politics of Liberation in America* (New York: Random House, 1967), 17.

2. "Minority Numbers in Athletics Administration," *NCAA News* (1994, August): 5, 13; Charles Farrell, "Black Collegiate Athletes Are being Double-Crossed," *USA Today*, 119 (1990): 18–30.

3. The Institute for Diversity and Ethics in Sport, "The Buck Stops Here: Assessing Diversity among Campus and Conference Leaders for Football Bowl Subdivision (FBS) Schools in the 2008–09 Academic Year," http://www.ncasports.org/Articles/2008-09_FBS_Demographics_Study.pdf (accessed December 8, 2008).

4. Farrell, "Black Collegiate Athletes Are being Double-Crossed," 18–30.

5. Kwame Nkrumah, *Ghana: The Autobiography of Kwame Nkrumah* (New York: International Publishers, 1957).

6. Ibid., ix.

7. This statement is a portion of the Preamble to the *Declaration of Independence*.

BIBLIOGRAPHY

2007 NCAA Division I Federal Graduation Rate Data. http://www2.ncaa.org/portal/academics_ and_athletes/education_and_research/academic_reform/grad_rate/2007/d1_school_grad_ rate_data.html (accessed September 30, 2008).

2008–2009 FHSAA Football Manual. http://www.fhsaa.org/fb/manual/0809_fb_manual.pdf (accessed October 5, 2008).

2008–2009 NCAA Division I Manual. http://www.ncaapublications.com/Uploads/PDF/ Division_1_Manual_2008-09e9e568a1-c269-4423-9ca5-16d6827c16bc.pdf (accessed July 27, 2008).

Aaseng, Nathan. *The Locker Room Mirror: How Sport Reflects Society.* New York: Walker, 1993.

"Academics and Athletics." *The Ann Arbor News.* http://www.mlive.com/wolverines/academics/ stories/index.ssf/2008/03/athletes_steered_to_prof.html (accessed June 24, 2008).

Adler, Patricia A., and P. Adler. *Backboards & Blackboards: College Athletics and Role Engulfment.* New York: Columbia University Press, 1991.

Ainsworth-Darnell, James W., and D. B. Downey. "Assessing the Oppositional Cultural Explanation for Racial/Ethnic Differences in School Performance." *American Sociological Review* 63, no. 4 (1998): 536–553.

Alesia, Mark. "Tourney Money Fuels Pay-to-Play Debate: Fewer Than 1% of Athletes Help Make More Than 90% of the NCAA's Money." *Indy Star.* www.indystar.com/apps/pbcs.dll/ article?AID=/20060401/SPORTS/604010509 (accessed April 6, 2006).

———. "'Special' Treatment for Athletes." *IndyStar.Com.* http://www.indystar.com/apps/pbcs. dll/article?AID=/20080907/SPORTS/809070375/1069/SPORTS0601 (accessed December 5, 2008).

Allahar, Anton L. "When Black First Became Worth Less." *International Journal of Comparative Sociology* 34, no. 1–2 (1993): 39–55.

Allen, Robert L. *Black Awakening in Capitalist America: An Analytic History.* New York: Doubleday, 1970.

Allen, Walter R. "Correlates of Black Student Adjustment, Achievement, and Aspirations at a Predominantly White Southern University." In *Black Students in Higher Education: Conditions and Experiences in the 1970s,* edited by G. Thomas, 126–141. Westport, CT: Greenwood, 1981.

———. "Black Student, White Campus: Structural Interpersonal and Psychological Correlates of Success." *Journal of Negro Education* 54 (1985): 134–147.

———. "The Education of Black Students on White College Campuses: What Quality the Experience." In *Toward Black Undergraduate Student Equality in Higher Education,* edited by M. Nettles, 57–86. Albany, NY: State University of New York Press, 1988.

Allen, Walter R., E. G. Epps, and N. Z. Haniff. *College in Black and White: African American Students in Predominantly White and in Historically Black Public Universities.* Albany, NY: State University of New York Press, 1991.

American Institute for Research. "Report #2: Methodology of the 1987–88 National Study of Intercollegiate Athletes." *Studies of Intercollegiate Athletics.* Palo Alto, CA: Center for the Study of Athletics, 1988.

American Institute for Research. "Report #3: The experiences of Black Intercollegiate Athletes at NCAA Division I Institutions." *Studies of Intercollegiate Athletics*. Palo Alto, CA: Center for the Study of Athletics, 1989.

Anderson, A., and D. South. "Racial Differences in Collegiate Recruiting, Retention, and Graduation Rates." In *Racism In College Athletics: The African-American Experience 2nd Ed.*, edited by D. Brooks and R. Althouse, 155–172. Morgantown, WV: Fitness Information Technology, 1999.

Anderson, Claud. *Black Labor, White Wealth: The Search for Power and Economic Justice*. Edgewood, MD: Duncan & Duncan, 1994.

Ashe, Jr., Arthur R. *A Hard Road to Glory: A History of the African-American Athlete 1619–1918*, 3 vols. New York: Amistad Press, 1993.

Banks, James A. "Approaches to Multicultural Curriculum." *Multicultural Leader* 1, no. 2 (1988): 1–3.

———. *Cultural Diversity and Education*, 4th ed. Boston: Allyn & Bacon, 2000.

Banks, James A., and C. A. M. Banks. *Multicultural Education: Issues and Perspectives*, 4th ed. New York: John Wiley, 2002.

Beckham Barry. "Strangers in a Strange Land: The Experience of Blacks on White Campuses." *Educational Record* 68, no. 4 (1988): 74–78.

Benford, Robert D. "The College Sports Reform Movement: Reframing the 'Edutainment' Industry." *Sociological Quarterly* 48 (2007): 1–28.

Bennett, Lerone. *The Shaping of Black America: The Struggles and Triumphs of African-Americans, 1619–1990s*. Chicago, IL: Johnson Publishing, 1975.

Berghorn, Forrest J., N. R. Yetman, and W. E. Hanna, "Racial Participation and Integration in Men's and Women's Intercollegiate Basketball: Continuity and Change, 1959–1985." *Sociology of Sport Journal* 5, no. 2 (1988): 87–106.

Betts, Raymond F. *Decolonization: Making of the Contemporary World*. New York: Routledge, 2004.

Bissinger, H. G. *Friday Night Lights: A Town, a Team, and a Dream*. Cambridge, MA: Da Capo Press, 1990.

Blackburn, Robin. *The Making of New World Slavery: From the Baroque to the Modern, 1492–1800*. London: Verso, 1997.

Black Coaches and Administrators. "The Number of Black Head Football Coaches in FBS Has Gone in the Erroneous Direction." http://bcasports.cstv.com/genrel/111208aaa.html (accessed November 17, 2008).

Black Coaches Association. "Scoring the Hire: A Hiring Report Card for NCAA Division I Women's Basketball Head Coaching Positions." http://bcasports.cstv.com/auto_pdf/p_hotos/s_chools/bca/genrel/auto_pdf/08-wbb-report-card (accessed November 18, 2008).

———. "Who You Know & Who Knows You: The Hiring Process & Practice of NCAA FBS & FBC Head Coaching Positions." http://bcasports.cstv.com/auto_pdf/p_hotos/s_chools/bca/genrel/auto_pdf/08-hiring-report-card (accessed November 18, 2008).

Blackmon, Douglas A. *Slavery by Another Name: The Re-Enslavement of Black People in America from the Civil War to World War II*. New York: Doubleday, 2008.

Blauner, Robert. "Internal Colonialism and Ghetto Revolt." *Social Problems* 16, no. 4 (1969): 393–408.

Bogle, Donald. *Toms, Coons, Mulattoes, Mammies, and Bucks: An Interpretive History of Blacks in American Films* (New York: Continuum, 1989).

Boskin, Joseph. "Sambo and Other Male Images in Popular Culture." In *Images of Blacks in American Culture: A Reference Guide to Information Sources*, edited by J. C. Smith, 257–272. New York: Greenwood, 1988.

Bourdieu, Pierre. *Distinction: A Social Critique of the Judgement of Taste*. London: Routledge, 1984.

———. "The Forms of Capital." In *Handbook for Theory and Research for the Sociology of Education*, edited by J. G. Richardson, 241–258. Westport, CT: Greenwood, 1986.

Bowden, Terry. "Uneven Playing Field." *Yahoo! Sports*. http://rivals.yahoo.com/ncaa/football/news?slug=tb-minoritycoaches062905&prov=yhoo&type=lgns (accessed November 11, 2008).

Bowl Championship Series on MSN. "BCS Bowl Facts." http://www.bcsfootball.org/bcsfb/facts (accessed October 28, 2008).

Brady, Erik. "Athletes' Academic Choices Put Advisers in Tough Balancing Act." *USA Today.* http://www.usatoday.com/sports/college/2008-11-20-athletes-advisers-cover_N.htm (accessed December 6, 2008).

Brand, Myles. "The Principles of Intercollegiate Athletics." *2006 NCAA State of the Association Address.* http://www.ncaa.org (accessed January 30, 2006).

Brewer, Britton W., and A. E. Cornelius. "Norms and Factorial Invariance of the Athletic Identity Measurement Scale." *Academic Athletic Journal* 15 (2001): 103–113.

Brigham, Carl C. *A Study of American Intelligence.* Princeton, NJ: Princeton University Press, 1923.

Brush, Michael. "3 Prison Stocks Poised to Break Out." *MSN Money.* http://moneycentral.msn.com/content/P105034.asp (accessed May 15, 2008).

Bynum, William F. "The Great Chain of Being after Forty Years: An Appraisal." *History of Science* 13 (1975): 1–28.

Cabrera, Alberto F., and A. Nora, "College Students' Perceptions of Prejudice and Discrimination and Their Feelings of Alienation: A Construct Validation Approach." *Review of Education/Pedagogy/Cultural Studies* 16, no. 3–4 (1994): 387–409.

Carmichael, Stokely, and C. V. Hamilton. *Black Power: The Politics of Liberation in America.* New York: Random House, 1967.

Carter, Akilah R. *Negotiating Identities: Examining African American Female Collegiate Athlete Experiences in Predominantly White Institutions.* Unpublished Ph.D. Dissertation. University of Georgia, 2008.

Case, Bob, H. S. Greer, and J. Brown. "Academic Clustering in Athletics: Myth or Reality?" *Arena Review* 11, no. 2 (1987): 48–65.

Chamberlain, Muriel E. *Decolonization: The Fall of the European Empires.* Malden, MA: Blackwell, 1999.

Chambers, Fredrick. *Black Higher Education in the United States: A Selected Bibliography on Negro Higher Education and Historically Black Colleges and Universities.* Westport, CT: Greenwood, 1978.

Chesler, Mark A., A. E. Lewis, and J. E. Crowfoot. *Challenging Racism in Higher Education: Promoting Justice.* Lanham, MD: Rowman & Littlefield, 2005.

Chronicle of Higher Education. http://chronicle.com/free/v54/i47/47a00102.htm (accessed April 22, 2008).

Cicourel, Aaron V. "Living in Two Cultures: The Everyday World of Migrant Workers." In *Living in Two Cultures: The Socio-Cultural Situation of Migrant Workers and Their Families,* 17–66. Paris: Unesco, 1982.

City-data—Madison, County Florida. http://www.city-data.com/city/Madison-Florida.html (accessed September 26, 2008).

Claerbant, David P. *Black Student Alienation: A Study.* San Francisco, CA: R&E Research Associates, 1978.

Clark, Kenneth B. *Dark Ghetto.* New York: Harper & Row, 1965.

Clement, Rufus. "Racial Integration in the Field of Sports." *Journal of Negro Education* 23 (1954): 222–230.

Coakley, Jay J. *Sport in Society.* St. Louis: C. V. Mosley, 1978.

———. *Sport and Society: Issues & Controversies.* New York: McGraw-Hill, 2004.

Coalition on Intercollegiate Athletics. "About COIA." http://www.neuro.uoregon.edu/~tublitz/COIA/aboutcoia.htm (accessed December 2, 2008).

———. "Academic Integrity in Intercollegiate Athletics: Principles, Rules, and Best Practices." http://www.neuro.uoregon.edu/~tublitz/COIA/AF.html (accessed December 2, 2008).

———. "Campus Athletics Governance, the Faculty Role: Principles, Proposed Rules, and Guidelines." http://www.neuro.uoregon.edu/~tublitz/COIA/policypapers.htm (accessed December 2, 2008).

———. "Charter of the Coalition on Intercollegiate Athletics." http://www.neuro.uoregon.edu/~tublitz/COIA/Charter.html (accessed December 2, 2008).

———. "Framing the Future: Reforming Intercollegiate Athletics." http://www.neuro.uoregon.edu/~tublitz/COIA/FTF/FTFtext&appendix.htm (accessed December 2, 2008).

———. http://www.neuro.uoregon.edu/~tublitz/COIA/index.html (accessed December 2, 2008).

CollegeBoard: 2008 College-Bound Seniors: Total Group Profile Report. http://professionals. collegeboard.com/profdownload/Total_Group_Report.pdf (accessed March 15, 2009).

———. http://professionals.collegeboard.com/data-reports-research/sat/cb-seniors-2008 (accessed March 15, 2009).

Conrad, Alfred H., and J. R. Meyer. "The Economics of Slavery in the Ante Bellum South." *Journal of Political Economy* 66 (1958): 95–130.

Cook, Philip J., and J. Ludwig. "The Burden of 'Acting White': Do Black Adolescents Disparage Academic Achievement." In *The Black-White Test Score Gap*, edited by C. Jencks and M. Phillips, 375–400. Washington, DC: Brookings Institution, 1998.

Cooper, John A., and E. C. Davis. "Athletic Ability and Scholarship: A Resume of Studies Comparing Scholarship Abilities of Athletes and Non-athletes." *Research Quarterly* 5, no. 4 (1934): 68–79.

Cox, Oliver Cromwell. *Race: A Study in Social Dynamics*. New York: Monthly Review Press, 2000.

Crissman, Jennifer L. "The Impact of Clustering First Year Seminars with English Composition Courses on New Students' Retention Rates." *Journal of College Student Retention* 3, no. 2 (2002): 137–152.

Crouse, James, and D. Trusheim. *A Case against the SAT*. Chicago: University of Chicago Press, 1988.

Crowley, John N. *The NCAA's First Century in the Arena*. Indianapolis, IN: National Collegiate Athletic Association, 2005.

Cruse, Harold. *The Crisis of the Negro Intellectual*. New York: William Morrow, 1967.

Cuyjet, Michael J. "African American Men on College Campuses: Their Needs and Their Perceptions." *New Directions for Student Services* 80 (1997): 5–16.

D'Augelli, Anthony, and S. Hershberger. "African American Undergraduates on a Predominantly White Campus: Academic Factors, Social Networks, and Campus Climate." *Journal of Negro Education* 62, no. 1 (1993): 67–81.

Davis, Billie. "Marginality in a Pluralistic Society." http://www.psichi.org/pubs/articles/ article_145.asp (accessed October 8, 2008).

Davis, David B. *Inhuman Bondage: The Rise and Fall of Slavery in the New World*. New York: Oxford University Press, 2006.

Davis, F. James. *Who Is Black? One Nation's Definition*. University Park: Pennsylvania State University Press, 1991.

Davis, Junius A., and A. Borders-Patterson. "Black Students in Predominantly White North Carolina Colleges and Universities, 1986: A Replication of a 1970 Study." *College Board Report No. 86–7* (New York: College Board Publications, 1986).

Davis, Laura R. "The Articulation of Difference: White Preoccupation with the Question of Racially Linked Genetic Differences among Athletes." *Sociology of Sport Journal* 7, no. 2 (1990): 179–187.

Dillow, Gordon. "Bright Lights, Big Money." *Register*. http://www.ocregister.com/ocregister/ news/columns/article_1338204.php (accessed November 12, 2006).

Diop, Cheikh Anta. *Pre-colonial Black Africa: A Comparative Study of the Political and Social Systems of Europe and Back Africa from Antiquity to the Formation of Modern States that Demonstrates the Black Contribution to the Development of Western Civilization*. Europe: Lawrence Hill Books, 1987.

———. *The African Origin of Civilization: Myth or Reality*. Europe: Lawrence Hill Books, 1989.

Douglass, Frederick Douglass. *Life and Times of Frederick Douglass*. New York: Collier Books, 1892.

Du Bois, W. E. B. *The Soul of Black Folks*. New York: Fawcett, 1961.

Duderstadt, James J. *Intercollegiate Athletics and the American University: A University President's Perspective*. Ann Arbor: University of Michigan Press.

Edwards, Harry. *Sociology of Sport*. Homewood, IL: Dorsey Press, 1973.

———. "The Black 'Dumb Jock': An American Sports Tragedy." *The College Board Review*, no. 131 (1984): 8–13.

———. "A Dual Challenge for College Sports: Demographic and Cultural Pluralism Must be Concurrent." *NCAA News* (1993, March 10): 4.

Eitzen, D. Stanley, and G. H. Sage. *Sociology of North American Sport,* 3rd ed. Dubuque, IA: William C. Brown, 1986.

Elliott, E. N. *Cotton Is King and Pro-Slavery Arguments,* 3rd ed. Augusta, GA: Pritchard, Abbott, & Loomis, 1860.

Ellison, Ralph. *Invisible Man.* New York: Random House, 1947.

Eltis, David. "A Brief Overview of the Trans-Atlantic Slave Trade." Voyages: The Transatlantic Slave Trade Database. http://www.slavevoyages.org/tast/database/index.faces (accessed February 21, 2009).

Ervin, Leroy, S. A. S., H. L. Gillis, and M. C. Hogrebe. "Academic Performance of Student Athletes in Revenue-Producing Sports." *Journal of College Student Personnel* 26, no. 2 (1985): 119–124.

Eskenazi, Gerald. "Arena of Big-Time Athletics Is Showcasing a Younger Act." *New York Times.* http://query.nytimes.com/gst/fullpage.html?res=950DE4D8103AF936A35750C0A96F948260&n=Top/Reference/Times%20Topics/Subjects/C/College%20Athletics (accessed November 23, 2008).

Evans, Gaynelle. "Black Students Who Attend White Colleges Face Contradictions in Their Campus Life." *Chronicle of Higher Education* (1986, April 30): 29–30.

Fanon, Franz. *The Wretched of the Earth.* New York: Grove Press, 1963.

———. *Black Skin, White Masks.* New York: Grove Weidenfeld, 1967.

Farrell, Charles. "Black Collegiate Athletes Are being Double-Crossed." *USA Today* 119 (1990): 18–30.

Farrell, Charles S., and P. Monagham. "University of Maryland Athletic Director Quits: Task Force Faults Sports Departments for Players' Ills." *Chronicle of Higher Education* (October 15, 1986): 45, 48.

Feagin, Joe. "The Continuing Significance of Racism: Discrimination against Black Students in White College." *Journal of Black Studies* 22, no. 4 (1992): 546–578.

Feagin, Joe R., H. Vera, and N. Imani. *The Agony of Education: Black Students at White Colleges and Universities.* New York: Routledge, 1996.

"FedEx BCS National Championship Game January 8, 2009: Postgame Notes." http://www.gatorzone.com/football/stats/notes/post/20090108200000.pdf (accessed March 2, 2009).

Feldman, Bruce. *Meat Market: Inside the Smash-Mouth World of College Football Recruiting.* New York: ESPN Books, 2007.

Fish, Mike. "Where Is the Justice?" *The Atlanta Journal-Constitution* (1997, March 2): E8–E9.

Fleming, Jacqueline. *Blacks in College: A Comparative Study of Students' Success in Black and in White Institutions.* San Francisco, CA: Jossey-Bass, 1985.

Florida Department of Education, Education Information & Accountability Services—Madison County School District. http://www.fldoe.org/default.asp (accessed September 27, 2008).

———. http://www.fldoe.org/eias/flmove/madison.asp (accessed September 27, 2008).

Fogel, Robert W. *The Slavery Debates, 1952–1990: A Memoir.* Baton Rouge: Louisiana State University Press, 2003.

Fogel, Robert W., and S. L. Engerman. *Time on the Cross: The Economics of American Negro Slavery.* Boston: Little Brown, 1974.

Foner, Philip S. "West India Emancipation Speech." *The Life and Writings of Frederick Douglass,* vol. 2. New York: International Publishers, 1950.

Fordham, Signithia. *Blacked Out: Dilemmas of Race, Identity, and Success at Capital High.* Chicago: University of Chicago Press, 1996.

Fordham, Signithia, and J. U. Ogbu. "Black Students' School Success: Coping with the Burden of 'Acting White.'" *The Urban Review* 18, no. 3 (1986): 176–206.

"Fox Earns 17.0 Overnight for BCS National Championship Game." http://www.sportsbusinessdaily.com/article/126777 (accessed March 2, 2009).

Frankl, Viktor E. *Man's Search for Meaning: An Introduction to Logotherapy,* 3rd ed. New York: Simon & Schuster, 1984.

Frazier, E. Franklin. *The Negro Family in the United States.* Chicago: University of Chicago Press, 1939.

Fredrickson, George. "Mulattoes and Métis. Attitudes toward Miscegenation in the United States and France since the Seventeenth Century." *International Social Science Journal* 57 (2005, March): 103–112.

Freeman, Mike. "Pro Football: Notebook; Upshaw Deplores the Plight of Black Assistants." *New York Times*. http://query.nytimes.com/gst/fullpage.html?res=9506EEDB163CF930A35751C1 A9669C8B63 (accessed November 3, 2008).

Friend, Tom. "Pro Football; for Manley, Life without Football is Impossible to Tackle." *New York Times*. http://query.nytimes.com/gst/fullpage.html?res=990CE5DC103DF935A15751C0A963 958260&sec=&spon=&pagewanted=1 (accessed February 26, 1995).

Fuller, Jr., Neely. *The United-Independent Compensatory Code/System/Concept: A Textbook/Workbook for Thought, Speech, and/or Action, for Victims of Racism (White Supremacy)*. Washington, DC: Library of Congress, 1969.

Funk, Gary D. *Major Violation: The Unbalanced Priorities in Athletics and Academics*. Champaign, IL: Leisure Press, 1991.

Gay, Geneva. *Culturally Responsive Teaching: Theory, Research, and Practice*. New York: Teachers College Press, 2000.

Genovese, Eugene D. *The Political Economy of Slavery: Studies in the Economy and Society of the Slave South*. New York: Random House, 1965.

———. *Roll, Jordan, Roll: The World the Slaves Made*. New York: Random House, 1974.

George, Nelson. *Elevating the Game: Black Men and Basketball*. Lincoln, NE: University of Nebraska Press, 1999.

Giddings, Paula J. *When and Where I Enter: The Impact of Black Women on Race and Sex in America*. New York: William Morrow, 1984.

"Given Half a Chance: The Schott 50 State Report on Public Education and Black Males." http://www.blackboysreport.org/ (accessed February 2009).

Gladwin, Thomas, and A. Saidin. *Slaves of the White Myth: The Psychology of Neocolonialism*. Atlantic Highlands, NJ: Humanities Press, 1980.

Goldstone, Lawrence. *Dark Bargain: Slavery, Profits, and the Struggle for the Constitution*. New York: Walker.

Gorn, Elliott J., and W. J. Goldstein. *A Brief History of American Sports*. Champaign, IL: University of Illinois Press, 2004.

Graduation Rate Data. http://web1.ncaa.org//app_data/instAggr2008/1_0.pdf (accessed March 10, 2009).

Grant, Carl A., and C. E. Sleeter. *Making Choices for Multicultural Education: Five Approaches to Race, Class, and Gender*. Columbus, OH: Merrill, 1988.

Gray, Lewis C. *History of Agriculture in the Southern United States to 1860*, 2 vols. Gloucester, MA: Peter Smith, 1958.

Gurung, Ghana S., and M. Kollmair. "Marginality: Concepts and Their Limitations." http://www.nccr-pakistan.org/publications_pdf/General/Marginality.pdf (accessed October 7, 2008).

Hall, M. Ann. *Feminism and Sporting Bodies: Essays on Theory and Practice*. Champaign, IL: Human Kinetics, 1996.

Hall, Stuart. *Race: The Floating Signifier*. Media Education Foundation, 1997.

Harries, Patrick. *Work, Culture, and Identity: Migrant Laborers in Mozambique and South Africa, c. 1860–1910*. Portsmouth, NH: Heinemann, 1994.

Harris, Othello. "African-American Predominance in Collegiate Sport." In *Racism in Collegiate Athletics*, edited by R. C. Althouse and D. D. Brooks, 51–74. Morgantown, WV: Fitness Information Technology, 1993.

Harvey, William B. "The Data Speak: No Rest for the Weary." In *Making It on Broken Promises: Leading African American Male Scholars Confront the Culture of Higher Education*, edited by L. Jones, 15–30. Sterling, VA: Stylus Publishing, 2002.

Herrnstein, Richard J., and C. Murray. *The Bell Curve: Intelligence and Class Structure in American Life*. New York: Free Press, 1994.

Herskovits, Melville. "What Has Africa Given America?" *New Republic* 84 (1935): 92–94.

———. *The Myth of the Negro Past*. Boston: Harper & Brothers, 1941.

Heuser, John, D. Gershman, and J. Carty. "University of Michigan Athletes' 'Safe Harbor' Is General Studies." *The Ann Arbor News*. http://www.mlive.com/wolverines/academics/stories/index.ssf/2008/03/athletes_safe_harbor_is_genera.html (accessed March 18, 2008).

"High School Football – A Growing Big Business." *Sport Business News.* http://sportsbiznews. blogspot.com/2006/09/high-school-football-growing-big.html (accessed October 11, 2006).

Hill, Susan T. *The Traditional Black Institutions of Higher Education, 1860 to 1982.* Washington, DC: U.S. Department of Education, Office of Educational Research and Improvement, National Center for Educational Statistics, 1985.

Himes, Cindy. *The Female Athlete in American Society: 1860–1940.* Unpublished Ph.D. Dissertation. University of Pennsylvania, 1986.

Himmelsbach, Adam. "First Impressions Can Create Unrealistic Expectations Basketball Recruits." http://www.nytimes.com/2009/03/10/sports/10recruiting.html (accessed March 10, 2009).

Hoover, Stephen M., M. Sayler, and J. F. Feldhusen. "Cluster Grouping of Gifted Students at the Elementary Level." *Roeper Review* 16, no. 1 (1993): 13–15.

Hosick, Michelle B. "Reform's Inroads Evident with APR Release." *The NCAA News.* http://www.ncaa.org/wps/ncaa?ContentID=331 (accessed December 2, 2008).

Huberty, Carl J., C. DiStefano, and R. W. Kamphaus. "Behavioral Clustering among School Children." *Multivariate Behavioral Research* 32 (1997): 105–134.

Hurtado, Sylvia. "The Campus Racial Climate: Contexts of Conflict." *Journal of Higher Education* 63, no. 5 (1992): 539–569.

Income, Earnings, and Poverty Data from the 2007 American Community Survey. http://www.census.gov/prod/2008pubs/acs-09.pdf (accessed February 23, 2008).

"Initiation Rites in American High Schools: A National Survey." *Alfred University.* http://www.alfred.edu/hs_hazing/ (accessed February 20, 2009).

Jackman, Mary R. *The Velvet Glove: Paternalism and Conflict in Gender, Class, and Race Relations.* Berkeley: University of California Press, 1994.

Jencks, Christopher, and M. Phillips. *The Black-White Test Score Gap.* Washington, DC: Brookings Institution, 1998.

Johnson, Peter A. "The Marginal Man Revisited." *The Pacific Sociological Review* 3, no. 2 (1960): 71–74.

Johnson, Norris R., and D. P. Marple. "Racial Discrimination in Professional Basketball." *Sociological Focus* 6 (1973): 6–18.

Jones, James M. "The Concept of Race in Social Psychology: From Color to Culture." In *Black Psychology,* edited by R. L. Jones (3rd ed.), 441–467. Berkeley, CA: Cobb & Henry, 1991.

Jones-Wilson, Faustine C., C. A. Asbury, M. Okazawa-Rey, D. K. Anderson, S. M. Jacobs, and M. Fultz. *Encyclopedia of African-American Education.* Westport, CT: Greenwood, 1996.

Jordan, Winthrop D. *White over Black: American Attitudes toward the Negro, 1550–1812.* New York: W. W. Norton, 1968.

———. *The White Man's Burden: Historical Origins of Racism in the United States.* New York: Oxford University Press, 1974.

Kallestad, Brent. "NCAA Gives Florida State 4 Years' Probation." http://rivals.yahoo.com/ncaa/football/news?slug=ap-floridast-cheating&prov=ap&ty (accessed March 10, 2009).

Kent, Raymond A. *Higher Education in America.* New York: Ginn, 1930.

Kiger, Gary, and D. Lorentzen. "The Relative Effect of Gender, Race, and Sport on University Academic Performance." *Sociology of Sport Journal* 3, no. 2 (1986): 48–59.

Kilson, Martin L. *Political Change in a West African State: A Study of the Modernization Process in Sierra Leone.* Cambridge, MA: Harvard University Press, 1966.

Knowles, Louis, and K. Prewitt. *Institutional Racism in America.* Englewood Cliffs, NJ: Prentice Hall, 1969.

Koch, James V., and C. W. V. Hill. "Is This Discrimination in the Black Man's Game?" *Social Science Quarterly* 69, no. 1 (1988): 83–94.

Kozol, Jonathan. *Savage Inequalities: Children in America's Schools.* New York: Crown Publishers, 1991.

Kunjufu, Jawanza. *Countering the Conspiracy to Destroy Black Boys,* vol. I. Chicago, IL: African American Images, 1982.

LaFromboise, Teresa, H. L. K. Coleman, and J. Gerton. "Psychological Impact of Biculturalism: Evidence and Theory." *Psychological Bulletin* 114, no. 3 (1993): 395–412.

Lapchick, Richard. *Five Minutes to Midnight: Race and Sport in the 1990s.* Lanham, MD: Madison Books, 1991.

———. "Think beyond the Competition: 2006–07 Racial and Gender Report Card." http://www.tidesport.org/RGRC/2007/2006-07_RGRC.pdf (accessed October 15, 2007).

Leab, Daniel J. *From Sambo to Superspade: The Black Experience in Motion Pictures.* Boston: Houghton Mifflin, 1975.

Lee, Jung Y. *Marginality: The Key to Multicultural Theology.* Minneapolis, MN: Fortress Press, 1995.

Lederman, Douglas. "Black Athletes Who Entered Colleges in Mid-80's Had Much Weaker Records than Whites, Study Finds." *Chronicle of Higher Education* (1991, July 10): A31.

———. "Blacks Make up Large Proportion of Scholarship Athletes, yet Their overall Enrollment Lags at Division I Colleges." *Chronicle of Higher Education* (1992, June 17): 30–34.

Lemire, Elise. *"Miscegenation": Making Race in America.* Philadelphia: University of Pennsylvania Press, 2002.

Lenaghan, Arlene. "Reflections of Multicultural Curriculum." *Multicultural Education* 7, no. 3 (2000): 33–36.

Leonard, Wilbert M. "The Sport Experience of the Black College Athlete: Exploitation in the Academy." *International Review for the Sociology of Sport* 21, no. 1 (1986): 35–49.

———. "Stacking in College Basketball: A Neglected Analysis." *Sociology of Sport Journal* 4, no. 4 (1987): 403–409.

Lévi-Strauss, Claude. *Race and History.* Paris: UNESCO, 1952.

Lipsitz, George, "The Possessive Investment in Whiteness: Racialized Social Democracy and the 'White' Problem in American Studies." *American Quarterly* 47, no. 3 (1995): 369–387.

———. *The Possessive Investment in Whiteness: How White People Profit from Identity Politics.* Philadelphia, PA: Temple University Press, 2006.

Logan, Rayford W. *The Betrayal of the Negro from Rutherford B. Hayes to Woodrow Wilson.* New York: Collier Books, 1965.

Loo, Chalsa M., and G. Rolison. "Alienation of Ethnic Minority Students at a Predominantly White University." *Journal of Higher Education* 57 (1986): 76–77.

Lovejoy, Arthur O. *The Great Chain of Being: The Study of the History of an Idea.* Cambridge, MA: Harvard University Press, 1936.

Loy, John W., and J. F. McElvogue. "Racial Segregation in American Sport." *International Review of Sport Sociology* 5 (1970): 5–23

Majors, Richard, and J. M. Billson. *Cool Pose: The Dilemmas of Black Manhood in America.* New York: Lexington Books, 1992.

Marable, Manning. "The Rhetoric of Racial Harmony: Finding Substance in Culture and Ethnicity." *Sojourners* 19, no. 7 (1990): 14–18.

———. *Beyond Black and White: Transforming African American Politics.* Brooklyn, NY: Verso, 1995.

———. *Speaking Truth to Power: Essays on Race, Resistance, and Radicalism.* Boulder, CO: Westview Press, 1998.

McIntosh, Peggy. "White Privilege and Male Privilege: A Personal Account of Coming to See Correspondences through Work in Women's Studies." Center for Research on Women, Wellesley College, Wellesley, MA, 1988.

———. "White Privilege: Unpacking the Invisible Knapsack." *Independent School* 49, no. 2 (Winter 1990): 5, 31.

McPherson, Barry D. "Minority Group Involvement in Sport: The Black Athlete." In *Sport Sociology,* edited by A. Yiannakis, T. D. McIntyre, M. J. Melnick, and D. P. Hart, 153–166. Dubuque, IA: Kendall/Hunt, 1976.

McWhorter, John W. *Losing the Race: Self Sabotage in Black America.* New York: Free Press, 2000.

Mead, Margaret, T. Dobzhansky, E. Tobach, and R. E. Light. *Science and the Concept of Race.* New York: Columbia University Press, 1968.

Meier, August, and E. M. Rudwick. *From Plantation to Ghetto.* New York: Hill and Wang, 1963.

Memmi, Albert. *The Colonizer and the Colonized.* Boston: Beacon Press, 1965.

Memmi, Albert, and R. Bononno. *Decolonization and the Decolonized.* Minneapolis: University of Minnesota Press, 2006.

Michener, James. *Sports in America.* New York: Random House, 1976.

Miles, Robert. *Racism.* London: Routledge, 1989.

———. *Racism and Migrant Labour.* Boston: Routledge & Kegan Paul, 1992.

Miller, Patrick. "The Anatomy of Scientific Racism: Racialist Responses to Black Athletic Achievement." In *Sport and the Color Line: Black Athletes and Race Relations in Twentieth-Century America,* edited by P. B. Miller and David K. Wiggins, 327–344. New York: Routledge, 2004.

"Million-dollar Coaches Move into Mainstream." *USA Today.* http://www.usatoday.com/sports/college/football/2006-11-16-cover-coaches-media_x.htm (accessed October 25, 2008).

Mills, C. Wright. *Sociological Imagination.* New York: Oxford Press, 1959.

Mingle, James R. "The Opening of White Colleges and Universities to Black Students." In *Black Student in Higher Education: Condition and Experiences in the 1970s,* edited by G. E. Thomas, 18–29. Westport, CT: Greenwood, 1981.

"Minority Numbers in Athletics Administration." *NCAA News* (1994, August): 5, 13.

Monroe, Sylvester. "Guest in a Strange House: A Black at Harvard." *Saturday Review of Education* 14 (1973, February): 45–48.

Murphy, Austin. "Goodbye, Columbus (Ohio State tailback R. Smith quits)." *Sports Illustrated* 75 (September 9, 1991): 46–49.

National Association of State Budget Officers. *2007 State Expenditure Report.* http://www.nasbo.org/publications.php (accessed March 5, 2009).

National Collegiate Athletic Association. *1999–00—2005–06 NCAA Student-Athlete Race and Ethnicity Report.* http://www.ncaapublications.com/Uploads/PDF/2005-06_race_ethnicity_reportf05055c6-deb3-45de-ab1c-cbeeb4c19584.pdf (accessed September 13, 2006).

———. "Academics and Athletes." http://www.ncaa.org/wps/ncaa?ContentID=8 (accessed December 6, 2008).

———. "Bylaw 10.3 and Related Cases." http://www1.ncaa.org/membership/enforcement/gambling/toolkit/chapter_4?ObjectID=42728&ViewMode=0&PreviewState=0 (accessed November 11, 2008).

———. "Defining Academic Reform." http://www.ncaa.org/wps/ncaa?ContentID=341 (accessed December 2, 2008).

———. "History." http://www.ncaa.org/wps/ncaa?ContentID=1354 (accessed November 20, 2008).

———. "Legislation and Governance Overview." http://www.ncaa.org/wps/ncaa?ContentID=18 (accessed November 18, 2008).

———. "NCAA Approves 31 Bowls for '06." http://www.ncaafootball.com/index.php?s=&url_channel_id=32&url_subchannel_id=&url_article_id=6676&change_well_id=2 (accessed February 21, 2007).

———. *NCAA Gender Equity.* http://www.ncaa.org/wps/ncaa?ContentID=286 (accessed April 3, 2009).

———. "Our Mission." http://www.ncaa.org/wps/ncaa?ContentID=1352 (accessed December 6, 2008).

National Consortium for Academics and Sport. *Racial and Gender Report Cards.* http://www.ncasports.org/press_releases.htm (accessed September 13, 2006).

"NBA Age Limit." http://hoopedia.nba.com/index.php/NBA_Age_Limit (accessed September 22, 2008).

NCAA Student-Athlete Advisory Committees. "Campus, Conference and Division SAACs." http://www1.ncaa.org/membership/membership_svcs/saac/campus-conf-div.html#campus (accessed November 12, 2008).

———. "What Is a Student-Athlete Advisory Committee (SAAC)?." http://www1.ncaa.org/membership/membership_svcs/saac/index.html (accessed November 12, 2008).

Nelkin, Dorothy. "A Response to Marginality: The Case of Migrant Farm Workers." *British Journal of Sociology* 20, no. 4 (1969): 375–389.

Nettles, Michael T. *Toward Black Undergraduate Student Equality in American Higher Education.* New York: Greenwood, 1988.

Nkrumah, Kwame. *Ghana: The Autobiography of Kwame Nkrumah.* New York: International Publishers, 1957.

Office of Postsecondary Education. *"The Equity in Athletics Data Analysis Cutting Tool."* Office of Postsecondary Education. http://www.ope.ed.gov/athletics/GetOneInstitutionData.aspx

Ogbu, John U. *Black American Students in an Affluent Suburb: A Study of Academic Disengagement.* Mahwah, NJ: Lawrence Erlbaum Associates, 2003.

Olsen, Jack. "Pride and Prejudice." *Sports Illustrated* 29, no. 2 (1968, July): 18–31.

Oshinsky, David M. *Worse than Slavery: Parchman Farm and the Ordeal of Jim Crow Justice.* New York: Free Press, 1996.

Parekh, Bhikhu. *The Concept of Multicultural Education: The Interminable Debate.* London: Falmer Press, 1986.

Park, Robert E. "Human Migration and the Marginal Man." *American Journal of Sociology* 33, no. 6 (1928): 881–893.

Parry, Jose, and N. Parry. "Sport and the Black Experience." In *Sport, Racism, and Ethnicity*, edited by G. Jarvie, 150–174. New York: Falmer Press, 1991.

Participation Rates, 1981–82—2006–07. NCAA Sports Sponsorship and Participation Rates Report Executive Summary. "Executive Summary." http://www.ncaapublications.com/Uploads/PDF/PariticipationRates20084232c5b7-6441-412c-80f1-7d85f3536a51.pdf (accessed November 12, 2008).

Pennington, Bill. "Reading, Writing and Corporate Sponsorships." *New York Times.* http://www.nytimes.com/2004/10/18/sports/othersports/18sponsor.html (accessed October 11, 2006).

Pew Centers of the States. *One in 31: The Long Reach of American Corrections.* http://www.pewcenteronthestates.org/uploadedFiles/PSPP_1in31_report_FINAL_WEB_2-27-09.pdf (accessed March 5, 2009).

Phillips, Ulrich B. *American Negro Slavery: A Survey of the Supply, Employment and Control of Negro Labor as Determined by the Plantation Regime.* New York: D. Appleton, 1918.

Philpott, Stuart B. *West Indian Migration: The Montserrat Case.* London: Athlone Press, 1973.

Phizacklea Annie, and R. Miles. *Labour and Racism.* Boston: Routledge & Kegan Paul, 1980.

Pieterse, Jan Nederveen. *White on Black: Images of Africa and Blacks in Western Popular Culture.* New Haven, CT: Yale University Press, 1992.

Play It Smart: A Program of the National Football Foundation & College Hall of Fame. "About Play It Smart." http://www.playitsmart.org/Play_about.php (accessed December 3, 2008).

"Poll Shows Gap between Blacks and Whites over Racial Discrimination." http://news.yahoo.com/page/election-2008-political-pulse-race-in-america;_ylt=Asi3cIqr1O5eLvV_F8zHqll2KY54 (accessed September 24, 2008).

Poulantzas, Nicos Ar. *Political Power and Social Classes.* London: New Left Books, 1973.

"Public School Report: Public School Information and Data." http://schools.publicschoolsreport.com/Florida/Madison/MadisonCountyHighSchool.html (accessed September 26, 2008).

Purdy, Dean, D. S. Eitzen, and R. Hufnagel. "Are Athletes also Students? The Educational Attainment of College Athletes" *Social Problems* 29, no. 4 (1982): 439–448.

Ramphele, Mamphela. *A Bed Called Home: Life in the Migrant Labour Hostels of Cape Town.* Athens: Ohio University Press, 1993.

Random House. *The Random House College Dictionary (Revised Edition).* New York: Random House, 1980.

Ransom, Roger L., and R. Sutch. *One Kind of Freedom: The Economic Consequences of Emancipation.* New York: Cambridge University Press, 2001.

Rediker, Marcus. *The Slave Ship: A Human History.* New York: Viking, 2007.

Reports of the Knight Commission on Intercollegiate Athletics. http://www.knightcommission.org/images/pdfs/1991-93_KCIA_report.pdf (accessed November 26, 2008).

Rescorla, Leslie. "Cluster Analytic Identification of Autistic Preschoolers." *Journal of Autism and Developmental Disorders* 18, no. 4 (1988): 475–492.

Rhoden, William C. "Athletes on Campus: A New Reality." *New York Times* (1990, January 8): A1.

———. *Forty Million Dollar Slaves: The Rise, Fall, and Redemption of the Black Athlete.* New York: Crown Publishers, 2006.

Riesman, David. "Some Observations Concerning Marginality." *Phylon* 12, no. 2 (1951), 113–127.

Ross, Karen. *Black and White Media: Black Images in Popular Film and Television.* Cambridge, MA: Polity Press, 1996.

Ross v. Creighton University, 957 F.2d 410 (7th Cir. 1992).

Sack, Allen. *Sport Sociology: Contemporary Themes.* Dubuque, IA: Kendall-Hunt, 1979.

Sack, Allen L. *Counterfeit Amateurs: An Athlete's Journey through the Sixties to the Age of Academic Capitalism.* University Park: Pennsylvania State University Press, 2008.

Sack, Allen L., and E. J. Staurowsky. *College Athletes for Hire: The Evolution and Legacy of the NCAA's Amateur Myth.* Westport, CT: Praeger, 1998.

Sage, George H. "Introduction." In *Racism in College Athletics: The African-American Athlete's Experience,* edited by D. Brooks and R. Althouse, 1–9. Morgantown, WV: Fitness Information Technology, 1993.

———. *Power and Ideology in American Sport: A Critical Perspective,* 2nd ed. Champaign, IL: Human Kinetics, 1998.

Sailes, Gary A. "An Investigation of Campus Stereotypes: The Myth of Black Athletic Superiority and the Dumb Jock Stereotype." *Sociology of Sport Journal* 10, no. 1 (1993): 88–97.

———. "The African American Athletes: Social Myths and Stereotypes." In *African Americans in Sport: Contemporary Themes,* edited by G. A. Sailes, 183–198. New Brunswick, NJ: Transaction Publishers, 1998.

Savage, Howard J. *American College Athletics,* Bulletin no. 23. New York: Carnegie Foundation for the Advancement of Teaching, 1929.

Schapera, Isaac. *Migrant Labour and Tribal Life: A Study of Conditions in the Bechuanaland Protectorate.* London: Oxford University Press, 1947.

Schermerhorn, R. A. "Power as a Primary Concept in the Study of Minorities." *Social Forces* 35 (1956): 53–56.

Scholar-Baller: Bringing Education to Sport and Entertainment. http://www.scholarballer.org/index.htm (accessed September 22, 2008).

Schulman, James L., and W. G. Bowen. *The Game of Life: College Sports and Educational Values.* Princeton, NJ: Princeton University Press, 2001.

Sedlacek, William E. "Black Students on White Campuses: Twenty Years of Research." *Journal of College Student Development* 40, no. 5 (1999): 538–550.

Sellers, Robert M. "Racial Differences in the Predictors of Academic Achievement of Division I Student Athletes." *Sociology of Sport Journal* 9, (1992): 48–59.

———. "Black Student-Athletes: Reaping the Benefits or Recovering from the Exploitation." In *Racism in College Athletics: The African-American Athlete's Experience,* edited by D. Brooks and R. Althouse, 143–174. Morgantown, WV: Fitness Information Technology 1993.

Sellers, Robert M., G. P. Kuperminc, and A. S. Waddell. "Life Experiences of Black Student-Athletes in Revenue Producing Sports: A Descriptive Empirical Analysis." *Academic Athletic Journal* (1991): 21–38.

Sertima, Ivan Van. *They Came before Columbus: The African Presence in Ancient America.* New York: Random House, 1976.

Shapiro, Beth J. "Intercollegiate Athletic Participation and Academic Achievement: A Case Study of Michigan State University Student Athletes, 1950–1980." *Sociology of Sport Journal* 1, no. 1 (1984): 46–51.

Shockley, William. "The Apple-of-God's-Eye Obsession." *The Humanist* 32 (1972): 16–17.

Smith, Earl. *Race, Sport and the American Dream.* Durham, NC: Carolina Academic Press, 2007.

Smith, Michael, and J. Ourand. "ESPN Pays $2.25B for SEC Rights." *SportsBusiness Journal.* http://www.sportsbusinessjournal.com/article/59824 (accessed October 25, 2008).

Smith, Ronald A. *Sports and Freedom: The Rise of Big-Time College Athletics.* New York: Oxford University Press, 1988.

Sperber, Murray. *Beer and Circus: How Big-time College Sports Is Crippling Undergraduate Education.* New York: Henry Holt, 2000.

Spivey, Donald, and T. A. Jones. "Intercollegiate Athletic Servitude: A Case Study of the Black Illini Student-Athletes, 1931–1967." *Social Science Quarterly* 55, no. 4 (1975): 939–947.

Staples, Robert. "Race and Colonialism: The Domestic Case in Theory and Practice." *The Black Scholar* 7, no. 9 (1976): 37–49.

Steeg, Jill L., J. Upton, P. Bohn, and S. Berkowitz. "College Athletes Academics Guided toward 'Major in Eligibility.'" http://www.usatoday.com/sports/college/2008-11-18-majors-cover_N. htm?POE=click-refer (accessed November 19, 2008).

Steele, Shelby. *The Content of Our Character: A New Vision of Race in America.* New York: HarperCollins, 1991.

Steward, Robbie J. "Alienation and Interactional Styles in a Predominantly White Environment: A Study of Successful Black Students." *Journal of College Student Development* 31, no. 6 (1990): 509–515.

Stichter, Sharon. *Migrant Labour in Kenya: Capitalism and African response 1895–1975.* Great Britain: Longman Group, 1982.

———. *Migrant Laborers.* Cambridge: Cambridge University Press, 1985.

Stonequist, Everett V. *The Marginal Man: A Study in Personality and Culture Conflict.* New York: Charles Scribner's Sons, 1937.

Storey, John. *Cultural Theory and Popular Culture: An Introduction,* 3rd ed. Harlow, England: Pearson/ Prentice Hall, 2001.

Suen, Hoi K. "Alienation and Attrition of Black College Students on a Predominantly White Campus." *Journal of College Student Personnel* 24 (1983): 117–121.

Suggs, Welch. "Jock Majors: Many Colleges Allow Football Players to Take the Easy Way Out." *Chronicle of Higher Education* 49 (2003): A33–A34.

———. *A Place on the Team: The Triumph and Tragedy of Title IX.* Princeton, NJ: Princeton University Press, 2005.

Sydnor, Charles S. *Slavery in Mississippi.* New York: D. Appleton, 1933.

Teno, Kevin M. "Cluster Grouping Elementary Gifted Students in the Regular Classroom: A Teacher's Perspective." *Gifted Child Today Magazine* 23, no. 1 (2000): 44–53.

"Texas High School Football Becoming Big Business." http://cbs11tv.com/business/texas.high. school.2.506554.html (accessed February 2009).

Thamel, Pete. "Top Recruit Weighs the Benefits of a Trip of Europe." http://www.nytimes. com/2008/07/08/sports/basketball/08hoops.html?ex=1373256000&en=abf7837f87e8ec38&ei =5124&partner=permalink&exprod=permalink (accessed September 22, 2008).

The Chicago Tribune. "Bannister Speculates on Sprinters." sec. 4, p. 7 (August 14, 1995).

The Drake Group. http://www.thedrakegroup.org/index.html (accessed December 2, 2008).

The Drake Group. "The Drake Group Proposals." http://www.thedrakegroup.org/proposals.html (accessed December 2, 2008).

The Institute for Diversity and Ethics in Sport. "The Buck Stops Here: Assessing Diversity among Campus and Conference Leaders for Football Bowl Subdivision (FBS) Schools in the 2008–09 Academic Year." http://www.ncasports.org/Articles/2008-09_FBS_Demographics_Study.pdf (accessed December 8, 2008).

The Knight Commission on Intercollegiate Athletics. http://www.knightcommission.org/about/ (accessed November 23, 2008).

———. "The Foundation's Interest." http://www.knightcommission.org/images/uploads/1991-93_ KCIA_report.pdf (accessed November 23, 2008).

———. *"A Call to Action: Reconnecting College Sports and Higher Education."* http://www. knightcommission.org/images/uploads/KCfinal-06-2001.pdf (accessed November 26, 2008).

The National College Players Association (NCPA). "Mission and Goals." http://www.cacnow.org/ our_mission.asp (accessed November 17, 2008).

———. "NCPA-Backed Lawsuit Makes Over $445 Million Available to Athletes." http://www. ncpanow.org/news_detail.asp?ArticleID=38 (accessed November 17, 2008).

The NCAA Minority Opportunities and Interests Committee's Biennial Study. "2005–06 Ethnicity and Gender Demographics of NCAA Member Institutions' Athletics Personnel." http://www. ncaa.org/wps/ncaa?ContentID=354 (accessed November 13, 2008).

The Sentencing Project. http://www.sentencingproject.org/ (accessed September 8, 2008).

The U.S. Department of Justice: Office of Justice Programs—Bureau of Justice Statistics. http:// www.ojp.usdoj.gov/bjs/ (accessed April 23, 2008)

Thompson, Chalmer E., and B. R. Fretz. "Predicting the Adjustment of Black Students at Predominantly White Institutions." *Journal of Higher Education* 62, no. 4 (1991): 437–450.

Torres, Kimberly, "'Culture Shock': Black Students Account for Their Distinctiveness at an Elite College." *Ethnic and Racial Studies* 31, no. 1 (2008): 1–23.

Turner, Renee D. "The Resurgence of Racism on White Campuses." *The Black Collegian* 16, no. 1 (1985): 18–24.

United States Court of Appeals for the Eighth Circuit. "C.B.C. Distribution and Marketing, Inc. vs. Major League Baseball Advanced Media, L.P. et. al." http://www.ca8.uscourts.gov/opndir/07/10/063357P.pdf (accessed November 12, 2008).

U.S. Department of Education. http://ope.ed.gov/athletics/ (accessed April 22, 2008).

———. Institute of Education Sciences—National Center for Educational Statistics. http://nces.ed.gov/programs/coe/2008/section3/table.asp?tableID=896 (accessed October 2, 2008).

Valenti, John, and R. Naclerio. *Swee' Pea and Other Playground Legends: Tales of Drug, Violence, and Basketball.* New York: Michael Kesend, 1990.

Weinberg, Ari. "The Business of Basketball: Biggest College Sports Arena Naming Deals." *Forbes.* http://www.forbes.com/2003/03/24/cx_aw_0320ncaa.html (accessed October 25, 2008).

Weir, Tom. "Hazing Issue's Lasting Impact Rears Ugly Head Across USA." *USA Today.* http://www.usatoday.com/sports/preps/2003-12-09-hazing_x.htm (accessed February 20, 2009).

Welsing, Francis C. *The Isis Papers: The Keys to the Colors.* Chicago, IL: Third World Press, 1991.

Wiley, Ralph "A Daunting Proposition." *Sports Illustrated* (1991, August 12): 27–25.

Willhelm, Sidney M. *Who Needs the Negro?* Garden City, NY: Doubleday, 1971.

Williams, Chancellor. *The Destruction of Black Civilization: Great Issues of a Race From 4500 B.C. to 2000 A. D.* Chicago, IL: Third World Press, 1987.

———. *The Rebirth of African Civilization.* Chicago, IL: Third World Press, 1993.

Williams, Eric. *Capitalism and Slavery.* Chapel Hill: University of North Carolina Press, 1994.

Wilson, Francis. *Migrant Labour in South Africa.* Johannesburg: The South African Council of Churches, 1972.

Wilson, William J. *The Declining Significance of Race: Blacks and Changing American Institutions.* Chicago: University of Chicago Press, 1978.

———. *The Declining Significance of Race: Blacks and Changing American Institutions,* 2nd ed. Chicago: University of Chicago Press, 1980.

Winebrenner, Susan, and B. Devlin. "Cluster Grouping of Gifted Students: How to Provide Full-time Services on a Part-time Budget." Teaching Exceptional Children 30 (Jan/Feb 1998): 62–66.

Wright, Bobby E. *The Psychopathic Racial Personality and Other Essays.* Chicago, IL: Third World Press, 1984.

Yancey, George. "Experiencing Racism: Differences in the Experiences of Whites Married to Blacks and Non-Black Racial Minorities." *Journal of Comparative Family Studies* 38, no. 2 (2007, March 22): 197–213.

Zahar, Renate. *Frantz Fanon: Colonialism and Alienation.* New York: Monthly Review Press, 1974.

Zimbalist, Andrew. "March Madness It Is, Economically." *Wall Street Journal.* http://online.wsj.com/article/SB123664681664078731.html (accessed April 3, 2009).

Zimbalist, Andrew. *Unpaid Professionals—Commercialism and Conflict in Big-Time College Sports: Commercialism and Conflict in Big-Time College Sports.* Princeton, NJ: Princeton University Press, 1999.

INDEX

29046032R00141

Made in the USA
Columbia, SC
19 October 2018